The Wounding and Healing of Desire

THE WOUNDING AND HEALING OF DESIRE

Weaving Heaven and Earth

Wendy Farley

WESTMINSTER
JOHN KNOX PRESS
LOUISVILLE · KENTUCKY

Book design by Sharon Adams
Cover design by Night & Day Design

First edition
Published by Westminster John Knox Press
Louisville, Kentucky

This book is printed on acid-free paper that meets the American National Standards Institute Z39.48 standard. ♾

05 06 07 08 09 10 11 12 13 14 — 10 9 8 7 6 5 4 3 2 1

Library of Congress Cataloging-in-Publication Data is on file at the Library of Congress, Washington, D. C.

ISBN 0-664-22976-X

To my teachers, especially Fay, Lynnsay, and Virginia,
and to the communion of women, living and dead,
that has kept alive a memory of the undiluted love of God.

Contents

Preface

When I was forty-one I lost the ability to read. During that time, I had a migraine that lasted for eighteen months. Unable to do much else, I listened to a lot of folk music, comforted by women singing about how hard life was, how intensely they loved, and how Jesus gave them strength to endure. Mostly I was comforted by the throbbing desire that was carried by the melodies they sang. Suffering opened my soul the way a meat cleaver severs gristle and bone, and few things could comfort me more than these yearning melodies. I was trying to get myself and my two children free of a husband I had been with for twenty years who had become dangerous to us. I spent those years not with books, colleagues, or students, but with lawyers, psychiatrists, social workers, and therapists.

When I wrote this book, I still could not read. Whatever was not in my head and immediately available to my memory could not be a part of my writing. As you might imagine, this felt like a terrible handicap, and the absence of all of my would-be conversation partners will no doubt be as keenly felt by my readers as it has been felt by me. I have written this book in a style at variance with the customs of the academic world, not out of disrespect for those customs but because I found myself exiled from that world by the conditions of my life. In preparing this manuscript for publication I have added endnotes for those texts and songs that are directly or indirectly alluded to in the text. Though a far cry from more customary methods of argumentation, they will hopefully give the reader some orientation to the traditions in which I have been immersed. I have made little attempt to connect what I say to others engaged in this conversation, either in the great wisdom tradition of the past or those writing now, mostly because it was not possible for me to do so. I have lived with theological texts—teaching them, reading them, writing about them—for not quite thirty years. The absence of all but a few direct references to these sisters, mothers, and fathers of the past and present has nothing to do with my disinterest in them. I could have written nothing without them. If you find strains of Augustine, Calvin, Schleiermacher, or feminist theologians, it is because they compose the background music of my mind. Even without my having direct access to them, they are present now in my thinking as generous ghosts of books I read a long time ago. I am also painfully aware of all of the things I have not read—things that, had I read them, would have changed and deepened my understanding. I would like to be the first among those who will point out the distortion this absence of conversation creates. The work of correcting and modifying the interpretations present in this work in light of a larger conversation will have to go on in the future, I hope with the help of my readers.

Yet I am also aware of the great gift not-reading has been to me. As a student of phenomenology, having read too much about the way reason works, it has been fascinating to observe my own scholarly mind deprived of the primary function of scholarship. Teaching texts with which I had some familiarity but could not reread in preparation for class felt like being a tightrope walker who looked down and saw no net. I found, though, that an act of integration and synthesis was occurring and that my mind was carried from the words and arguments to the matter of the text itself. I was reminded of Bonaventure's words, which direct the reader to the intention of the writer rather than to his work: "The sense of the words rather than the rude speech, of truth rather than beauty, of the exercise of the affections rather than the erudition of the intellect."[1]

Bonaventure is reminding us that the subject matter of theology is a reality beyond any word or argument. The words and arguments on the page of even the most brilliant theologian's work are only rough attempts to carry mind toward that reality. Having trained my whole life in reading texts, not-reading gave me a different kind of access to these same texts. I began studying religious practices with Buddhist, Christian, and yogic masters, and these experiences forced me to reevaluate radically what I had thought about the nature of reason, of epistemology, and of the relationship between what ancient writers wrote and what they did. As a good Protestant it did not occur to me that metaphysics had a root in bodily contemplative practices and that in the absence of these practices metaphysics makes almost no sense at all. That Buddhist and Christian metaphysics are efforts to move back and forth across the line between cataphatic (naming God) and apophatic (negating names) experiences that arise out of practice had not really occurred to me. The soteriological significance of metaphysics collapsed into system building when the only access I had to the texts was through reading them.

Just before the lights went out on my reading, I had begun to read the women contemplatives and became aware of them as a kind of underground railroad of theology that had kept alive certain aspects of Christianity for thousands of years, even if the institutions of the church and the canonical texts maintained other aspects of Christianity with much greater historical visibility. Women theologians have written outside the standards of the academy all through history up until sometime after I was born. We women have relied on whatever learning we could acquire, our native intelligence, our experience, and community with one another. Even twenty years ago this literature was not considered theology and is still not accepted as such in most places where theology is taught. What a terrible defrauding of our understanding of what theology is and of the beauty of Christian faith this exclusion has been.

There is also a terrible diminishment of theology when the oral tradition of these communities is not integrated with the study of a textual tradition. Even while writing in the genres of and according to the standards of the "fathers," feminist theologians struggle to maintain such distinctive values as the importance of experience and community and an awareness of the untidiness of reality and its recalcitrance to abstractions and universals. Feminist theology must push against the genres and sources of the tradition in order to say what must be said. In this struggle we are in a similar position to that of womanist and African-American writers who must augment the traditional sources of theology with song, literature, oral tradition, and experiences that are generally not recognized as having any significance to academic theology.

Not-reading not only gave me a different kind of access to texts I have known, loved, and taught for years, but it also drove me to new sources. I found that the deep symbols of song and folktales open up possibilities for theological reflection that are absent when one remains within the lineage of traditional theology. The ransoming of humanity looks different when its symbolic structure is juxtaposed to the root symbols in a story like "The Polar Bear King" than when it is placed in a progression of atonement theories. Dwelling in the symbolic realm of folk tales reminds us of a depth dimension of religious imagery that is sterilized and amputated when it is forced into authoritarian doctrines. These alternative sources also contribute to a sense of what theology looks like from "the underside of history." The nature of desire and of wounding, anguish, and transformation cannot be exhausted by the canon of scholars. Dwelling in the expressions of these things that accumulate anonymously in song and story weaves theology together with one of its crucial sources: the wisdom and experience of people who are not themselves academics. If theology cuts off its roots from practices, stories, and song, from the accumulated experiences of the ages, then how can we pretend that what we say has anything to do with human life?

Deprived of the usual access to philosophical theology, I have been reminded that theology is not primarily texts but a kind of desire that employs thought as a religious practice. I feel grateful to the women who have been writing for thousands of years, creating and preserving theological wisdom while remaining almost completely invisible. I am glad that my loss of reading has driven me to find this underground community, and it is my hope that this oddly constructed book may be a bridge that helps to carry some of this wisdom into more mainstream theological discussions.

I have not made any real attempt to address the current methodological and metaphysical climate, which is particularly sensitive to the absurdities of trying to make general claims about the human condition. A discussion of method is out of place here. But a few comments might help interpret the kind of status I think claims about human experience might have. I think of what we write as part of a dialogue. I am able to write what I write only by resting on what others say and do. This work, for example, does little to help us interpret the social and political difficulties we are enduring, but it does presuppose this work as it is being done by others. I feel I am free to explore certain dimensions of theology because I have already been shaped by the work of others and because others are doing this indispensable work. In a real, interpersonal dialogue we can change what we say as we go along because we understand something better in light of what others say, criticisms they make, and perspectives we offer one another. A book has an artificially static character. It cannot change in light of a conversation. "Truth is a living animal," Plato observed in the *Phaedrus*, so writing is ill-equipped to deal with it. This is only one reason that I am in complete agreement with criticisms of those who claim to have deciphered a universal in human experience that would be recognizable and acceptable to everyone evolutionary biologists classify as *Homo sapien*. Yet whom would I exclude from a compassionate response to suffering? If conceptual uniformity is neither possible nor desirable, there remains something that inspires us to care for suffering others whoever they are.

What follows is no more an attempt at a universal claim for Christianity or human experience than a poem is. If, in its extremely particular and idiosyncratic unfolding, anything resonates with a reader, it can do so because sometimes particular expressions of a point of view can have this connecting effect. Sometimes people write things that resonate with many people, across cultures and historical boundaries. The acknowledgment that writing arises from a particular culture, epoch, gender, and so on is still an effort to communicate beyond the solipsism of particularity. I am not sure a writer should be in the business of predetermining to whom their writing might prove interesting.

After all, we all write as completely unique persons, shaped by all kinds of cultural realities beyond ourselves, trained in ways that make some things more visible and others much less visible. Each of us can see things and say things in ways no one else would, and this shared insightfulness is part of the sweetness of our interdependence. At the same time, it means that we all see only by way of distortions and partiality, and these limitations make the process of dialogue, criticism, correction, and the creation of alternatives equally integral to our interdependence.

I bear witness to a power that is stronger than what binds us. In this book I use more or less Christian names for this power: the Divine Eros, named as a trinity the Good Beyond Being, the Beloved, and the Holy Spirit. But this power has a thousand names and none that capture it. Studying other religious traditions makes me much more immediately aware of how little the power of redemption respects the confines of faith. When we say that we are created in the image of God or that our true nature is Buddha nature, we are saying that this power is essential to us and cannot be ultimately defeated or defiled. I believe that a holy spark burns in each of us that cannot be quenched. It is characteristic of the contemplative dimension of all religious traditions to attribute this reality to all beings without exception. Even in this postmodern epoch I feel inclined to try to open my own eyes to this unbearable beauty we all possess. I am hoping that the poor words I write here might help to stir up others to remember the power of their desire and find the resources, communities, teachers, and traditions that will feed it in their own lives. But because words fail, I have included references to music that carries a longing that may reconnect you with your own.

Acknowledgments

All of us exist and flourish only in utter and complete interdependence on others. Acknowledging even the limited sense of my dependence on others that allowed this book to come into existence would be an almost infinite task. A few crucial names come to mind, however. I am deeply grateful to Laurie Patton, the Chair of the Department of Religion, for her astonishing generosity and wisdom. It is not every academic chair who can figure out what to do with a faculty member who cannot read and can do little else that is academically useful. Without her kindness and support I do not know what would have become of me. This gratitude extends to all of the members of the Department of Religion who tolerated the years of my disability with grace and kindness far beyond anything that one could reasonably expect or hope for. The collegiality among the faculty at Emory is a great treasure, and it was tested to an unusual degree. I can hardly say how indebted I am to the good hearts of my colleagues.

Scholars, because we depend so heavily on books, can forget the importance of the living wisdom of other people. It is hard to footnote what I have learned from the wise women around me. But they have contributed as much to what I have learned as all the books I have read. I have learned not only from their insightful words but also from their living example that the contemplative life can be a potent force of transformation. Most of these women are not themselves writers. However pale the refraction of their example in my writing, I would like to acknowledge my gratitude and indebtedness to them. Fay Key, Director of the Green Bough House of Prayer, is a great teacher in the tradition of the ammas (mothers) of old. Reverend Lynnsay Buehler has been a gracious and wise guide. Bobbi Patterson, Roberta Bondi, and Peggy Court-right have been strong supports and good friends in our practice together. I am deeply grateful for the presence of Virginia Apperson in my life and the wells of wisdom from which she has helped me. Tara Doyle illustrates for me the fruits of Buddhist practice through her friendship and her life.

For the same reasons, I would like to express my gratitude to my teachers at Loseling Institute of Buddhist Studies. I am especially thankful for my friendship with Geshe Lobsang Negi, my first teacher in this tradition. I am, in a different way, deeply indebted to Rizong Rinpoche, whose teachings of Tibetan Buddhist practices transformed my life. Both of these men embody the teachings of Tibetan Buddhism in ways that, before I met them, I did not really believe possible.

There is a certain, narrow sense in which the presence of children in one's life not only does not help a book to be written, but actively undermines it. I have a seven-year-old daughter adopted from China, Liz; two birth children, Paul, eleven, and Emma, fourteen (all children are born, of course, but only two of mine were born to me); and a stepdaughter, Joanna, fifteen. My heart was flayed open by my love for these four, and without them, this book would not exist. A song or pregnant silence rather than words is called for to try to express my gratitude to my beloved Maggie. Without her, whatever funnels of grace might have been around me in my world could never have reached me. So, not only for the book, but for my new life, I am unspeakably thankful to her.

Introduction

Human consciousness plunges into depths to which we normally have little direct access. We might think of consciousness through the image of a spiral. At the top of the spiral are thoughts, emotions, decisions, and so on that we consciously experience. Spiraling down through consciousness is to enter level after level of memory, desire, terror, and habit. The traumas we have endured structure our experience but hide themselves here. The motivations that guide our actions but violate our self-image live here. Awareness of the intolerable aspects of our lives take up residence here: constant degradations at work; grief over our endangered or dead children; the gap between our treasured piety and our despairing doubts over the goodness of God. Even if these things rise to consciousness, we cannot feel them. We can only look at them like amputated limbs that have no connection to us.

Spiraling down deeper, we find the places where the ingrained habits of our spirit dwell: intuitiveness, fear, unfelt rage, cheerfulness. Everything we have known and felt, every intolerable experience or too-intense joy remains with us, sedimented along this spiral staircase of our mind. Spiraling down deeper still we come to an incandescent fire that has the power to burn away every obstacle to love. When, like Dante, we pass through this sweet, excruciating fire we come to the great emptiness where the divine image burns beyond light and darkness in a purity and luminescence that nothing can stain.

Desire is the thread that runs from this emptiness through fire, and through all the hidden recesses of our minds. We may not see it, a tiny star-flower hidden among the weeds and trash and bolder flowers that bloom in our consciousness. But if we catch a glimpse of even the tiniest flash of this holy desire, we have found our way home. This desire does not require that we know the way home or that we master virtues that enable us to walk a way of perfection. Desire does not wait until we are free of illusion and anger. Desire itself will guide us, past and through all of our mistakes, pain, losses, and moments of despair. If we can connect with even the smallest hint of this desire, which emanates from the divine image deep within us, then nothing, not even ourselves, can break this thread that leads us home. Desire does not protect us from the difficulties of the world. Far from leading us away from pain, it leads us through the demon-haunted wilderness that blocks us from the courage to love the world, to feel compassion for its aches, and to delight in its beauty. Desire does not prevent pain, but it ameliorates the tyranny of pain. With the confidence of true lovers, we can, like Psyche, throw ourselves into nothingness and find ourselves held up by Eros. Living in the world is difficult, and we hide from ourselves, from one another, and from the gracious Beloved that longs for us so earnestly. Desire is the emissary of the Beloved, and it lends us the courage and strength and hope we need for this work of healing. Desire allows us to journey down the spiral staircase of our minds, through everything we have hidden away, until we remember who we are and can again repose in intimacy with the Beloved, the infinitely compassionate one, and remember that we have never really been separated at all.

The work that follows focuses on dimensions of the human spirit that Protestantism, especially in the Reformation traditions, has tended to ignore. One of the virtues of at least some strands of contemporary Christianity is its attentiveness to issues of justice in the social and political realms. Because Christians are called to a vocation of love, and love is grieved by suffering, and much suffering is caused by injustice, attention to justice is integral to Christian practice. Attention to the interior landscape of human beings is not a rejection of the claims of justice. To the contrary, attention to our interiority deepens our capacity for justice. Or rather, it roots justice in the well-spring of compassion. Justice without compassion can make demands on us but fail to feed us. It can tend toward self-righteousness or hatred of opponents. There is nothing individualistic about seeking to understand why it is so much easier to feel indifference or disdain for others than to love them. Attention to interiority can resuscitate our capacities for relationship and ignite in us the desire for compassion and delight in life. In this sense it is integral to the desire for justice.

My milieu is Protestant and academic, and it seems to me that this interior dimension of human being is largely absent from the conversations I know. Yet "spirituality" is on the shelves of every bookstore—under New Age Religions, Buddhism, Self-help Manuals, and Psychological Analysis. Our need to understand our spiritual life is quite intense, all the more so as our consumer culture defrauds us of spiritual existence and as patriarchy and homophobia drive many away from religious communities. The Christian tradition has enormously rich resources for interpreting our condition and generating practices that heal our wounds. Emptying Christianity into a narrow pattern of sin and redemption denies us the enormous wisdom this tradition has for interpreting the ways that we as individuals and communities are bound to unloving, destructive patterns of life and relationship. The focus of this book is therefore on the obstacles we bear within us that prevent us from even wanting justice. The focus is not on sin but on the wounds that bind us to self-hatred, paralysis, meaningless self-sacrifice, illusion, misdirected patience, rage, violence, and the mutilations of affliction.

I write as a Christian and feminist theologian but my adoration of the blessed Trinity compels me to seek that beauty and power in all of the cosmos and in every religious tradition. It seems to me a kind of blasphemy to constrain the power we name as Christ only within a Christian church, as if the infinity of love could tie itself to a narrow lineage of thought and history. Christ laid on us only one commandment, that we love one another. But imprisoned and wounded by the difficulties of life, we find this the most impossible of all. Instead, we throw up any number of obligations: to believe a certain way, to hold certain political views, to uphold particular moral positions, and so on. This impulse to despise ourselves and one another is so deeply rooted in our religions that we forget that nothing that forms us in hatred has anything genuinely religious in it. These impulses, even—or especially—when inculcated by Christianity itself, are only more wounds, more signs of the bondage that holds us so far away from our capacity for compassion. Perhaps reflecting on the interior dynamics of bondage and liberation will help remind us that there is only one freedom and one command and they are the same: to know ourselves beloved of God and to allow that love to flow within and through us toward all the world.

The nature of mind is a mystery that neither theology nor science dissolves for understanding. Perhaps some of the images and ideas that follow may be useful to conceive of the depth and self-contradictions of our minds as we consider ways we are bound and ways we can become free.

1

Wounded by True Love

Desire for Things Lost

What is the soul of a man [sic]. . . . It's nothing but a burning light.
Traditional Folk Song

And so it is that all things must desire, must yearn for, must love the Beautiful and the Good . . . each bestirs itself and all are stirred to do and to will whatever it is they do and will because of the yearning for the Beautiful and the Good. And we may be so bold as to claim also that . . . the divine longing is the Good seeking good for the sake of the Good. That yearning which creates all the goodness of the world preexisted superabundantly within the Good and did not allow it to remain without issue.
Pseudo-Dionysius, "The Divine Names"

That we are but incarnate flames of desire is well known to anonymous folk singers and anonymous desert ascetics alike. Plato, too, recognizes desire as a fundamental power of the soul. In the *Symposium* he weaves a ladder integrating "earthly" Aphrodite with the "heavenly" Aphrodite that allows the soul to ascend to direct tasting of beauty and to descend to the companionship of friends at a drinking party. In the *Phaedrus* desire is what enables the soul to feast on truth. Desire culminates in an intoxicated longing for beauty itself. Throughout the dialogues, desire moves back and forth from heaven to earth, tasting the Good Beyond Being even as it perambulates through the world of dinner parties, flirtations, political intrigue, and prison cells. Augustine describes desire as a weight that draws our hearts more irresistibly than gravity draws our bodies. Will power is weak against the force of desire. If we wish to change what we do, we must change what we desire. The power of desire is such that only a stronger desire can displace desire.[1] Noticing that our temporary satiations seem only to inflame our restlessness, Augustine follows Plato in identifying desire with a longing to possess the Good forever.[2] For him it is only the Good itself that can calm and satisfy desire: "Our hearts find no peace until they rest in you."[3] For him, much of our misery is bound up in the power of small desires to obscure our great desire.

What is this desire that afflicts us with a merciless restlessness and the torment of insatiable thirst? A lover tantalizingly beyond reach may be a happy fate for figures on a Grecian urn, but for those of us who live, the goad of desire leaves us instead

> . . . a heart high-sorrowful and cloy'd,
> A burning forehead, and a parching tongue.[4]

Beyond every enjoyment, which becomes wearying even in its possession or whose loss is foreshadowed in the relentlessness of death, the heart longs to consummate its desire with the sweetness of unending happiness. But unending life is not our fate; neither does the world dedicate itself to our happiness. We are not reconciled to life as it is given to us: full of boredom and trivialities that stun the spirit, anguish we cannot digest, pleasures we cherish but cannot hold. Our actual experience and our capacities for understanding or satisfaction remain achingly incommensurate. Desire resides in this gap. Desire is a light in us, a "burning light" that cannot be completely extinguished. Desire is the great seal on our souls, marking where we have been "oned" with God in the instant of our creation.[5] This oneing has nothing to do with the peculiarities of our individual lives, our particular hopes and longings, the afflictions and misfortunes we suffer. "Caught up in this world of many things," we seem to have wandered far from this "precious oneing."[6] But however far we seem to have wandered, desire is the beautiful, scathing brand that reminds us who we are and to whom we belong. This desire does not live on the surface of our minds, waxing and waning with particular wants and needs. It is the core and substance of our existence, the warp of our lives that stretches us from heaven to earth. We weave the particularities of our lives against this warp, and in this way the sacred and the profane, the ordinary and the holy, become one cloth and one flesh.

There are a million or more ways to wrestle with the nature of personhood or the peculiarities of our minds or the difficulties of our fate. Desire is the clue we will be tracking here. We will begin by looking at the way people sing of the poignant yearning that undergirds desire. Thinking about all of the ordinary things people long for opens us to a memory of the depth and mystery of our hearts, because we long not only for this or that thing but for happiness itself, for wisdom, and for love that abides. This kind of desire, which the things of the world do not completely satisfy, also tells us something about ourselves. When we look at leaves on trees, they appear to us green and lovely, but when the sun hits them just right, they glint like stars fallen to earth. Desire is like this. Surging underneath our ordinary desires is a brilliant desire that makes us glisten like stars. Beginning with folk music, we will listen to the testimony of philosophers and poets, some famous and some anonymous, who witness to the bitterness and sweetness of desire.

THE TESTIMONY OF FOLK MUSIC

Like philosophy, folk music is aware of different kinds of desire: for goods in life, for goods beyond life, desires that are harmful, desires that are nourishing. But I suspect that beginning with a categorization of desire would be misleading. The feeling tone that underlies the varieties of actual desires is that of longing. Longing is the motion of the heart toward that which it does not or cannot possess. Our deepest desires are not always known to us, but our longings are their light footsteps in the snow. If we follow them carefully, we might be led deeper into the hidden structures of our heart. It is the phenomenon of longing itself that will lead us. The CD that was formulated to accompany this writing was conceived as a way to convey the actual matter of longing in a way that writing can rarely do.[7] Longing is rooted in the heart, and music speaks much more directly to the heart than words can. Admittedly, not everyone is moved by "roots" music, but the haunting melodies of such songs carry the memory of that "burning light" in us much more directly than any of these words of mine.

Desire for Home, Community, and Love

We want to be happy, but life heaps difficulties on us. Folk music constantly rehearses this enduring, intolerable reality. Because of the vitality of our sexuality, we are condemned to the "Magdalene Laundries," prisoners of endless penitence.[8] A war we know nothing about steals our husband or severs our limbs. The coal company steals our land, and the court system allows it. Our babies die. We want the difficulties of life to make sense, but no particular significance or ultimate meaning can be read off of pain. Most of us have lived within some religious system that gives accounts of these things. But the intensity of our loves and the claims of mortality break efforts toward coherence. The shattering of coherence and the ache of loss are expressed in folk songs simply as longing:

Hame, hame, hame; hame would I be;
Hame, hame, hame, in my own country;
Where the birch and the pine
And the bonnie rowan tree,
They are all blooming fair
In my own country.[9]

Did this Scot leave his home for a job? Was he exiled for a political crime? Did she cross the ocean looking for a better life? Did he beat a hasty retreat when he found he had gotten his girlfriend pregnant? We do not need to know any of these things in order for the poignancy of melody and word to trigger the ache in our own souls. Whatever power cleaved the narrator from home, yearning is like a hemorrhage, bleeding a longing that cannot be stanched. There is something, some place or memory, where the "heart will e're remain." But the heart must remain forever exiled from its home.

There is a place of rest for this anguished heart, but that place is not available. It is known and felt only by the inexorable distance of time and space. Yet no matter how far one wanders or however long one tarries, there will be a glint of light that will "shine upon them yet—in my own country." It is not a mere fantasy or bauble that has captured this heart. It is something real and lovely, "blooming fair," that continues to bless others, if not oneself. Seeing, in one's mind's eye, that glint that yet shines upon them soothes and intensifies the yearning. The solidarity of souls makes it possible to take comfort in knowing, even feeling, that this precious thing exists and is enjoyed by others. But it also keeps alive the sharpness of yearning: we feel the exile all the more because we cannot dismiss it or doubt it. We feel rootedness of those who remain behind. We feel the wind on their cheeks carrying the scent of heather. We know the preciousness of "home" because we feel it through the experience of others. Deep, deep down, our souls are all knit together, and we cannot go so far astray that this solidarity is completely broken. However far beneath our conscious experience, awareness of the preciousness of home remains alive because we are connected to others who have not lost their home. Or so it seems to desire.

Empirically, not everyone longs for home; some long just as fiercely to get away from home. The tenderness of a folk song does not arise only from nostalgia about how wonderful everything is back home. Whatever the particularities from which this nostalgic longing arises, it continues to wound our hearts because it is also nostalgia for something no one has ever experienced. It sinks into that place where we recognize ourselves as "wayfaring strangers, traveling through this world of woe." Yearning makes us all sojourners, like all of our ancestors (Ps. 39). Our actual solidarity is with all of homeless humanity. It is desire that connects us to something beyond experience. Desire insists that it has some memory, some hint or clue, some incontrovertible evidence of a light glinting through darkness that shines on our heart's home. It is there, precious and perfect, even if we must remain exiled from it.

Home is only one of the icons desire puts before us to give concreteness to inchoate longings. Although actual communities are filled to overflowing with strife, harshness, absurdities, trivialities, injustices, violence, pettiness, and so on, folk music continuously mourns the loss of community. Many folk songs express anxiety about being a "stranger." Again, this is not just about the empirical anxiety of being in a new place. We long to be known and recognized. We want to be "seen." There is something chilling about being a stranger to those around one: to be invisible to one's own family, to be unseen by society. There is a sense in which we hardly exist without recognition. There is also a sense in which we remain strangers throughout our lives even to those who love us most.[10]

This longing for eyes that see us and faces that recognize us is desire's insistence that the communion of saints is not a fantasy but our actual condition. We feel the solitariness of life so poignantly because desire insists that communion is available to us. There is an unbreakable circle that undergirds the losses of life. One of the dominant images I have run across in Appalachian music is the reconstitution of family and community "on the other shore." "Here in the Vineyard of Our Lord" illustrates this as well as any.[11] It begins with a sturdy appreciation of living, and laboring in the vineyard of the Lord continues to describe the faithful worship and loyalty to God.

But this song of praise is interrupted by the plaintive concern that, though we are faithfully reading, singing, praying, our hearts remain "deeply wounded." Praise is interrupted by recognition that even the "ransomed church of God" is severed by death. The little community that gives us solace in the midst of life's troubles is itself torn up by the implacable claims of mortality. Desire moves into the breach: the deep wound even the "faithful" receive is not mortal. Desire conjures a picture of a community that does not meet only to be severed, but sings "one sweet chord forever." This is not everybody's fantasy of everlasting bliss, but it is an image through which we try to fill the gap between the communities we actually experience and those our soul craves.

A third example of desire's refusal to accept the limitations of life is probably the most familiar. Songs about falling in love, being betrayed by love, losing love, betraying love, feeling divided over lovers, aging with one's beloved seem more plentiful than any other kind of song. The intensity of feeling that can rise up between lovers makes it the preeminent example of desire in Western culture.

And if I live to see next spring
Ain't gonna laugh at any old thing
Gonna save up all my jokes and tales
And I won't tell a one while your gone
'Til I'm there with you in any old place
And I see your smile and touch your face
Saving my tales for you, my heart for you
I'll be waiting for you to come home, waiting for you to come home.[12]

This may not be the stuff of high tragedy, but most of our longing and losses are not. They are as invisible and as unbearable as this cotton farmer's love for someone gone away. Her absence could last until next fall, through winter, through next spring. Where is she that she is gone for so long and for such an indeterminate length of time? We know nothing about it. We only know he is saving everything until she is back. The best he has to offer her, his jokes and tales, are dormant without her. Everything precious is for her, and it is nothing in her absence. Love can be like that: life is flat when the beloved is gone. Everything that seemed significant and fine turns to ashes. Maybe this is why the plight of lovers is so often the icon of all desire, especially the desire for God. More than other desires, that between lovers connects us to the fire within us, melts our ego boundaries, and possesses the urgency of life and death. The divine image in us is fire, and lovers imitate it with particular verisimilitude.

Folk songs are about concrete desires: home, family, congregation, a beloved. This is part of what makes them carry the feeling of longing. Longing aches for some particular loss or absence. We can recognize the sweetness and bitterness of desire in its particular objects. But longing does not empty into its objects. I do not mean that the anguish of lost home, community, or love is not intense and entirely real. These longings stir a dream-like memory of desire and pain that exists beyond actual, particular desires and a structure of desire that is not limited by objects of any sort. Desire for particular things is intense because its taproot is infinite desire.

There is a river of yearning, carried as much by the melodies as by the words, that runs deeper than any particular longing. These songs, in all of their particularity, are at the same time the faint trace of some other barely heard, scarcely remembered tune. They evoke some half-remembered "trip to Bountiful" where we were loved and surrounded by a peaceful, beautiful land. Such a memory is not rooted in our actual experience. Abused or orphaned children can long for a mother they never had; their hearts "remember" that the absence of a caring mother is a deprivation. Refugees or mall children can feel, even if they cannot know, that to be raised without a culture, community, or roots is to be defrauded of something crucial. The degree to which any life receives the things it needs to flourish varies enormously, but in no life is experience adequate to desire. This memory is not nostalgia for something we humans experience, either individually or corporately. It is desire, ever needy, ever resourceful: desire for the impossibility of happiness.[13]

Desire and Death

Folk songs are about particular longings. But over the edge of the horizon against which the objects of desire recede lies the world's final answer to all desire: death. The human mind does not tolerate this answer amicably. Acceptance that the soul which animates the body dies when the body dies has not been typical of human cultures. What becomes of this animation is not known or agreed on: ongoing existence in a dark, shadowy underworld; reincarnation; salvation by grace; continuing presence in nature; the tripartite divisions of heaven, purgatory, hell. More recently, this imagery has been dismissed as myth or mystification, even criminalized, as in totalitarian regimes in the Soviet Union or China. It is not part of the purpose of these reflections to take a position on what becomes of this animating force upon the body's death. But the ubiquity of images and appeals to heavenly rest, happiness, and communion suggests that ordinary objects do not have the capacity to express all of the complexities of desire. "There'll be no more crying/dying there." This is the promise that concludes the book of Revelation: our crying and dying will end in a new heaven and new earth. God will dwell with the people and will "wipe every tear from their eyes./Death shall be no more" (Rev. 21:4). That the two things which most universally mark our condition are felt to be the most alien is an astonishing paradox and not without its dangers. Liberation theology is born in contexts not only of great oppression but also of religious indifference to suffering. People will die anyway. It is the work of the church to look after their *spirits*. This is only one example of the political pliancy of eschatological imagery and belief. But this danger does not make them go away. They remain with us, as they have for tens of thousands of years, in part as clues to the desires of the human heart. If we think of heavenly imagery as the poetry of great desire, and not only as the opium of oppressed persons, something of the brilliance of the human soul may appear before us.

Christianity, in its folk music and in its classical theologies, employs a strong duality to talk about our destiny and our nature. Heaven is above; the earth below. In heaven there is no dying or crying. Earth is a "barren land," a "prison" from which we will "fly away." It is a "weary land," a world of "trouble and sorrow here below." While we live in exile from our true home, we are "pilgrims" and "strangers"; we are "climbing up the rough side of the mountain." This duality of heaven and earth is a misleading emphasis in Christianity. To the extent that "heaven" is portrayed almost exclusively in the future tense, it conceals the way heaven is intrinsically woven to earth at every minute.

Yet these are images from the songs black people and white people have sung to describe something about their experience. Folk traditions come out of communities where the rawness of suffering and oppression is immediate and unconcealed. Crying and dying cannot be easily postponed or disguised. The dualism of these songs is in part a beautifully courageous tenacity in the face of life's difficulties; it is a way of testifying to something about the human being that is not reducible to suffering and death. But courage to endure in the midst of suffering begins with the unadorned fact of suffering.[14] Classical theology and reform liturgy justifies rather than encounters suffering. Before suffering can speak or cry out, it has been steamrolled by an aggressive theology of sin and guilt. By contrast, folk songs, both secular and religious, testify to suffering as a fundamental condition of human life. In this they are more ruthlessly honest than classical theology. In "Sweet Sunny South," both the words and a mournful tune carry knowledge of death's irreversible power:

> And I know that the faces and forms I have loved
> Now lie in the cold mossy ground;
> But still I'll return to the place of my birth
> For the children have played round the floor.
> And I know that no matter how long I may live
> They will echo their footsteps no more.[15]

The poignancy of a song like "Sweet Sunny South" contrasts with a greater level of intensity when the visceral horror of death is set out in conversation with death personified:[16]

> O yes, I've come for to git your soul
> Take your body and leave it cold.
> I'll drop the flesh from off'n your frame
> The earth and worms both have their claim. . . .
> O Death, O Death please give me time, to fix my heart, to change my mind.
> Your heart is fixed and your mind is bound
> And I have the shackles to drag you down.

Death and catastrophe can come in an instant. "Come all ye tenderhearted," begins another song, telling the story of a mother who crosses over a hundred yards or so to the next cabin to borrow some liniment, but on her return finds her own cabin in flames:

> She cried, O lord my babies are gone and I'm the one to blame.
> She cried, Alas they sleep wrapped up in a red hot flame.

She bursted all asunder and the flames roared over her head.
Their little bones laid on the ground.
They both laid face to face,
Each other did entwine, each other did embrace.[17]

These are not the words of fantasy and wish fulfillment, or of pathological guilt and unworthiness. Their juxtaposition to songs about heaven suggest that the image of heaven does not simply pass over the realities of life. In them a "myth of punishment" has not rendered suffering inarticulate and alien to anything Christianity has to say about life, death, or the work of Christ. The courage to acknowledge the ferocity of suffering and to bring this knowledge directly into Christian life is a great gift to our understanding of Christianity's capacity to speak to the disorder of life. But they also give one some sense of why a counterbalancing image of reality is called for. The brutality of life experience is qualified by the sweetness of life "beyond." Whether songs make cheerful promises that we will soon meet our Savior or they mournfully await "the gospel train [that] is coming and don't you want to go, and leave this world of sorrow and trouble here below?"[18] they provide an antidote to the suffering by looking to another world where suffering comes to an end.

But hope can be thin gruel if its promises can nourish us only when we die. However intense the desire for a life without suffering, dying seems a high price to get it. "Everybody wants to go to heaven, but nobody wants to die." Someplace between the testimony to suffering and the longing to be free from suffering is a firm desire to *live*. I wonder if these songs touch the taproot of desire not primarily as a hope for reward but because they tell us part of the story about what is happening right now. How is it that I, a miserable, bad-tempered nobody, could imagine that the most sublime and universal power of all reality would have anything to do with me? I cannot be "welcomed home" so enthusiastically by my Savior if he is not cheering me on, loving me, strengthening me *right now*. The delight my Savior has in me tells me a great deal about who I am.

These songs about dying are mostly about living, about how we "go from day to day." They are about who we are right now. The hope is not all ahead; the hope is the actual experience of "holding to God [Her] mighty hand." Right now, right here, we know that Christ will "walk around my bedside": when I am praying, when I am sick, as well as when I am dying. This present tense is about ways everyday life is knit with divine power. But nostalgia for a different life is also a way of resisting the identity that affliction and persecution stamp upon me. Suffering is not only pain; it is also a name we are forced to bear. Affliction gives us the names "Not Pitied" and "Not my people" (Hos. 1:6, 9). I must bear the pain and the identity suffering inflicts on me. My heart is "sorely wounded." My boss is a sadist; my children, stolen. The world holds up a mirror to me, and I look ravaged, black circles are under my eyes; I look haunted and empty. The world tells me I am a worthless cracker, a nothing woman, an impotent sharecropper. I take all of that into myself, and I hate the person I am who has inexplicably invited and deserved this treatment. I take in all of the ugliness of the human form: oppressed, mistreated, cruel, enraged, terrorized, greedy, weak, ignorant, disfigured, contorted by pain, remorseless. It flows right back out of me as my own paralysis, self-loathing, and hatred. But when I hear these songs and when I sing them in my kitchen or as lullabies to my children, something else flickers in me. I know myself as more than all of these distortions. I may not be able to believe it as deeply as I believe the other things, at least not yet. But it flickers in me like a dimly burning wick that will not be quenched (Isa. 42:3). My "real" identity may be concealed in the future tense, "in the sky, Lord, in the sky." But I know that real identity is part of me right now.

Pictures of heaven are among the root symbols of our desires, and our desires have to do with who we are while alive on this earth. One of the deepest components of the desire to be happy is a desire to know ourselves to be *worthy* of happiness. Augustine, Luther, and their brethren believed our deep poison was the sin of pride. But I suspect that deeper than any pride we suffer is the anguished uncertainty that we deserve happiness. History tells those on its "underside" how worthless and impotent they are. But those who dwell in history's penthouse apartments carry the worm of self-doubt within them as well. We require the trappings of wealth and power because it is too hard to believe that permanent, stable, inexhaustible happiness belongs to us. One reads of executives arrested for their illegal activities. One, hired to create ways of concealing debt, pleads innocent. The deeds to his half-dozen houses are confiscated; his many million dollars, frozen; his passport, taken. The bosses that hired him, praised him, and rewarded him turn state's evidence. He faces decades in federal prison, yet brilliant as he is, he refuses to cooperate. How could he cooperate? Surely he would cease to exist altogether if he conceded. These folk songs have another story. Nothing the world can do to us changes who we are: beautiful jewels, friends of Christ, flames of happiness.

DESIRE WITHIN AND BEYOND THE WORLD

Christianity often describes the movements of desire in terms that are denigrating to the world. The desire for heaven is "good," but there is something wrong with the world and something wrong with us that we desire its fruits so fervently. Churches often encourage us to orient our desires to God, who alone can satisfy them and to eternal life that is the only "time" when they can be satisfied. The moralistic insistence that we desire only God and eternal life can be quite unhelpful. It tends to carry a misleading interpretation of our nature and our desire. It is also a terrible distortion of the sacred and holy mystery that dwells beyond being and pervades all that is. The representation of heaven and earth as opposing objects of desire is false but contains a crucial insight. There are ways of inhabiting desire that are deeply harmful to ourselves, the world, and one another.

Desire within the World: The Unsatisfactory Character of the Goods of the World

The restlessness of desire does not come from any poverty of goods offered by the world. The heart pours itself out toward the infinite variety of experiences through which we come into relationship with the world. Our senses call us outward toward the world's physical beauty and order—to food, sounds, and pleasure. The interesting things presented to us by our senses invite further exploration. We discipline our understanding to respond to a world that endlessly confronts us with possibilities and dangers. Every culture shapes and trains reason so that it can more or less successfully engage its environment. But the need to attend simply to physical survival hardly dents the capacities of reason. Those dimensions of the environment that are accessible to our senses and minds are intertwined with dimensions that impinge on our awareness but defy understanding. We can trace our heritage back generations, but how did it begin? Where did the world come from; why does it exist? We see the flesh rot off the bones of people we knew, but what became of their animating spirit? Why do people act so foolishly? What possesses us to go to war? Why do the stars move the way they do? We want to understand as well as survive, but the cosmos does not explain itself. We fill the breach with stories, myths, holy writings, science, rituals, philosophies. But with all of these things presented by sense, mind, and tradition, desire remains unsatisfied.

We extend our encounter with the world beyond sense and mind, beyond survival, and we create symbols through our creativity. The great artists of every culture magnificently testify to the range of the human spirit as it shapes sounds, colors, movements, and ideas. Creativity allows us to deepen our awareness and expressions of the loveliness and agonies we experience. But creativity is just as much a part of all of us as are sensing and thinking. We make something new when we modify a biscuit recipe, hang a door just right, or discover how to calm a child's nightmares. Human beings engage the world through the million ways we can imagine what does not exist and then make it exist. When work becomes drudgery, a terrible calamity has befallen the human soul. Through our creativity, life is brightened by novelty and beauty. And yet, as much as creativity sweetens life, it does not put an end to desire's poverty.

The itinerary of desire peregrinates into chambers of heart and mind opened by personal and social relationships. Through these relationships, we become human ourselves. Every form of love, as it is present or distorted or absent, offers itself to desire: that of siblings, family members, mothers, children, soul sisters, friends, colleagues, fellow citizens, companions, neighbors, kinfolk, teachers, lovers, spouses, co-religionists and so on. Beyond the relationships of intimacy are those that connect us to larger chunks of society and culture: clubs, tribes, neighborhoods, political groups, artistic groups, denominations, ethnicities, gender, countries, regions, humanity. All of these relationships can give us great joy. But they do not quench desire.

When we try to understand ways in which desire for things in the world is unsatisfying, we must remember how beautiful the world is and how rich and lovely are the goods that reside in the world. We love the things in the world, yet inevitably everything in the world betrays us: everything is subject to the laws of death and change. "All people are grass, / and their constancy is like the flower of the field. / The grass withers, the flower fades" (Isa. 40:6–7).

Augustine berates himself for grieving so inordinately at his mother's death. But how can love of one another and love of life itself be "inordinate"?[19] We love not as creatures destined for death, but as beautiful, immortal souls that could not possibly die. Should our love be more restrained? More tepid? We desire happiness, but we suffer; we desire life, but we die. It is as if we somehow landed on the wrong planet, one alien to our nature. We complain deep inside ourselves, as if we were all characters in Kafka's novel *The Trial*. We have been wrongly accused. We are innocent. We are not the sort of people who should be convicted and executed. Something is terribly wrong.

The inordinate strength of our love of the things in the world takes on a different face when we think of trying to satisfy this love. A consumer culture is an oversized example of the misery brought about by an effort to still desire with possessions. In the decades since the end of World War II, the wealth of most Americans has dramatically increased. TVs, cars, dishwashers, and so on have become virtually essential items in every household. New and better ones are essential to anyone who can afford them. Plastic toys are cheap and readily available; they grow in our houses like mold. We are surrounded by astonishingly useless things that promise beauty, love, security, happy families, lovely homes, sex appeal, national pride, and every other major and minor good.

Yet these promises are accompanied by stress relievers necessary to cope with the physical consequences of anxiety, pollution, and depression. We suffer as a culture from a pathological refusal to notice the ways in which this way of life is destructive of our own society, other societies, and the natural world itself. Polluted water and air, decimated environments, disappearing species, disappearing cultures, the generation of poverty, the use of repression, even war are necessary to continue the flow of cheap goods.

The world offers us an unending variety of material and nonmaterial goods: life, creativity, understanding, wisdom, love, community, spiritual practice, pleasure, beauty, zest, novelty. But still the heart hungers for more time with a beloved, a greater variety of pleasures, peace with others, peace of mind, more and better friends, more exciting discoveries and entertainments, better sciences, and so on. We want deeper understanding, fresher beauties, sweeter honors: the heart hungers for something more than all the world and a new pair of skates.

Desire is insatiable not because the goods of the world are too few, too uniform, or too bland. Desire burns through the goods of the world, even though these goods are not false or intrinsically unsatisfactory. The dissatisfaction of desire arises from desire itself; it cannot be satisfied with any finite thing or even an infinite number of finite things, and the attempt to achieve satisfaction can be destructive. Desire is not like physical hunger. There is a correlation or proportion between physical hunger and its satisfaction: one hungers, then eats, then is satisfied (until later). Desire is simply desire. It yearns, but it never eats; it delights in things but is never satisfied. It might be thought that desire turns to heaven because it discovers that the earth is a meretricious fraud. But desire does not so easily despair of the world. It has as its companion a desire beyond the world, a desire expressed in religious symbols and hopes.

Desire Beyond the World

Desire shatters the economy of things; it disputes the tyranny of objects. IT longs for the great emptiness, which is beauty and love without limitation. Christians call this "God" because we need some word to specify our desire. But any name draws desire back into the economy of objects and is therefore both an expression and a violation of desire. In this deeper dimension of desire we are carried from the beautiful, wonderful things of the world to realities that do not have a direct "earthly" manifestation. When desire begins to thirst for more than the world can directly offer, it does not have to leave or reject the world; it simply goes in more deeply. As desire concentrates its powers, it recognizes the two-fold beauty of the earth. The world is filled with familiar goods and difficulties that we all know. It is good in and for itself even with its hardships. The world is also an opening, a sacrament of something beyond itself. The world is both itself and a doorway to the Divine Eros. A yearning for something "beyond the world" has the paradoxical character of being both a renunciation and an intensification of desire. Or rather, renunciation *is* an intensification of desire.

A crass example may provide an analogy. A hard-drinking, girl-chasing fraternity boy, much to his surprise, falls in love. He renounces the pleasures of nightly carousing with his buddies for time with his beloved. He renounces the pleasures of seduction for the joy of intimacy. He renounces the self-perception that construed his drinking and carousing as emblems of success and allows a different sense of himself to emerge. These renunciations may invite ridicule from his buddies. They may see the change in their friend as a sacrifice of the things the world so freely offers. But his renunciation is an intensification of and deepening of the human capacity for joy and happiness. The awakening of desire "beyond the world" may or may not require a renunciation of a way of life. It may or may not involve changes in habits of eating, drinking, loving, or working. But it will involve a deepening capacity for joy. Weaving desire for and delight in the things of this earth together with desire for the deeper dimensions of reality illuminates the things of this world in a way that makes our enjoyment of them richer.

Desire for reality, for the mystery creation speaks when it sings out, "I am not God, but God made me" is intrinsic to desire.[20] It pulses out of the divine image in us. But it is known to us through the mediations of religious traditions. Convents, monasteries, lay orders, retreat houses, fasting, good works, prayer, meditation, and study are examples of how religions set aside ways of life for those who experience this quickening of desire. But the desire for reality is by no means restricted to those with obvious religious vocations.

The difficulty in reflecting on this dimension of desire is that it does not have a clearly defined object, although it seems to burn brighter and brighter as particular objects are burned away. "Reality" is at once too bland and too bold to say much about this new dimension of desire. Desire's most passionate pull is by "something" that lacks any face or word that conveys what it is. The Holy of Holies is empty. It is approached only through the symbols, traditions, wisdom, distortions, practices, and philosophies of the world's religions. These are quite various. Our desire and our knowledge, such as it is, is shaped by the tradition we inherit. It is our traditions that give us some language for orienting our desire. Without these traditions, desire is like an arrow shot with enormous power but without much direction. Traditions enable us to speak together about this desire and to find ways to live more deeply into this desire.

Reality is beyond being, beyond word and concept, but we pursue it with mind and emotion, with word and concept, and in communities that are flawed and limited. Desire lives at this border, fed by the tradition in which it finds itself and pushing beyond it. If it is lucky, it will fly back and forth along this border, drinking the wisdom of tradition and entering the silence that cannot be called back into words. But religious traditions are sometimes tempted to stand in for the Holy of Holies, forgetting that Holy Mystery is represented by emptiness, by crucifixion and an empty tomb. Under these circumstances, it is easy for desire to be caught like a bird in a net, its wings fouled and twisted, no longer free to cross back and forth between silence and word. Desire may also find itself so amputated from tradition and community that it wanders in a void with nothing to orient it, to shape or discipline it. Desire must find ways to navigate its bitter and sweet paradox: it moves toward but also always through and beyond every object, including the objects presented by religious traditions.

Noticing how desire attaches to things within and beyond the world in ways that can be destructive invites us to conceive of a different way of desiring. That is, the problem with desire is not that it desires the wrong objects: the problem is that it relinquishes its erotic structure for the economy of possession. Desire, ever restless, ever yearning, ever hopeful, does not seek heaven to still its lust for pleasure eternally and completely. It does not stoically await paradise. It desires to live and to love the earth. Holy desire, radiating from the divine image, does not need to pass beyond the world. Wisdom protects desire from the illusions that binds us to things, in hopes they will be an antidote to our misery. Desire within the world neither rejects nor attaches to the goods of the world. It delights in them as they are: lovely, perishable, temporary, replete with faults. Desire, in love with impossibility, enables us to see creation as it really is: living and open, always lit by the beauty and compassion of God.

When the goods of the world are recognized for what they are, they neither hold the key to our happiness nor require rejection or hatred. Desire does not pass beyond the goods of the world but inhabits them without attachment. God approves of the gift of the littlest angel, the rough box containing a butterfly wing or a white stone, because it contains the things of the world. It is the emblem of the beautiful, perishing world that God, in the person of Her Christ, will love and also regretfully have to leave.[21] This is the poignant joy of desire within the world: loving what must inevitably perish.

This holy desire is betrayed by the suffering the world also inflicts. We human beings are too fragile to bear up under the painfulness of life. The power to keep the holy fire of desire lighting and delighting in the goods of the world but not attaching to them is weak in us. Psyche answered the call of Eros and threw herself into the void where Eros could catch her. Eros enabled Psyche to travel beyond the border of the possible. From the time she threw herself into nothingness at the sound of his voice, through all of the tribulations inflicted by Aphrodite, Eros held open the space between what was and what, impossibly, could be. Because Psyche possessed the courage to live in that open space, she gave birth to Joy. Desire is this absurdity that holds open the infinity of possibility. Ever optimistic, ever resourceful, desire tells us what it sees as it speeds ahead on its divine wings. What we cannot see, desire describes, and then it goads us to travel on until we have given birth to Joy.[22]

It is hard for us to follow the way of Psyche. The power to maintain a delight in the world without demanding that it satisfy desire is weak in us. Psyche answered the call of Eros, but this leap beyond what we see and touch and know is terrifying and dangerous. We tend to cling with all of our might to the roots and scrabble of rocks at the edge of the abyss. We want anything but to fall in. One more box of building blocks, one more good deed, one more night out, one more, one more—"one more" will stay the hand of the executioner who would shove us into that abyss. Terror and pain are heavy burdens. It is hard to be lifted by Eros's wings when we are so heavy laden.

"THE BUSH WAS BURNING BUT WAS NOT CONSUMED"

The earth itself, the cosmos in all of its unending beauty, cannot contain reality or satisfy desire's thirst. Thousands of years of wisdom and revelation hardly dent the mystery distinguished as "religious." The inadequacy of the cosmos and of religion to our desire is not their flaw but their immense beauty. The economy of proportionality, correlation, of *possession* is not the economy of desire. Reality does not empty into anything; it is not ever finished or complete. Drawn to reality, desire lives in the world and loves the world and the wisdom of its traditions, yet constantly moves beyond these things. But desire is not destitution; it is not homeless wandering. Desire, precisely by *not* possessing what it desires, is infinitely more deeply connected to its beloved. Relationship to any object is by its nature superficial; it cannot touch us deeply. To the extent that other people become objects of our needs, fears, and longings, our relationship to them is likewise limited. In desiring beyond the world we do not desire a different object or even a different kind of object. Nor do we desire "unselfishly." What we desire is not an object of any sort, and holy desire is not the sort of thing that desires objects, even holy ones. The infinity of personhood expands to the infinity of goodness; the more sweetly it is quenched, the more insatiably it thirsts. "Love attracts love. But my love is not even a drop in the ocean. To love you as you love me, I must borrow your own love—it is the only way which will satisfy my desire."[23] Desire flows to desire and from desire. As it moves within and beyond the world, the bonds of desire to what it loves cannot be severed. This is the intoxicating sweetness of intimacy on which desire feeds. Desire carries us beyond the objects that can be possessed to an intimacy that is possible when this structure of object and possession has been left behind.

The great beauty that is ourself is drawn to the great beauty that is God, just as a roe is drawn to water in the desert. With nothing but our thirst to guide us, we who have "been scorned and 'buked'" walk past and through the beauties of the desert always onward toward the Great Beauty. This beauty beyond all knowing and naming pulls us out of ourselves and toward ourselves and in doing so pulls us most intimately and scathingly toward the world. It is impossible to be drawn to the beauty of Christ without entering more vividly into the beauty of everything else.

The emptiness of all form, name, order, structure, or image that is the Great Beauty reminds us to hold lightly all of our names for it. As images of the Great Beauty, we, too, are empty of name and form, order and structure. Entering this holy emptiness, we go toward the beauty of God and toward the beauty of all of God's beloveds: everything that is. It is the unquenchable luminosity of our being that we thirst. In our thirst we are images of the power that thirsts for the beauty of every existing thing. In our emptiness we unite with all beings, like streams that mingle underground, even while the desert above makes them appear separate.

In our affluence and boredom, in our suffering and deceptions, we must always remember who we are: flames of Christ. But this memory is hard to revive. Our beauty has been betrayed before we ever knew we possessed it, and it is a weary journey to recover from this mischance. Consciousness is like an endlessly deep ravine, almost all of it obscured from us. We are often tempted to believe that the roles we play in society and family, or our reason, will, and emotion, are all of us. But these are usually only the last traces of ourselves before we dive into the deep; they are as often as not deceiving masks rather than true portraits. It is the wisdom of Buddhism to know that our normal condition is one of illusion. It is the wisdom of Christianity to understand that we are so wounded we do not know who we are. So it is as deluded and wounded lovers of Christ that we follow our hearts desire.

2

"Knit and Oned to God"

A Christian Story of Bondage and Transformation

> We were all created at the same time: and in our creation we were knit and oned to God. By this we are kept as luminous and noble as when we were created. By the force of this precious oneing we love, seek, praise, thank and endlessly enjoy our Creator.
>
> *Julian of Norwich*, Showings

Desire testifies to the divine image in us and to the great and precious beauty that is in us and cannot be blotted out. Yet it remains our nature to suffer and to fantasize about freedom from suffering. A great deal of cultural life, certainly the bulk of consumer culture and much of religion, gives us fantasy as meat and drink. We are told that if we buy enough things or believe the correct things, our suffering will cease. We long to be free from suffering, and we eat this advice like candy. But our longings are not satisfied, our sufferings do not decrease. Suffering and the overwhelming desire to be free from suffering cloud our senses and our minds. But we long not only for relief. We also long to know who we are. We long for beauty that is not meretricious and for love that does not betray us. There survives in us human beings a desperate desire for truth. This desire is a burning light in us. It is the image of God in us. It is that part of us that cannot be destroyed or tarnished, although it can be hidden. This book is testimony to that desire.

Like all beings gifted with any degree of sentience, we suffer. The good suffer along with the bad; the weak, with the strong; the young, with the old. We flee this fact in our lives and we justify it in our theologies, but it remains a foundational truth of our experience. Because we cannot bear the omnipresence, tyranny, and unfairness of suffering, we are compelled to find relief in fantasy. We distract ourselves in a thousand different ways: work, alcohol, exercise, busyness, entertainment, dogmatic beliefs, moralism. Christianity has taught us we suffer because we have fallen into sin and that at some level, our sufferings are justified. Like the abused and traumatized, we feel guilty for suffering inflicted upon us. Guilt is, perhaps, less intolerable than awareness that we inhabit a cosmos in which we are deeply and fundamentally vulnerable no matter what we do. But theologies of cosmic guiltiness are also fantasies that obscure the horrific reality that suffering cannot be justified. At the same time, while this guiltiness may preserve God's honor, it disguises from us the infinitely sweet and unstained depths of divine love.

In fleeing the reality of our situation in fantasy, we are like Ged, a wizard of Earthsea, who spends much of his life fleeing darkness. But at last he knows that it is only by going *toward* it that he will become free. Setting off in the direction of the darkness that haunts him, his companion asks why they must leave so soon the place they have arrived. Ged responds, "Not soon—late. I have followed too slow. It has found a way to escape me and so doom me. It must not escape me, for I must follow it however far it goes. If I lose it I am lost."[1] We discover both the possibilities of our actual condition and the magnanimity of the Divine Eros by turning toward the truth of suffering, not away from it.

Awareness of how deeply we suffer is possible because it arises out of an intuition of something more fundamental to us. Deeper than the distortions of our lives is a beauty and luminosity that makes suffering seem an utter contradiction to our true nature. This luminosity is known by many names: the image of God, Buddha mind, Atman is Brahman, or, in Lincoln's words, "the angels of our better nature." Each name implies something slightly different about the source and destiny of this luminosity, yet these differences are small compared to the wisdom traditions that share in discerning this deep beauty beneath the appearance of so much suffering and distortion. Suffering seems to us intolerable in part because it comes to us as a betrayal. Against all the evidence of our senses, our history, and our knowledge of the natural world, we experience suffering as something foreign; it seems to us *unfair*. As Simone Weil says, when afflictive suffering penetrates to the heart of even the hardest or most cynical of persons, something cries out in them, "Why am I being hurt?"[2] This indomitable sense of injustice is a barely visible trace of a beauty in us that testifies against any and all justifications of suffering. The implacable voice in us that cries out so piteously and foolishly, "Why am I being hurt?" arises from the image of God in us. Even when it can only be provoked by our own suffering, this cry testifies to the last remnant of awareness that to defile the loveliness of a creature defiles at that very moment the beauty of God. This cry comes from an unstainable luminosity beside which suffering seems like vandalism.

We can begin with that ridiculous cry—Why should we not be hurt when every other creature that ever existed has been hurt?—and track it backwards, through and beyond names and images to the silent mystery that is the fountain of every good. However obscured the divine image may seem, the desire for good—even if it is only the desire that I not be hurt—remains in us like a silver thread that leads us back to genuine self-knowledge. The desire for our own good is the incognito of the holy desire that radiates unceasingly from the divine image. The desire with which our Mother and Lover Christ desires us is the same desire with which we seek whatever we identify as good. But our pitiful, blind eyes do not always recognize in our small and large yearnings or in the restless wandering of our souls a desire for the source of our beauty, the source of our incredible joy. Generally speaking, our desire for good can be separated from the oppressions of pain and pleasure only with enormous difficulty. But Christ's desire for us breathes through this constriction of desire, opening it to yearn toward the *source* of good.

Constricted and ego bound, desire is simply a cry not to be hurt but when it is expanded by the breath of the Divine Eros, it is an intuition of the tender sympathy that binds together every being. The pleasures available to egocentrism and the desperation to be free from suffering are tiny hints of the incomparable delight that is the foundation of our being: our identity with the Beauty Beyond Being that makes us "one flesh" with every creature. The divine image gives rise to a flame of desire that burns without consuming. Its roots are the desire for good, and it arises through all our desires out to the cravings of egocentrism. This flame reaches out toward the world and purifies whatever it touches, never breaking the unity of image and its source. Desire weaves all the dimensions of our life together so that everything becomes holy ground (see Exod. 3:2, 5). In this way, our hatred of suffering becomes a thread back to the source of our deepest joy, and our isolating pleasures open to communion. This flame or thread of desire is understood in a Christian context as the longing of the soul for God. Longing does not remove suffering from our lives, but it can transmute it. Desire weaves together heaven and earth, negating neither but enriching each.

We are bound to countless forms of suffering, but our desire beats against this cage like a bird longing for freedom. These two realities fundamentally condition the experience of being human: suffering and this unstainable good that longs for freedom. Religions attest in their myriad ways to these twin features of our life and try to give some account for our deeply contradictory nature. The reflections here are guided by the Christian version of this story.

DESIRE AND THE CHRISTIAN NARRATIVE: CREATION, FALL, REDEMPTION, AND ESCHATOLOGY

The framework for these reflections is Christian theology, even though the emphasis placed on suffering is less characteristic of much classical Christian thought. To help orient the reader, I will begin by locating the ideas developed in these pages within the structure of a Christian narrative.

The piety and metaphysics of Christianity change dramatically as they are expressed in the theologies of Julian of Norwich, Schleiermacher, Calvin, or Augustine; in the liturgies of AME Baptists, Spanish Inquisitors, early Celtic monasteries, Russian Orthodox of the seventeenth century, Nigerian villages, or affluent Presbyterian congregations; or in the art of Dante, Dostoyevsky, or Giotto. But there is a kind of skeletal structure that can be recognized in Christianity's diffuse and contradictory expressions. We are created good, in the image of God. The human race is, however, fallen, and history remains locked in the evils consequent upon this fall. With the advent of Christ, the incarnation of the divine, our condition opens to new possibilities of transformation and reconciliation. Redemption does not end either the painfulness or the sinfulness of our lives, but there is a fundamental hopefulness to the cosmos that is figured in the symbols of eschatology, that is, of heaven or end times. For Christians, creation, fall, redemption, and eschatology are deep structures that give some account of the human condition and the bizarre workings of our psyches. The key moments of this story occur beyond the bounds of recorded time. To know who we "really" are we must go back to a beginning before history and go forward to a time and place beyond history. There are many good reasons to dismiss this extrahistorical thinking (particularly in its more literal forms), yet without symbolic expressions of who we are, we are destitute and deceived by the literalism of fact. It is not the work of theology to preoccupy itself with this narrative as describing literal events in human history. Instead, theology uses this narrative as a prism that sheds different kinds of light on the incomparable puzzlement of human life.

Of Sin and Bondage

Who are we that we suffer so? That we deceive ourselves so extravagantly? That we yearn so passionately for home, love, and happiness? Symbols of creation and eschatology give us golden moments before and after history so that we are not simply lost to the ugliness of evil and suffering. They interpret who we are when the chaos of our lives would make us think ourselves more worthless than the lowliest worm. But the actual stuff of life has to do with what goes on here and now. Unhappily, even if we are made in the divine image and bound for glory, we find ourselves caught in a history demented by evil. We ourselves are constantly engaging in patterns of belief and action that are quite destructive to ourselves and to everything else. Sin and its chief consequence, the bondage of the will, are Christianity's primary ways of interpreting this ugly reality. As a cornerstone of the narrative of Christianity, sin provides a core explanation for the fact that life is so rife with evil and suffering.

We suffer because we are a fallen race.[3] The evil we see around us in the world and within our own hearts is the inheritance of a bondage to evil that has become the defining feature of humanity. We have turned aside from God, and history is the long story of the punishment that follows that turn. The story of the fall is filled in by theologians who analyze sin as the distortion of spirit. As sinners we are inordinately in love with the things of the earth and forgetful of our relationship to the One who created us. The great psychological genius of someone like Augustine or Luther lies in the recognition of the ways we are incapacitated, unable to see clearly what would make us happy or to act in ways that might contribute to genuine happiness. Unfortunately, Augustine, the Reformers, and their ilk make this great insight almost completely indigestible by linking this strange incapacity to guilt and punishment.

Much recent theology turns the language of sin toward injustice in order to retain the power of the symbolism of sin yet call attention to the destructiveness of social evil.[4] This move focuses our attention, as it should, on social and political structures and institutions that degrade human beings and generate violence, hatred, and oppression. This focus on institutional evil is a powerful and essential part of any adequate understanding of the Christian narrative. It has its roots in the exodus of slaves from Egypt and is continued in the Hebrew prophets and throughout Scripture until John of Patmos sees a brilliant vision of cosmic peace that condemns the atrocities of the Roman Empire. Interpreting injustice as sin serves as a much-needed reminder that injustice and the structures that carry it blaspheme the divine image. Every form of interpersonal harm—racism, patriarchy, domestic violence, hate crimes, poverty, war, exclusions of gay and lesbian people, and everything that encourages us to despise another person or group of people or the earth itself—is violence and therefore heresy. Using the language of sin assists us in seeing the seriousness of injustice and to understand it as a religious and spiritual problem rather than a matter of political opinion.

The language of sin, however, can also seduce us into living out of one of Christianity's deepest and most infected wounds: the impulse to divide humanity into a duality, the saved and the rejected. We seem justified not only in our anger and pain and in our efforts to change institutions and political systems. We seem justified also in our hatred of the oppressor and in our judgment that oppressors are beyond the pale of divine or human reconciliation.

The temptation to condemn utterly offers a dangerous spiritual practice. It nourishes our incapacities to love and is therefore harmful to ourselves. It also hides the wounds hidden in those who exercise their power in obviously harmful and destructive ways. This does not mean that compassion lacks a wrathful dimension, but it does mean that wrath is only a moment of spiritual practice and not its final destination.

Interpreting the fundamental human condition as sin not only reinforces our pleasure in casting judgment; it also limits our perception of how we are bound to harmful ways of life. Those aspects of our life unrelated to guilt are not covered by a theological or spiritual interpretation. Those addicted to caregiving and unable to nourish themselves in body or spirit are understood to be "good" and their lives opposed to "sin." But the ways that this addiction is destructive to us or serves to pacify resistance to patriarchal images of women, or blocks the flow of the Divine Eros through us, are obscured. When our bondage to harmful ways of life is understood as sin, there is little opportunity to track the destitutions of spirit except under the aegis of guilt. In order to understand the distortions in the lives of the brokenhearted, they must be brought under the category of sin. This is the advance by some Christian feminists who add to the "sin of pride" the "sin of weakness."

In this view, sin is not only the distortion of arrogance and strength but also the weakness whereby those who are downtrodden or lacking in confidence or who allow themselves, wittingly and unwittingly, to be exploited by oppressive forces bind themselves to small and distorted expressions of their beauty and power. It is not the will of God that women, for example, manifest only tiny scraps of the good within them. Grace is evident when this weakness is overcome and the strength of women shines more brightly. Retaining the language of sin allows feminists to remain in the central symbolic structure of Christianity, yet for myself the symbolism is too tightly woven with the theme of guilt to express adequately the variety of ways we suffer. When we extend sin to include weakness or use it to condemn utterly the obvious wrongdoer, the deeper dynamics of bondage that constrain us to patterns of self-hatred and cruelty continue to operate.

This obsession with sin that gradually absorbed more and more of Christian theology and piety provides us with a distorted and harsh way of understanding our bondage to suffering and destruction. The language of sin does little to nourish the compassion for ourselves and for one another that is one of the clearest signs of the presence of the Holy Spirit. To conceive of our primary identity as sinners makes it all the more difficult to reconnect with the soul's power for love and joy. Worst of all, it maligns the Divine Eros and shuts the magnificence of divine love into a narrow box of judgment, anger, and grudging forgiveness. Sin misrepresents who we are and most of all who God is. As Julian of Norwich says after receiving her divine "showings," "pain condemns and punishes" but in God there is no wrath but only an "abundance of love, for grace transforms our dreadful failing into plentiful and endless solace; and grace transforms our shameful falling into high and honourable rising; and grace transforms our sorrowful dying into holy, *blessed* life."[5]

This paradigm of sin, punishment, and forgiveness is not the only way Christians have understood the anguish of our lives or our capacities for cruelty. Within Christianity itself other ways to describe how we are paralyzed and dominated by harmful forms of life survive. Many of the great women writers of medieval Europe describe our lack of self-knowledge and our ignorance of our true situation to be the source of our greatest anguish and incapacity. Teresa of Avila reminds us how seldom we consider "what good qualities there may be in our soul, or Who dwells within them, or how precious they are."[6] Julian of Norwich likens us to devoted servants, fallen in a ditch. Bruised, weakened, confused in our minds, our worst agony is that we are unable to see the infinitely consoling and tender love that is just inches from our face, if only we could turn and see it.[7] We perceive neither the love God bears for us nor the luminosity and beauty of our desire. It is this ignorance above all that binds us to destructive ways of life and burdens us with unbearable misery. These women remind us that our deepest difficulty comes from our ignorance of our actual condition. Another aspect of our difficulty is the dynamic of bondage as excavated by the desert ascetics and other masters of contemplative prayer.[8] By dedicating themselves to interior prayer, the desert fathers and mothers came to possess great insight into the psychological roots of our suffering. Using the language of the "passions," the desert mothers and fathers describe the power that our own minds possess to block the flow of divine love through us.

Following these other traditions within Christianity, the approach taken here is to interpret our addiction to the causes of evil and suffering as bondage arising out of the deep woundedness of existence. The depth and seriousness of this bondage can hardly be overestimated. It has ramifications in every aspect of our life: psychological, physical, spiritual, domestic, political, social, religious, and cultural. The scope of this bondage is broad and deep, penetrating into the hidden places of our psyche and spirit, far beneath our conscious awareness. In this sense Augustine, who refers to human beings as "poisoned wells," and John Calvin, who determines that we are "wholly depraved," are correct. The scope of our bondage is inclusive. But the association of bondage with guiltiness is to be avoided, if only because it invites us to a hard-heartedness toward ourselves and others completely out of keeping with our call to love God and neighbor.

Both the impulse to judge ourselves or others as guilty and the impulse to divide humanity according to some scheme by which some are right and others rejected are resisted here. Instead, we are trying in these pages to understand something about the dynamics of bondage itself. At many levels of human life, these dynamics are particular to persons with experiences unique to themselves and to groups of people who experience particular temptations and vulnerabilities. Being bound to a consumer way of life or drunk with rage and cruelty have different causes and conditions than being bound to an owner as an indentured servant, concubine, slave, or serf, or being subject to a group of people because of one's caste, religion, or minority status. But when the Buddha formulated the Four Noble Truths or when Job cried out that we humans are "born to suffer as the sparks fly upward," they were thinking about ways in which we are all bound together in dynamics of suffering that precede and inform particular forms of suffering. It is to that level that these reflections are aimed. Considering ways that we share a common humanity in our suffering, difficulties, and faults does not negate the need for more particular understanding and response to harmful situations. But it might allow us to feel more compassion for ourselves and the others caught "on the fangs of affliction."

Creation and Eschatology

Theologians and Bible readers know that, deeper than the sin and bondage that trap us, we are created in the image of God. Creation in the divine image is paired at the other end of time with the claim that the soul will not die but be raised up to heavenly glory. These are two ways of saying that there is something in us irreducible to the difficulties and distortions of our lives. We possess a sublime beauty and nobility that is not subject to the predations of time. There is an intuitive power to this counterintuitive self-portrait. It flies in the face of the actual events of life, and it requires that we understand ourselves with reference primarily to dimensions of time and space outside of history and experience. We live in a literal-minded era: things must either be historically true or not true at all. This literalism deprives us of the whole realm of the symbolic. In an effort to reconnect with the intuitive power of this counterintuitive self-portrait, we turn not to the high road of theologians but back to folk music.

As suggested in the last chapter, folk songs remain a potent source of symbolism: "It don't matter where you bury me, I'll be home and I'll be free." "Ain't no grave gonna hold my body down." These songs about heaven are all mixed up with love songs, empty-bed-blues songs, drinking songs, my-husband-is-a-drunkard songs, prison songs, my-children-were-burned-alive songs, work songs, coal mining songs, I-wish-I-were-a-single-girl-again songs, and homesick songs. The juxtaposition of the hardness of life and the beauties of heaven may suggest that eschatological songs are nothing more than a fool's hope, patriarchal rejection of earth-bound life, or opiates for miserable people. All of these might be true. But they seem also to be windows into a kind of refusal to let oneself and one's community be emptied into the realities lamented in the children-burned-alive songs and another-man's-done-gone songs. Eschatology lines up with creation to deprive suffering of the exclusive right to describe who we are. The defiant and courageous insistence that we are made in the image of God and destined for glory is a remarkable flaunting resistance when so little in the actual environment lends any support to these outrageous claims. It is an amazing and wonderful aspect of our minds that we can look at ourselves and, seeing slaves and former slaves, soot-stained miners, haggard mothers, sickly children, betrayed women, cruel bosses, drunks, gamblers, unwed mothers, murderers, cads, or impenetrable institutions of power, still say that we *really* are jewels in Christ's crown.

Creation, fall into suffering, and eschatology overlap and together illuminate fundamental dimensions of our experience. When the common realities of life are backlit by assertions that we are made in the divine image and are sparkling, beautiful diamonds on their way back to their proper setting, we can see things about ourselves that suffering and pleasure cannot teach us.

Redemption and Contemplation

Within the Christian story, the moment of transition from the burden of sin to the restoration of our destiny is the incarnation and passion of Christ. A characteristic understanding of the passion story is that God the Father is so angry at humanity or so honor bound by divine justice that nothing but a blood sacrifice will restore relations. God the Son innocently suffers torture and death so that we, who deserve both, get off the hook and can sneak into heaven hiding in the skirts of Jesus. But because even after this death the grandeur of divine justice still must be displayed, the redeeming death of Christ only works for a relatively small portion of humanity. The elect or faithful or Christians or true Christians go to heaven; the rest of humanity is tortured throughout eternity in an endless death camp called Hell.

For modern thinkers, the idea that one person, even a divine one, could die for everyone else's sins is hard to understand. It is easier to ignore this language when it comes up in the liturgy. For those with a lively sense of ethics, theologies of atonement are worse than archaic; they are heinous and disgusting. That a father-god would demand a blood sacrifice is revolting. That no coherent account of a guilt sufficient to justify eternal torment has ever been given renders the whole story a disgusting mess. That even this death of God is efficacious for a handful chosen for salvation and is insufficient to save humanity calls into question the sincerity of God's desire to save humanity. That the beauty of the Gospels is lost to this hideous, hate-mongering, divisive splitting up of humanity into saved and damned is as ugly a piece of theology as I know.

In addition to this disappearance of the passion narratives into violent theologies, the name of Christ often becomes synonymous with the church's pigheaded cruelty toward women, women-loving women, men-loving men, dissenters, Jews, and all other non-Christians. For women and homosexuals it is the name that justifies our exclusion from the call to ministry and our enduring degradation as secondary humans. For Jews it is the name that justifies any and all acts of anti-Semitism. For non-Christians and dissenters, it is the name for the condemnation of millions of peoples to hell, and, when we have the political power to do so, it is the name that justifies the destruction of cultures, the plundering of the earth, and the reduction of non-Christians to servitude or death. The church has so blasphemed, trivialized, and monopolized Christ's name for holy power that it seems entirely unrecoverable.

But here again, when one turns to less opulent presentations of Christianity, when one turns to women, contemplatives, and folk singers on history's underside, a different picture emerges. Christ is a name that surges up from below: in the writings of women whom the church has excluded from its communion, in the songs of slaves and coal-miner's daughters, in the actions of frumpy housewives who save their children from violence. In the fourth of the Harry Potter novels, *Harry Potter and the Goblet of Fire*, "Mad-Eye Moody" is imprisoned in a small trunk over the course of many months while an imposter takes his place and works great mischief, disguised in the identity of this hero. We might think of the name of Christ in this way: imprisoned by the church and only too often forced to do the work of destruction and hatred. But even confined in this way, the Divine Eros continues to come to the outsiders and the afflicted, continues to break the hold of their enslavement, and even, sometimes, continues to do so bearing the name and face of Christ. Because of this underground community of Christ's lovers, it is possible to return to the incarnation and passion and see if they yield other meanings than those of atonement and division.

Redemption is fundamentally about power. It is the power that begins to unbind every form of bondage and to unblock everything that resists that flow of the Divine Eros through creation. A woman locked in a marriage that is destroying her body and soul, a woman blind to her danger and inert to her suffering, does not need to be forgiven. Nor does she need a companion in suffering. She needs power sufficient to open her eyes and give her the strength to protect herself. A community so addicted to consumption that it foregoes virtually every other pleasure and responsibility needs the intercession of a power great enough to reveal and tame the addiction. "God" is the place-holding word for the power that interrupts the tyranny of evil in all of its forms. It is not that belief in Jesus makes redemption available. It is rather the reverse: when the always-unbelievable miracle of release from evil burns through a psyche, a family, a church, a community, a political situation, or the endless chaos of nothingness, Christians give it the name handed to us through our tradition. The eternal and limitless power of Good Beyond Being is everywhere and always; it cannot coincide with the story of Jesus of Nazareth or the church sprung up in his name. But that is the shard of power that illuminates the corner of space and time Christians inhabit. For Christians, this beyond-being intensity of power is manifest in the face of Christ and in Her beloved, wild sister Sophia, the Holy Spirit, but the nature of this power remains puzzling and frustrating. The birth and passion of Christ are the implacably subversive symbols for the unbridgeable distance between the power that redeems and the power of Caesar. When we expect the power of redemption to mimic the power we see around us everyday in fathers, judges, rulers, warriors, or captains of industry, it is because we have not yet been able to digest the shocking images of power we celebrate every Christmas and Easter.

When we conceive of our condition to be one in which we are bound to suffering and to destructive ways of life, redemption can be understood as the process by which this bondage is relieved. When we think of the story of Peter's release from prison (Acts 12), we might crave a similarly dramatic release. Occasionally we might find some temporary satisfaction. But it is not just our bodies that are confined to prison it is also our psyches and spirits, our communities and churches. The work of redemption is the long and slow work by which all of the layers of our hearts and minds and community are opened to the flow of the Divine Eros. The once-and-for-all forgiveness that Christians celebrate in the passion of Christ might be understood not as something that happens within God but something that happens within us when we become aware of the impossibility of turning God away from us, so precious are we to God. We are united with the erotic power that is God. This is our nature and nothing can change or undo that unity. We do not have the capacity to undo the unchanging and infinite love of the Divine Eros. But this holy power is largely unavailable to us or distorted by its expression through the cruelties and foolishness of history.

The "person and work" of Jesus Christ is not something that happens in God but something that happens in us.[9] Contemplation is one way of understanding some of the ways this ever-present reality is metabolized in us. It is the desire to live more fully out of our "precious oneing" with the Divine Eros as this unity swims toward explicit awareness. Put another way, contemplation is an intoxication of desire, which is one of the ways Christ calls her lovers back to herself. The gradual disintegration of all obstacles between ourselves and the Beloved was described as a "dark night of the soul" by one of Christ's great lovers, St. John of the Cross. As all forms of bondage slowly lose their grip, powers of the soul become more available. This release is the descent of personhood to the powers appropriate to it, powers that flow from the divine image in it: compassion, delight, wrath, freedom, courage, and peace. These powers are intensified as the unity between the soul and Christ is unveiled. A contemplative path is lit by desire. It is the weaving together of heaven and earth that is not simply eschatological but a central practice of living Christian faith.

The Christian Narrative Revisited

The images of creation, fall, redemption, and eschatology present in Scripture, music, and theology are "deep symbols" that give some account of this intertwining of separation from and intimacy with the Divine Eros. These symbols describe suffering and bondage as characteristic of our actual condition while holding before our eyes an awareness that these do not define who we are. These symbols are important because they do more than explicate our situation. They make us aware of our bondage to harmful ways of life so that we will not be condemned to forgetfulness forever. In retrieving our ancient wisdom we are invited not only to deeper understanding. We are invited to reignite the desire that is banked within us but cannot stop burning. For the purposes of these reflections, contemplation is understood as the desire to awaken from our dark sleep. This desire for awakening has been described by contemplatives in many traditions, and it is nourished by practices of contemplation. Contemplation is not a work by which we are saved; it is desire and practice that awaken us to the salvation that always surrounds us and everyone else. Focusing on contemplation, this text is perhaps closer in spirit to more ancient theologians, for whom theology was not only thinking but "tasting"; women and men for whom the desire to understand God and themselves was a practice that carried them into the womb of God and back into the world with an intensified compassion.

In the transpositions developed in the next chapters, sin ceases to be the primary thing we need to know about ourselves. But creation, fall, redemption, and eschatology remain deep symbols for our nature and condition. There is a light in us that cannot burn out or become tarnished or destroyed. This light is disguised from us, hidden by the layers of suffering and difficulty we experience. But it can be reignited as desire for the Divine Eros. This desire does not overcome suffering, but it does transform it. The path of contemplation is one way in which this desire takes root in us. Taking advantage of the wisdom of folk singers, contemplative women and men, and desert ascetics (among others) alters the way we understand the structure of the Christian story. The brilliance of our creation and the beauty of our destiny are caught now on the "fangs of affliction." The world is a hard place, and distortions, injustices, and cruelties preceded us and bind us to them. Harm done to us solders itself to the deepest recesses of our psyches and makes us its slave. Harm we do to others habituates us to a spiritual poverty that seems impossible ever to escape. This bondage refracts from the microcosm of the human mind throughout the increasingly complex orders of societies and cultures. We are mercilessly distracted from our heart's desire and more lost in ignorance of our true selves than fabled kings and queens who are reared as orphans and servants, far from the nobility of their birthright. But in all of this there is nothing, not even something as thin as cigarette paper, that separates us from the tender mercy that intoxicates the Holy Trinity. We may feel separated and feel darkness around us, but we cannot create any real separation between ourselves and the Beloved, or our mighty sister, the Holy Spirit, or the Beauty Beyond All Being.

STRUCTURES OF PERSONHOOD: EGOCENTRISM TO *VAJRA* PRIDE

Christian theology offers this grand narrative that endeavors to orient us to the broader and deeper dimensions of our lives. In addition to these deep symbols, classical theology offers also a kind of spiritual psychology that explores the interior dynamics that hold us in bondage. Put most simply, under the impact of sin the desire that is properly ordered to love God has become twisted so that it attaches itself *inordinately* to the goods of this world. This is not to say that enjoying the goods of this world is in and of itself sinful. But because the structure of desire is itself disordered, we relate to the world in ways that are harmful to us while forgetting or distorting our awareness of the one good that most deeply satisfies us. Because of this disordering of desire we are like alcoholics who cannot simply enjoy a glass or two of wine but instead destroy our lives through our addiction. The root addiction is not to any particular thing in the world but to our own egos, and through this addiction our relationship to everything else is ruined. The sin of "pride" is just this: it is not the annoying excess of self-confidence that afflicts some people. Pride in this sense is the inordinate attachment to our own egos that displaces God as the center of our life and happiness. The psychological and spiritual fruits of redemption include the breaking of the hold of pride so that we are free to love God and neighbor as we should. In this way genuinely satisfying happiness is possible.

Unhappily, the insightfulness of this spiritual portrait of humanity is marred by the implication that the cure for pride is humiliation. Likewise, the cure for excessive pleasure in the world is to denigrate the goods of the earth and our pleasures in them. Too often the dismemberment of the ego has been offered as the antidote to egocentrism. For people who have experienced only too much powerlessness and humiliation in their actual experience, this antidote can be spiritually fatal. For women in particular this opposition between pride and "self-sacrifice" has proven exceptionally unenlightening and often noxious and debilitating. But all beings suffer, and it is a harsh and loveless description of any of us. Nonetheless, there remains enormous wisdom in these traditions that have tracked the source of our spiritual misery to particular ways we experience the *self*. The scheme that unfolds in the following chapters is a variation on this theme: particular forms of egocentrism burden us and tyrannize us in ways that block the flow of the Divine Eros through us. Releasing our powers is not humiliation but something more akin to what the Tibetan Buddhists call *vajra* pride.[10] This is a serenity that is rooted in our self-awareness as vehicles of the Great Compassion. Egocentrism is loosened not by the mutilation of the ego but by the empowering of the ego by the Divine Eros, that is by the Holy Ones whom Christians name in trinitarian fashion: Good Beyond Being, Beloved, and Holy Spirit.

In order to try to sort out what is harmful egocentrism from what might become a healthy form of personhood, a distinction can be drawn between egological existence and egocentrism. Human beings, like every form of sentient being, are conscious because we are rooted in a particular center of experience. Persons are conscious of being recognizable centers of identity. My body, my memories, my dreams, my ideas are *mine* in a way nothing else is. No sympathy, empathy, compassion, or solidarity can extinguish the difference between my experience and my most intimate awareness of someone else's experience. Our sense of identity, our sense even of existing at all, arises with an awareness of ourselves as a particular self. We might think of this as the egological structure of personhood. That is, our experience is located in a particular ego. Without this centeredness of consciousness, it is hard to see what a person would be. In fact, sentience itself is probably egological. Any being capable of any degree of awareness turns toward what it needs and seeks to avoid what is harmful, as a plant turns toward light and aims its roots around obstacles. Further, we are not free-floating minds but egos embodied in flesh and blood, woven into the network of nerves, hormones, cells, and genes that are uniquely ours. These bodies of ours are not neutral automatons but organisms rich with feeling responses to everything that happens to us, to what we think and want, to what thwarts us. Feeling tones are woven into our being through everything we consciously and unconsciously experience. We desire things we perceive as good; we fear things we perceive as harmful; we get angry when we are threatened. We experience pleasure, fear, and anger not only as fleeting emotions but as deep, often unconscious, dispositions that shape our relationship with the world.

It is natural and appropriate that our awareness of our own embodied self is much more vivid than our awareness of other things. This vividness is a good thing: hunger makes us feed ourselves; pain makes us remove our hand from the fire. When these responses are damaged by illness of one sort or another, one's very life can be at risk. The evolutionary demands to survive, together with the fact that we have nerve endings, emotions, and spirit to perceive pain and pleasure, joy and harm, make the intensity of my own experience inevitable. But this is where the difficulty comes. It seems nearly impossible to avoid the slide from the particular vividness of my own experience to the feeling that my ego is the center of the cosmos. This is not to say that many of us actually believe this. The literal belief in this egocentrism is a pathology diagnosed as narcissism in our therapeutic age or as solipsism in a more philosophical one. But the fact that we do not believe it does little to undermine the organizing feeling of our own experience as more real, more central, and more important than anything else. In point of fact, my pains, ambitions, hopes, sorrows, fears—my life itself—are not one iota more important than anyone else's. I can easily write those words and even believe them. But the smallest pain or inconvenience drives from my mind the difficulties others are suffering. I believe the environment is truly threatened and the quality of the air in Atlanta is poisoning us all. But I do not sacrifice the convenience of driving around or subject myself to the misery of an unair-conditioned summer, let alone pour out my life in unfettered compassion for all beings.

Because we are pinned to the intensity of our experiences, the necessary and good egological structure of consciousness slips into the destructive illusion of egocentrism. The hold of this illusion on me survives my knowledge that it is an illusion completely intact, without a mark on it. From this root illusion flow deep patterns of destructive beliefs and behaviors. Augustine was, in a sense, right: the motion of the soul toward self-absorption constitutes its "fall." Although Augustine usually associates pride with inflated self-worth, at one point in *The City of God* he notes that the fall of the angels occurs because of a moment of panic, a kind of existential terror when they realize that they could be separated from the love of God.[11] This moment of panic was such that it turned their attention from God to themselves and constituted the fall that propelled Satan out of paradise and filled the world with demons intent on our destruction. That is, even Augustine perceived that the deepest root of self-absorption was not inflation but pain. The intensity of our desires, our fears, disappointments, suffering, and grief is too great for us to bear. It is as if the strength of our experience outstrips the capacity of our embodied spirits to endure it. Our fall is into more pain and bondage as we struggle with unsuccessful attempts to mitigate the painfulness of egological consciousness.

The illusion of egocentrism modifies the feeling tones that accompany our conscious and unconscious awareness. Anger becomes a disposition of rage; fear becomes a disposition of terror and powerlessness; pleasure becomes addiction. But the illusion of egocentrism can be weakened, perhaps even broken, by the unleashing of the Divine Eros. *Power* is required to counter the fragility of personhood and the painfulness of experience. Through the always inexplicable miracle of grace, divine power transforms egocentrism into kenotic *vajra* pride, that is, the self-emptying confidence and joy of erotic compassion. Consciousness remains egological, but it opens out from itself with much greater vitality. The flow of psychic and spiritual energy is not trapped, swirling in on the ego. Eros allows the flow of energy to break out toward others, toward the world. This is not a "sacrifice" of personhood but its liberation. As the hold of egocentrism weakens, feeling tones are released from their bondage and subjugation. Passions become powers of the soul. Terror is transposed into freedom. Rage becomes the divine energy of compassionate wrath. Addiction becomes eros: loving delight that others exist. Egocentrism whispered the despairing lie that we are alone. But as the isolation of egocentrism breaks down, the deep intimacy we share with the Beloved and through the Beloved with every being becomes part of our lived experience. Resting in the communion of saints eases the painfulness of isolation and fills us with vitality. The tenderness and joy of connection mediates power to us, and what was impossible in our ego-bound terror now flows from us as spontaneously as beauty shines off the flower.

In brief, that is the schema that underlies the following chapters. Personhood is organized by awareness located in a particular ego. The vividness of this awareness produces the illusion that we exist alone, trapped with our ceaselessly nagging fears and hopes, sufferings and desires. In this way we are bereft of the consolations of companionship, sharing only faint shadows of the joy of intimacy or compassion in suffering. Our emotional and spiritual life degenerates into a struggle with passions that bind us ever more tightly to our sorry attempts to ease our pain. But as the ever-fresh rivers of the Divine Eros flow through us, this illusion and its debilitating consequences dissipate. Our natural powers for joy and compassion, the strength of our courage, and the light of wisdom trickle through the bars of our prison. Our egos, mutilated by egocentrism, convalesce as *vajra* pride shines through them.

3

The Passions: Wounds of Love

Remember Holy Mother
That never was it known
That anyone approached Thee, out of pain,
And found within Thy Beauty
The silence of a stone
And took her sorrow to the night again.
This confidence inspires me
To stand before Your shrine:
A child of sorrow and despair.
I lay my small petitions
Upon this throne of Thine
And light the golden candles with my prayer.
Let not a holy justice
Arouse Thee to despise
The depth and terror of my misery.
Pity the dreadful blindness
Of these unseeing eyes.
Mother of Jesus, hear and answer me.
                                    Miserere

How is it that these flames of desire live out lives of such drudgery, triviality, suffering, affliction, pettiness, cruelty, and ignorance? How is it that we run so hard in the opposite direction from the happiness we crave? We are lovers of the world and are wounded by this love. We are lovers of Christ, but our power to love is wounded. Much of the suffering we experience is imposed on us—

oppression, poverty, grief, illness, work, lack of work, the untold millions of disasters that befall us. In turning to the passions, we are not displacing these causes of human misery. The passions show us how deeply these sufferings bite into us, wounding and poisoning us. They are one way we can interpret how the things that happen to us are appropriated by us in destructive ways. The distortions accomplished by passions make us unwilling, and often unknowing accomplices to our pain.

St. Paul cries out the frustration so deeply embedded in our condition: "I do not understand my own actions. For I do not do what I want, but I do the very thing I hate" (Rom. 7:15). It is as if we are enthralled to some alien power, incapable of doing the good we crave, constantly demanding the very poison that torments us. We are aware of making decisions and choosing things that we consider goods. But when we are able to look at the basic patterns of our lives, we find them mired in pain and difficulty. In Atlanta, thousands of people drive beautiful cars with fine audio systems on roads so clogged that a twenty-minute drive is expanded to an hour or more. The air is so polluted that many days of the year school children cannot go outside to play. People wear beautiful clothes as they work eighty or so hours a week at a job that exhausts them physically and spiritually. The outward signs of affluence, power, and success conceal the disintegration of health, family life, connections to community, and even a capacity for joy. Equally invisible is the price the rest of the world pays in low-wage labor and poisoned water, land, and air for our affluence. We drink more, amuse ourselves, buy things: sad, *ersatz* pleasures for creatures who bear the flame of the divine image. Another kind of example is the child who was abused in small or severe ways. Sometimes when such children grow up they find themselves in relationships that replicate ways they were hurt as children or accomplish on others the horrors that terrorized them. What could be more irrational than to injure oneself over and over again? But the entropy and blindness of affliction binds us like an inexorable fate. Even noticing the paradoxes of these compromised lives and wishing for another way to live are often of little avail. This impotence toward what is healthy and addiction to what is harmful makes it seem as if someone else were in charge of our actions. "It is no longer I that do it, but sin that dwells within me" (Rom. 7:17).

Christianity and Buddhism are both built around an intuition that we are strangers and dangers to ourselves. We act in ways that are completely inappropriate to our desire for happiness. We are bound to misery that we conceal from ourselves by a thousand distractions and comforts that further numb us to the reality of our situation. Our capacities to give and receive love are bitterly damaged. All of these are ways of saying that our fundamental condition is one of bondage and illusion. Describing some of the dynamics of what desert ascetics called the "passions" is one way of trying to untangle this web of illusion, even while we still inhabit it.

WHAT THE PASSIONS ARE NOT

There is no readily established contemporary vocabulary for trying to draw the strangeness of our condition up to consciousness. We reason, we choose things, we feel things; psychologists and therapists remind us of our unconscious. But outside of trauma theory, it is hard to understand this bondage to unhappy ways of life so well known to Shantideva and St. Paul. In these modern times, reason, will, and emotion are the main constituents of our understanding of persons, and these are understood to be "free." Determining how crazy a person has to be before he or she is no longer held criminally responsible for his or her actions is one of the few senses in which this freedom is understood to be limited. The wisdom of religious traditions as well as reflection on our own social and psychic experience tell a different story.

The "passions" is an ancient name for some of the ways in which our own psyche helps to trap us in patterns of behavior that block us from our deepest joy. Since the time of the desert ascetics and medieval theologians, the word *passion* has come to mean different things. I employ this terminology as it was used in the ancient world and not according to its more contemporary connotations. In this earlier literature passions are not necessarily conscious feelings; we are for the most part hardly aware of them. They do not inhabit the upper surfaces of self-consciousness, but tracking them can help expose those parts of us that engage in this odd but nearly universal addiction to harmful ways of life. There is a weirdness and inaccessibility to these dynamics of our spirit, so we begin by suggesting what the passions are *not*.

After the Romantic movement, the word *passion* has taken on a largely positive connotation, meaning something like intense emotion or a great commitment to something wonderful, if slightly bizarre. It is therefore necessary to say first of all that the passions in this earlier sense are not emotions. A Tibetan monk, Geshe Lobsang Negi, in comparing cognitive psychology to Buddhist psychology, noted that there was no word in Tibetan that corresponded to the English word *emotion*. It occurred to me that there was not such a word in classical theology either. Theologians described many aspects of our minds: passions, desire, affections, the voluntary and involuntary, intellect, concupiscence, will (free and bound), appetitive will, intellectual will, virtues, vices, habits. This tradition gave theology a way of reflecting on the extreme complexity that characterizes the human mind. Emotion does little to capture this complexity. Emotions usually refer to uncontrived feeling states of which we are consciously aware. Emotions are part of the vitality of life and contribute to our awareness of reality. The passions, by contrast, may or may not arise to an explicit feeling state. Passions refer not to emotions but to distortions of our psyche and spirit that block out a clearer understanding of reality. Passion has passivity as its root; it is something that is *suffered* involuntarily. Passions have the connotation of bondage and uneasiness. They exemplify the way the soul can become twisted and turned in on itself and alienated from the world around us.

The distinction between passions and emotions can be made more confusing by the association ascetics made between the passions and anger, lust, jealousy, greed, vainglory, and so on. This list may imply that passions are emotions, but that would be misleading. Anger and so on are passions when they move beyond passing emotions and take deep root in the soul, distorting mind, spirit, freedom, embodiment, agency, and, most of all, love. Passions have deeper roots than emotions. They trouble the soul. Unless they are clearly distinguished from emotions, the association of the passions with bondage and disorder might imply emotions themselves were bad, irrational, out of control—as Enlightenment thinkers sometimes say. This, too, is an interpretation to be avoided. Emotions cover a range of feelings, including many that are positive. Emotions are an essential part of our orientation to reality. To feel sorrow in the face of suffering or joy when something wonderful happens reflects the power to respond to truth. The emotional dimensions of love, joy, enthusiasm, pity, or sorrow are not passions.

As we proceed to reflect on what the passions are, it is crucial to remember that they are not emotions. They sink deeper into the soul than emotions and are, in this literature, always understood as a kind of bondage and painful disorder.

The passions are also not vices. The feelings the ascetics associated with passions can be considered vices: anger, lust, jealousy, and so on, and passions can be expressed as vices. Habits of pettiness, drinking and whoring, stealing, lying, violence, and so on usually do not possess souls at peace with themselves. But then preoccupation with vice and virtue, moral and immoral behavior can itself be a vice. The ascetics identified other passions as well, that we would not think of as vices, such as acedia and sadness.[1] The passions muffle and distort holy desire; melancholy and virtues can do this as easily as can vices. The infinitely accommodating teacher, the doctor who works eighty hours a week, and the obsessive volunteer who cannot refuse even the most trivial and thankless requests all may contribute to the well-being of others. They may be pleasant and kind people. But they may be in thrall to unrealistic expectations that they can and should perfectly meet everyone's need; they may be exorcising some imagined guilt; they may lack the "skillful means" that would enable them to shine with erotic power while resting in tranquility. They may be able to take care of everyone except themselves, so the divine image in them becomes dim and scarred. These distorted efforts to "do good" are neither emotions nor vices, but they are related to the passions. The passions have in these cases choked the intended virtue. If we think of the health of the soul only in terms of virtues and vices, we are less likely to see how the passions can use even our virtues in harmful ways. Passions distort everything they touch, including our emotions and our genuine impulses toward good. It is not our virtues but the divine image in us that matters. The passions are obstacles to the shining of this holy luminescence.

THE DESERT ASCETICS ON THE PASSIONS

It must have been strange for small groups of men and women who fled the civilization of Rome and Byzantium for the desert. A demon-haunted wilderness of hunger, thirst, stinging insects, lions, and loneliness seems an unpromising sanctuary. Yet they left behind them a literature that embodies significant psychological wisdom and testifies to something in the desert that could succeed in reigniting the fire of love. Having renounced so much, these athletes of spiritual discipline knew better than most of us the hidden and contorted passions that flourished long after "the world" had been overcome. The imagery of the desert ascetics is often quite alien, even offensive, to those of us with contemporary and feminist sensitivities. But their wrestling in the desert gave them an understanding of how the psyche hides from itself. As the soul cleared, the passions' ability to use everything against the holy desire for God could be better perceived. Their language can sound moralistic, but they are not concerned with being nice, well-behaved boys and girls. They have more affinity with *Vajrayogini:* they had huge energy to expose and overcome every obstacle to love.[2] They believed that one could not go one inch closer to God without at the same time loving people that much more. It was love that fired and fed them in the desert, as seen in Dorotheus's image of the circle:

> I give you an example from the Fathers. Suppose we were to take a compass and insert the point and draw the outline of a circle. The center point is the same distance from any point on the circumference. Now concentrate your minds on what is to be said! Let us suppose that this circle is the world and that God himself [sic] is the center; the straight lines drawn from the circumference to the center are the lives of men [sic]. To the degree that the saints enter into the things of the spirit, they desire to come near to God; and in proportion to their progress in the things of the spirit, they do in fact come close to God

and to their neighbor. The closer they are to God, the closer they become to one another; and the closer they are to one another, the closer they become to God. . . . See? This is the very nature of love. The more we are turned away from and do not love God, the greater the distance that separates us from our neighbor. If we were to love God more, we should be closer to God, and through love of him we should be more united in love to our neighbor; and the more we are united to our neighbor the more we are united to God.[3]

The men and women of the desert believed that great asceticism contributed to this love. But their asceticism did not translate into harshness toward one another, at least those were not the examples used to teach others the way of the desert. According to Dorotheus, the holy ones of the desert acted like mothers of unruly children, ruling them with sweetness and patience.[4] Dorotheus gives us an example of this in the story of the Abba who was summoned with great boisterousness by the monks to come to a brother's cell because he was hiding a woman there. "Knowing that the brother had hidden the woman in a large barrel, he went in, sat down on it, and told the others to search the whole place. And when they found nothing he said to them, 'May God forgive you!' . . . when [the Abba and erring monk] were alone he laid on him the hand with which he had thrown the others out, and said, 'Have a care for yourself, brother.' Immediately the other's conscience pricked him . . . so swiftly did the mercy and sympathy of the old man work upon his soul."[5]

The ascetics were focused on vivifying love. As psychologists of souls and masters of skillful means, they were interested in results. This focused attention brought to light the primary obstacles to love: their own passions and most especially the passions that survived the renunciation that brought them to the desert in the first place. Those of us who have no desire for the desert or for asceticism can still find their understanding of the psyche helpful as we notice the way we ourselves are bound by obstacles that prevent us from loving ourselves, one another, the world, and the Holy Mystery.

Ascetic renunciation begins with leaving "the world" for the desert. We have seen in the previous chapter that compelling "the world" to satisfy our deepest desires can lead to trouble and unhappiness. But breaking free of the expectation that "the world" be adequate to our desires is extremely difficult. There is a commonplace dimension of desire that transforms the beauty of the world into objects of pleasure and fear. Addiction to pleasures of "the world" can distract us with greed. This in turn can make us jealous of those who have more, angry when our goods appear threatened, and unjust when it suits us. The ammas and abbas of the desert began by renouncing this source of temptation as a first step in the pitched battle against the passions that sullied their love of God and neighbor. Pseudo-Macarius identifies renunciation of normal social life as the first of two kinds of spiritual struggle. We are bound to "material affairs of this world, meshed by various earthly bonds and seduced by the evil passions."[6] These prevent us from loving the Lord, believing, and praying as we would wish.[7] Until such a person

> frees himself from the earthly passions with all his heart . . . he will not know about the deception of the hidden, evil spirits and about the hidden evil passions. He remains a stranger to himself, as one who is unaware of his wounds. He has hidden passions and yet he is not aware of them. He is still given over to exterior things and willingly consents to the preoccupations of the world.[8]

The significant point here for nondesert ascetics is that attachment to the pleasures and pains of normal human life (work, family, buying things, comfort, and so on) is a problem not primarily because these things are evil. These things are a problem because they conceal from us our deepest wounds. They are like pain relievers that prevent us from recognizing how serious an injury or illness really is.

Because it was not really "the world" that was the root of the problem, renunciation of the world did not itself bring ascetics the tranquility of spirit and abiding love they desired. This first stage of renunciation merely cleared ground so that the deeper wounds and obstacles to love could begin to appear. Renunciation of "the world" did not give the ascetics mastery over passions; it only allowed them to begin the journey to freedom. Like St. John of the Cross's "dark night of sense," renunciation is a preliminary practice that prepared them for the more difficult "night of the soul." It is only after the "earthly passions" are calmed that the depth and terror of the passions can be exposed. A renunciation of the more obvious desires and fears allows deeper patterns of addiction and terror to be seen. The ascetics had a keen eye for how quickly "spiritual" addictions replaced "earthly" ones. They saw how (relatively) easy it might be to renounce worldly honors and dedicate ourselves only to fasting, vigils, and austerities. But then we bask in the honor this brings us. Or someone else gives up all of his or her wealth. But then "suppose there is a good tool to which we become attached. We allow that miserable tool to have the same affect on us, as Abba Zosimos says, as if it were a hundred gold sovereigns."[9]

The structure of the passions remains but is transferred to a different context. This is not to say that renunciation was insincere or that the desire to embody God's love to all humanity was superficial. But the desert ascetics understood the complexities and depth of the psyche as well as the determination of the ego to remain in control. As Pseudo-Macarius put it, there is an "infinite depth of the human heart. There are found reception rooms, bedrooms, doors and antechambers, many offices and exits. There is found the office of justice and injustice. There is death and there is life. There takes place upright business as well as the contrary."[10] This mixture is hard to see when absorbed in daily occupations. It is hard to call out our interior shadows when we want so desperately not to see them. The ascetics knew that they had to travel through many chambers of the mind before love could inhabit the "infinite depth of the human heart." For the ascetics, in order to get to the level of the psyche where they could renounce everything that blocked their capacity to love, they had to first renounce their preoccupations in society.

There is a very thin, choking vine that wanders all over my back yard. It is hard to see; I notice it when I am weeding because it is covered with tiny thorns that bite into my hands. It is easy to pull out. I can pull it out by the yard and feel I have accomplished a great deal. But on one occasion I tracked that tiny, thin string of thorns back to its roots. I spent over an hour digging it up. It would let go of a big chunk of root, concealing the huge ice-berg-like root that remained. I was amazed at the cleverness of this plant: so modest and unobtrusive, so good at hiding, a trickster that feigned defeat even while its gigantic root remained serenely intact. The ascetics might recognize these tactics as ones they were familiar with as they wrestled with their passions.

All of the austerities in the world did not in themselves break the hold of the passions to block the ascetics from the love they desired. They could identify particular vices, but they discovered negative emotions, vices, and bad habits had much deeper roots. They learned to combat not only the bad habits, "but the unruly passions which cause them and are their roots."[11] Realizing the limitations of making peace with vices and addictions made it possible to begin a second struggle. As Macarius put it, even the person who

> really has rejected the world and has taken effort to cast from him the weight of this earth and has thrown off the vain passions and desires of the flesh, of glory, of authority, and of human honors, and has withdrawn from them with his whole heart . . . and has stood manfully in the service of the Lord and has persevered wholeheartedly in body and soul, such a person . . . discovers the opposition, the hidden passions, the invisible bonds, the unseen warfare, the battle and interior struggle.[12]

In an echo of Zen meditation, Evagrius Ponticus describes how this struggle is undertaken: "If there is any monk who wishes to take the measure of some of the more fierce demons so as to gain experience in his monastic art, then let him keep careful watch over this thoughts." Nothing displays our distortions as clearly as our own minds. Because of this, "the demons become thoroughly infuriated with those who practice active virtue in a manner that is increasingly contemplative. They are even of a mind to 'pierce the upright of heart through, under cover of darkness.'"[13] The quieter the mind becomes, the more intense and horrific are the "demons" that are released from its depths. Like the thorns in my backyard, the passions may feign defeat. But as the ascetics of the desert traveled further down the spiral staircase of mind, they found the deep roots of the passions—the "demons"—more, not less, ferocious as they were dragged from their hiding places. There is in us great resistance to the eros that frees us from our preoccupation with ourselves and opens us to love.

The journey inward is dangerous and painful, and the ascetics of the desert were wise enough to know these difficulties were only magnified by unbroken solitude. They were wise not only in noticing the sneakiness and subtly of the passions, but also in being aware of how important it was to be spiritually gentle with oneself and lean on the help of others. Passions can fill us with terror, so they admonished, "Let us make provision for protecting this power of our soul by praying to Christ in our nightly vigils, and also by applying the remedies we spoke of above."[14] They leaned heavily on one another and the collective wisdom of their community, finding wisdom and safety in the guidance of spiritual masters.[15] They leaned heavily on Christ, seeking to conceal nothing of their struggle from Him.[16] The ascetics exhibited astounding tenacity in their enthusiasm to uproot every obstacle between themselves and love. They understood that this was possible through their own determination and practices and through the power given to them by Christ: "Having armed himself [sic] by all prayer and perseverance and supplication and fasting and by faith, he will be able to wage war against the principalities."[17] The fruit of this struggle was love, "which has the role of showing itself to every image of God as being as nearly like its prototype as possible, no matter how the demons ply their arts to defile them."[18] Asceticism contributed to a clarity that allowed them to perceive and renounce their own passions. But these practices were only for this: to see the image of God in every person clearly and spontaneously, no matter how it might be dulled down by affliction and passion.

The depth and tenacity of the passions, and their chameleon-like agility remind us that we are not dealing with something we can turn away from through a simple act of the will. Nor are we up against something that we overcome by being "good." It is the restructuring of the ego itself that is effected by the passions. Study of the passions exposes hidden places of woundedness. In doing so, they lead us to a deeper understanding of the healing and transformation the divine Eros opens for us. This is why they are worth recovering.

REVISITING THE PASSIONS

Reading the ascetics is necessarily a work of translation: the refrains concerning asceticism, renunciation, humility, pride, perfection, and the dangers of hell are less helpful than the psychology that frames these themes. Using a psychology of the passions to reflect on ways in which holy desire is betrayed branches away from the ascetics' own understanding of the passions. But beginning with them gives us some vocabulary for thinking of the distortions, betrayals, and bondage to which the holy desire of our spirit is subject.

Investigation of the passions suggests how the ego is restructured by harmful illusions—most deeply, the illusion of egocentrism. One way of thinking of this is that the illusion of egocentrism effects a root distortion of personhood. Normal feelings become distorted into passions. This is not a symmetrical distortion: a feeling of fear does not become the passion of terror. Passions are not more intense or more destructive variations of emotions. They are different in their character. Normal feelings of fear, anger, and pleasure are familiar emotions that arise and pass away. The effect of a feeling of anger at a colleague or friend will vary, but the emotion itself leaves few ripples in one's consciousness or in the relationship. Pleasures of eating ice cream or wading through warm sand and tide likewise arise in experience and pass away, perhaps leaving the traces of a pleasant memory. Being afraid of a bad storm or a scary-looking stranger may leave a bad taste, but these do not in themselves leave deep scars. These are not passions. They are normal feeling states that arise in the ordinary flow of life because we are psychic, spiritual, embodied persons and feelings are intrinsic to our way of being alive.

Egocentrism carries normal feeling states deeply into the structures of consciousness. Here they solidify into habitual patterns of relationship to oneself, the world, and all reality. As psychic and spiritual habits they are no longer normal feeling states that arise and pass away. They are no longer discrete feeling states at all. As passions, they precede and infiltrate the divisions of mind, body, will, emotion, feeling, and sensation. Tyrannized by the passion of terror, one will reason out of terror, make decisions on the basis of this terror, relate to other people and events through terror. All of this can happen even in the absence of a felt emotion of fear, let alone terror. The passions are neither emotions nor faculties. They inhabit that imprecise dimension of mind in which reason, will, and emotion blend in indeterminate integration. They are not easily called into conscious awareness but instead slide up and down the spiral staircase of mind. The next chapter will examine these dynamics in more detail. At this point, it will have to be sufficient to say that passions are deeply rooted in the fundamental distortion of egocentrism. They might be expressed in emotions, opinions, beliefs, or actions. But they may also be emotionally invisible, even as they dominate one's life.

The ascetics noticed that it is good to control vices, but the root of spiritual bondage and misery does not lie there. They were also aware of the way passions could conceal themselves as virtues. A monk or nun may be famed for heroic fasting, but closer discernment might show that this fasting was not God intoxication but "vainglory." The sweetness the ego finds in praise can survive many years in the desert and feed off respect for one's amazing asceticism as easily as off marvel at one's amazing ability to consume shots of whiskey without throwing up. Passions cannot be recognized by the emotions, vices, or virtues that trail after them. A feeling of pleasure may obscure rage or terror. An apparent vice like irascibility may be the fire of justice. Constant work may not be diligence but rather numbness and escapism. Because of this remarkable ability at deception and concealment, the mothers and fathers identified *discernment* as the crucial virtue of a contemplative life. It is not by fasting or not fasting, hard work or laxity, effervescent emotion or apathy that the passions could be recognized. The health of a soul had to be identified by more subtle signs, most notably serenity and spontaneous love. In trying to follow these interior masters of prevarication, we will pursue the passions along three tracks: passions as "habits," the distortion of consciousness by egocentrism, and the ego's craving for relief from pain. In the next chapter, we will study the passions through three examples: terror, rage, and addiction.

Habits and the Passions

The passions are not fleeting experiences but deeply rooted dispositions that shape the way we orient ourselves in the world. To better understand ways that passions shape our consciousness while remaining largely inaccessible to our self-awareness, an analysis of *habits* might be helpful. In classical theology habits were understood to be not simply repeated actions but the way in which all of our human capacities take on solidity over time so they become so automatic and spontaneous they seem to be a kind of second nature.[19] The capacities of mind are extremely diverse. But these capacities remain generic potentialities before they become concrete through experience and action. This is true even of something as simple as vision. When we are born, we see patches of color and light. Over time our vision gains the capacity to give shape and meaning to these patches that greet our eyes. Our eyes are habituated into the power to see objects. As adults it may seem that the inability of larger things to fit into smaller things is a visual perception, but in fact it is habituated knowledge gained through trial and error.

Likewise we habituate our muscles and sense of balance to walk and later to kayak, meditate, play tennis, or dance. We habituate our minds and muscles to transform the virtually infinite array of possible sounds and movement into language. According to the culture and subcultures in which we find ourselves, mind will be made further concrete with capacities to read our environment, whether a jungle, desert, urban street, or intensely politicized family structure. The generic power to reason, imagine, and create is made concrete and useful to us when we learn astrology or how to hunt seals, weave complex tapestries, memorize multiplication tables, follow the reasoning of medieval theologians, interpret a landscape, cook, or mediate conflicts. Our generic power of agency becomes concrete when we learn to control our tempers, or use tantrums to frighten people, or fast, seduce, tell lies, act courageously, cry manipulatively, and desire more or less culturally appropriate goods.

Most of what we actually think, do, desire, and repress is so deeply habituated it does not arise into conscious awareness. Our habits can take on the character of a second nature, and we no longer make any particular effort to organize and respond to the world in ways characteristic of ourselves and our culture. This is extremely convenient. We do not have to recreate from scratch the ability to see or walk, to understand Thomas Aquinas, or notice the feelings of those around us. If we had to identify carefully each musical note and then try to connect our fingers to the place on the instrument that made that sound, we could never make music. But because these mental and physical abilities can be habituated, we can. We no longer have to throw ourselves on the floor and cry because the meeting is running late and we are hungry. We probably do not even notice that we have to resist this impulse or that such an impulse exists in us at all. But this control is a habit that was formed, sometimes with great effort, long ago.

Having a head located at the top of our body and being subject to gravity are more or less unchanging aspects of our existence. But many other things that shape us as individuals and societies exist in a zone between unchanging essences and arbitrary, momentary decisions or experiences. Our psychic, emotional, spiritual, and somatic life is constituted out of habits. Unlike the placement of our head on our body, habits can be changed. In contrast to a decision about what to cook for dinner, they can be difficult to change. Habits are in between. They are difficult but not impossible to change. The advantage to this is that useful habits can stay with us with almost no effort. Even a habit that has been put aside for a while can be quickly revivified. Learning a language is difficult, but relearning the same language ten years later is much easier, even if one was not aware of remembering it. The habit of the language was neither lost nor retained in conscious memory. Eventually one can read or speak a second language without being aware of any effort at all. At this point, it is a deeply rooted habit, virtually a second nature. Habits can be acquired quickly or slowly. For some, learning to read or multiply or controlling one's rage comes easily; for others, painstakingly. Deeply embedded habits become apparently permanent and integrated parts of who we are. They not only are firmly rooted capacities but also seem essential to our self-identity. A mother who can respond with consistent good humor to the vicissitudes of parenting may be understood by herself and those around her to be virtually identical to the patience she exhibits. A habit of despair or depression can feel like such an indelible dimension of oneself that it seems impossible to alleviate it.

Habits can be more or less deeply rooted. But even when one begins to recognize them, they are likely to be difficult to change. They have formed a rut in our souls and we cannot simply change our minds about them. Helpful and harmful, deeply and shallowly rooted, habits structure us: body, spirit, emotion, soul, and mind. The more deeply they are sedimented in us, the more difficult they are to change. As Dorotheus says, "it is one thing to pluck out a small weed and quite another thing to uproot a great tree."[20] This makes overcoming a habit that is harmful to us, like smoking or race prejudice, unreasonably difficult.

Identifying passions as habits is a way of pointing out the way they precede and coordinate conscious action, thought, and desire. If we become habituated to stress and anxiety, the muscles in our back and neck and shoulders may become a series of knots. Our muscles may have become so constantly and deeply tense that it seems the natural state of a human body; we remain unaware of the way this somatic tension is affecting our health. Our capacity for joy and laughter gradually flattens out. Our tears stop flowing as we dull down our emotions to accommodate a burden of sorrow that is long past healing. Mind, body, and emotion will conspire as rage or grief, jealousy or addiction dominate us.

At another level, passions become second nature and seem to be an essential part of our identity. The more they have entwined themselves with one's self-identity, the more difficult they will be to dethrone. Passions blend with self-identity, though not in the sense that we conceive ourselves as terrified or enraged. These may be the last things we associate with ourselves. But we do incorporate the effects of these passions into our self-understanding. We act out of a preconscious feeling of the world as threatening or unjust. The myriad ways in which this predisposition to the world shapes our responses solidify in the very structure of our ego. Without knowing why or even thinking about it, we never, ever use public transportation. Somehow this has been swept up in a general feeling of danger that has nothing to do with public transportation or anything else of which we are consciously aware. We may not associate not-using-public-transportation as a marker of our personality. We certainly do not think of terror or even fear as such a marker. These remain invisible. Yet the organization of our life out of these effects of passions remains both crippling and constitutive of our sense of identity.

There is a kind of brain tumor that fastens onto the spinal cord and sends out tiny strands all around itself. This is a particularly terrible kind of tumor because it is virtually impossible to trace all of its tiny tendrils and free the brain from them. They are hard to track and are attached to such fragile parts of the brain that any misstep is as crippling as the tumor itself. In a similar way, the passions embed themselves in our egos, most deeply as the illusion of ego-centrism itself.

The Passions and Egocentrism

The passions reflect ways our psyches navigate a world that is difficult and confusing. In trying to understand why we are so vulnerable to such unhelpful psychic habits, we might remember how intensely our ego experiences the world. We share many things with other people, but one's pains and pleasures, kinesthetic memory, cognitive processes, memories, desires, and way of integrating new things are all "mine." They are unique to the individual, unrepeatable, and largely inaccessible to anyone else's direct experience. This uniqueness is part of the dignity of personhood. The ego is the central location and synthesizer of all of this. It exists in constant, pervasive relationship to its world but takes in the world and organizes it in ways peculiar to itself. The ego has a great stake in continuing its existence and protecting itself from too much pain. Classical theologians have thought of this preoccupation of the ego as the sin of pride. Evolutionary biologists conceive of it more as the pre-programmed drive to survive that allows species to succeed. In either case, the ego is primarily aware of its own experiences and dedicated to making those experiences as positive as possible. This is the job of the ego; we would be hard pressed to survive without the ego's interest in our physical and psychological survival. But because of the inordinate assaults on our well-being that are omnipresent in human life, the ego makes alliance with the passions to keep unbearable pain at bay. In this tragic alliance, the natural vividness of the ego slides into the illusion of egocentrism.

The ego has to spend a lot of energy coping with the pain. The mind has a thousand or so tricks for numbing and hiding psychic pain: denial, repression, suppression, distraction, drugs, exercise, dissociation, fanaticism, obsessive work, and so on. Because of the agility of the mind in avoiding pain, we are able to lodge much of our pain in our body, and this ties our consciousness all the more vividly to our own experience, at the expense of awareness of other people. Emotional pain hurts our bodies; we experience "heartache" or nausea. Meditation, supposedly so "spiritual," requires a strong body and carries with it somatic changes ranging from decreased blood pressure to physical bliss, panic attacks, sweating, and so on. In addition to somatic dimensions of experience, the body bears the brunt of much psychic pain. One trick for easing pain is to shunt it off to the body: headaches, ulcers, muscle tension, stomach aches, preterm labor, high blood pressure, weak immune systems, and rashes can all be signs that the body is dutifully bearing the psyche's burdens. At the same time, much of what the psyche has to hide and numb is the violence to which the body is subjected from illness, accident, and assault.

The ego organizes its existence as embodied experience. Whatever resources mind has for avoiding pain, there is not much to soften the intensity of the body's experiences or to neutralize the price the body pays for being the last refuge for pain. The deceptions, moralizing, and ignorance that the psyche has available to it are denied the body. I can say, think, believe, and act out of the belief that I am not being hurt by my care for a psychically disturbed and often cruel member of my household. But my body will bear all the misery, confusion, anger, and reality rending that I cannot bring to consciousness. Embodiment gives an intensity or vividness to "my" awareness that is virtually unmatched. The work of the ego in navigating these convolutions is ridiculously complex. But, in the end, the intensity of embodied experience gives the ego little choice but to take "my" experience extremely seriously. None of this has much to do with whether I am kind, mean, compassionate, selfish, or reclusive. These are all secondary to this normal feature of personhood: *my* experience, however convoluted my awareness, is more real to me than anything else.

Naturally, in light of the vividness of my own experience, other things cannot impinge on my awareness with the same strength and urgency. If I fall in love and am delirious with delight, I can care about the news that a typhoon just wiped out whole villages, leaving thousands homeless and desperate for water, medical care, and lost family members. I can understand that my newfound happiness is neither more real nor more important than the sufferings of these strangers. But I cannot help but be more aware of my own happiness and to care about it much more than all of their suffering put together. In fact, I may not have fallen deliriously in love. Perhaps I am chopping vegetables as I listen to the news report. The knife slips, and I graze my finger. It bleeds. My regard for the typhoon victims vanishes completely as I find a paper towel to wrap up my scratch.

My intellectual knowledge that I am not one iota more important or real than anyone or anything else does not translate into felt experience. In the absence of an immediate awareness of others as vivid as my awareness of myself, I will constantly act out of this root experience of the brilliance of my own experience and the comparatively pale, tepid, and inessential reality of everything else.

Given this disparity between the intensity of my own and the vagueness of others' experience, it takes what seems to be a superhuman accident of grace, luck, desire, and good karma to avoid the slide to egocentrism. The Buddhists say that the great compassion of a bodhisattva is like a person who holds his or her own hand in the fire of another's suffering. But, speaking for myself at least, if I were holding my hand in the fire I cannot imagine being aware of anything but wanting it *out*. Only then might I (*might* I) get interested in pulling someone else's hand out of a fire. I can agree that my hand is not more important than anyone else's. I can even agree that this other person might be much more important, virtuous, and indispensable than I am. I can appreciate the beauty of altruism and anticipate the rewards of agapaic love. But to feel the burning of someone else's hand as equal in significance to the burning of my hand is something else again. To live as if it were of equal or even more importance does not seem possible. This is the central illusion to which we are all subject. We know we are not the center of the universe, but in our piteous state, it is impossible for us to live this truth. This illusion is not an overt posture of narcissism. It does not exclude genuine compassion for others. It has nothing to do with the moral desirability of unselfishness or self-sacrifice or humility. It is the gap between what we experience and our actual situation. We live in radical, intimate connection to everything else—as intimate as drops of water in the ocean. We are fires that image God. But our experience continually burdens us with the terrible news that we are more real than anything else; we are tyrannized by the painfulness of our lives and the loneliness to which our illusion condemns us. Egocentrism is like the dentist's drill that has slipped past the reach of Novocain. When that happens, our own pain is all we can experience. There is a sense in which this is a dimension of our ordinary experience. Because of the intolerability of ordinary and extraordinary forms of suffering, egocentrism conspires with the passions because they promise to alleviate pain.

Pain Relief

We are beings out of balance. The intensity of our experiences produces a gap in which the strength of our spirit is outstripped by the conditions of our existence. It is natural that we seek consolation and cling desperately to whatever seems to bring relief. The passions move in as pain bearers. They are comrades of the ego, and, like it, befuddled by the vividness of "my" experience. The passions represent those parts of us that are hostile to the characterization of egocentrism as "illusion." Through them we believe the ego is the rightful heir, the Sun King, and we detest those who say it is a usurper. The passions are soldiers, not "in the army of the Lord," but for the ego, to defend it against all comers and to relieve all unnecessary pain. Devoted to their cause, they have no need for honors or fanfare. They know that their usefulness lies in their ability to conceal themselves. They are the Special Forces, the ninja warriors of the ego.

Dorotheus of Gaza describes the painfulness of the passions by imagining hell as the state of being turned over to them without anything to distract us from them:

> Through this body the soul gets away from its own passions and is comforted; it is fed, it drinks, it sleeps, meets and associates with friends. When at last it goes out of the body it is alone with its own passions and, in short, it is tormented by them, forever nattering to them and being incensed by the disturbance they cause and being torn to pieces by them so that it is unable to remember God.[21]

When we think of Dorotheus's description of hell as undiluted presence to one's passions, it may seem counterintuitive to identify them as painkillers. But holding this paradox in our minds may be a particularly helpful clue to their nature. They appear to us as something that will ease our pain, but they exact a high price for their pain-relieving powers. In this, the dynamics of passions are eerily similar to those of drug addiction. It is hardly necessary to point out that drugs are harmful to mind and body and that the life of a drug addict is far from enviable. Yet we still turn to drugs to soften the painfulness of life and to displace suffering with pleasure. The unbearable burden of reality becomes too much and release into illusion feels not only preferable but essential. It is the nature of many drugs to be addictive. It is in our nature to attach very quickly to things that bring us relief. The combination of these two trajectories of addiction is quite powerful. This addictive tendency of drugs is present in those that bring relatively minimal relief, like cigarettes, chocolate, or caffeine, as well more violent drugs like cocaine and heroin. Of course, not all of us are heroin addicts, and it is easy to be dismissive of the "weak" who cannot take reality and so turn to drugs. It is true that not everyone turns to drugs, mild or strong, to soften the blows of the day. But there are very, very few who are not addicted to pain relievers that are as addictive and destructive as drugs. This may seem an exaggeration. But we are probably at least as far removed from the luminosity at our hearts as the most degraded drug addict is removed from the pleasures of "normal" life.

Egocentrism is not a benevolent illusion but rather a source of difficulty and pain. The "I" that experiences the world so vividly is not a monstrously inflated ego but a raw nerve exposed to a great deal of mental and physical suffering. Much of the work of psychic and social formation is to enable this raw nerve to survive its often inhospitable environment. This work is all the more complex because the world is not only dangerous but also unbearably beautiful. The relationships we enjoy, the creativity we express, the longings for spiritual refreshment, all prevent us from simply raising barriers between ourselves and the world. We face the impossible task of opening our spirits ever wider to beauty, friendship, love, and knowledge while protecting ourselves from assault and danger. The passions are spiritual, psychological, and social responses to this impossibility. Like cocaine or cigarettes, they do not provide real nourishment. The passions are destructive and sometimes morally unattractive. But they are nonetheless attempts to cope with contradictions inherent in our existence.

We suffer passions. They are the torment of hell. Yet they present themselves to us as pain relievers. When we feel anxious that we are worthless or our work is no good or we are not loveable, this deep-down pain can be intolerable. Jealousy raises up to succor us. It displaces pain with the insistence that we are just as good and deserving as anyone else: our virtues are as bright, our work as brilliant, our good looks as enticing. Jealousy is not as enjoyable as delight or satisfaction, but it is much better than anxiety and self-doubt. It distracts us from our more genuine and painful feelings. This is an example of a particular response mostly at the level of emotion.

But passions do not ride into battle only at moments of difficulty. If this example were extended to become a habitual modus operandi, it would mean that we were more or less continually shielded from anxieties of this sort. Instead of noticing these feelings, one throws up the constantly rehearsed reassurance that one is "just as smart!—no, much smarter, than the next person!!! They just made their way ahead because of—family connections, good looks, good luck, lack of integrity. . . ." We can gnaw on our jealousy with a kind of rough contentment; it gives us a degree of satisfaction that dims our awareness of our limitations and our frustrations at our failures (real and imagined). Over time the relief we experience in this way becomes indispensable to us. It seems like a natural buoyancy of our spirit, and we hardly notice we feel it. The reassurances, the excuses, the jealous anger at others are barely registered in consciousness but run on continuously, like white noise in the background of our mind. One might even have mastered the social etiquette of appreciation of others. "Jealous? Me? Absurd!" But still the soothing record hums its comforting refrain. We may gain a reputation as unusually confident, even arrogant. In this way, a passion sinks into the background but continues to shape how we feel and respond to the world. In shielding us from genuine pain, the passions are like narcotics, and, like narcotics, are befuddling because they shield us from reality. We know less about who we are, what we feel, and who other people are because we know these things through the anesthetizing mediations of passions.

Much of human life can be understood as addiction to patterns of life that ease pain but are physically and spiritually debilitating. They give the appearance of help but conceal their price. This theme of a hidden price is common in folktales. The Grimm brothers record the story of "The Girl without Hands."[22] A poor miller, now reduced to gathering wood for a living, is promised by a stranger enormous wealth in exchange for what stands behind his mill. Nothing but an old apple tree stood behind the mill, so the deed was easily done. Unhappily, the miller's daughter was standing behind the mill just then, and he had inadvertently traded his daughter away for fabulous and exaggerated release from toil. One can sympathize with the miller. What impoverished person would not want to trade a useless apple tree for wealth? Should we know that a deal this good must contain a hook? Maybe if we were strong and in our right senses we would be more wary. But the passions entangle us when we are already disoriented by pain. When the pain is bad enough, we almost do not care what is behind the mill, as long as our pain can be relieved.

4

"Caught on the Fangs of Affliction":

Terror, Rage, and Addiction

For those whose minds are slack and wandering
Are caught between the fangs of the afflictions.
                    Shantideva, The Way of the Bodhisattva

Passions are habituated obstacles that take root in the human soul, blocking us from our heart's desire. These obstacles are probably as various as are individual persons; they are also affected by the cultural and social worlds we inhabit. Rather than attempt a catalog of passions, it might be more helpful to examine the structure of three exemplary passions. To help us keep in mind that we are reflecting on destructive passions and not healthy emotions, I use the terms terror, rage, and addiction to identify three root passions. These might be considered root or exemplary passions in the sense that they help us interpret distortions common to the human spirit.

Buddhism and Christianity both notice that amidst the infinite plurality displayed by beings, a deep structure is present in all sentient creatures: any creature that can be aware of feeling at all seeks what it wants and avoids what is harmful.[1] Desire and anger are common expressions of these root orientations to things in the world: we want what we want, and we are angry when we are thwarted. Both anger and desire can quickly deteriorate into harmful relationships to others, in part because they both intensify our experience of ourselves. In our desires and their frustration our ego becomes like a sore we cannot help but worry. At least some writings of the monastic traditions of Buddhism and Christianity reflect awareness of this structure by giving pride of place to anger as the most destructive passion.[2] This is closely followed by disordered desire. The *disorder* of desire is designated in Buddhism as "attachment" or "craving" and in Christianity as "concupiscence." Monastic traditions set a premium on patience, detachment, renunciation, and asceticism because these were perceived as powerful antidotes to egocentrism. In monastic practice, anger and distorted desire are subjected to these practices so they will wither away, allowing deeper rivers of compassion and love to flow.

Recognizing the great power anger and desire have over us, we can appreciate the wisdom of these monastic traditions in identifying them as possessing the mother lode of egocentrism. At the same time, we can observe ways in which this wisdom itself becomes distorted. Limitations in the way these passions have been understood do not neutralize the potential destructiveness of anger and distorted desire, but they mean we must learn from both the wisdom and the distortions of the past as we try to understand these things for ourselves. Distortions are present both in what is said and what is unsaid. Humility is conflated with humiliation; natural and healing impulses are rejected as sinful desire; "patient" acceptance of cruelty or deadening self-sacrifice are confused with love. Even when we correct these explicit distortions, the implication remains that the fundamental distortion of the ego lies in its inflation. Feminists and others have brought to our attention how unhelpful this view is.[3]

In gratitude that this feminist insight has been added to a more ancient wisdom, I am adding "terror" to rage and addiction as a root passion. When we add terror to these two other passions, we are able to see that timidity represents another type of bondage that extinguishes spiritual power. Including terror along with rage and addiction might help us sort out the bondage and distortions of a passion from the ostensible virtues of humility, patience, and self-sacrifice. Understood in this way, terror is a way of extending the work of womanists and feminists to distinguish between the vulnerabilities that arise from weakness and those that arise from strength. But monastics understood rage and addiction not just as common human vices but as structural distortions of the human spirit. They are more like a skeletal structure of the ego that is overlaid with particular virtues and vices, fears, hopes, and capacities. The intensity with which craving and anger modify our awareness is not an accidental structure but is present in virtually all forms of sentience. In egocentrism, these twin drives take the form of the passions of addiction and rage. Unlocking this bondage is not a matter of overcoming a bad habit. It is a matter of reconstituting the ego. When we think of root passions in these terms the addition of terror is a way of saying that fearfulness and unworthiness are also part of the skeletal structure of egocentrism. The significance of fear as a structural aspect of the ego is suggested in Tillich's analysis of courage as the root orientation of faith and in the inclusion of courage as one of the cardinal virtues.[4] But even these literatures do little to help us understand or develop compassion for the paralysis of the soul brought about by a sense of terror or unworthiness. The inclusion of terror as a root passion is an effort to rectify this gap in our understanding.

Like rage and addiction, terror pins us to our ego so we can experience little self-transcendence. When we are terrified, it is hard to think and feel outside the experience of terror. It demands our complete attention, diminishes our awareness, and distorts our entire sense of reality. When we leave it out of the religious imagination, we are forced to interpret our spiritual lives as if our main problem were a strong, overweening ego dominated by impulses of pain and pleasure, when in fact so many of our difficulties arise from self-hatred, fear, anxiety, and the misapprehensions that flow from these.

When we consider the omnipresence of suffering, it should come as little surprise that patterns of terror are embedded in our spirits and psyches. From the first shocks of hunger and pain that assault us as infants, awareness that we have landed in an unreliable environment is branded on our bodies, hearts, and spirits. When we leave this root tenor out of our reckoning, we may imagine that our egos are more perverse than they actually are. Perhaps even more tragically, we are inclined to conceive of the Holy Mystery as angry and alien. The sweet goodness of the Divine Eros is twisted into a cruel and violent paterfamilias, whose demand for perfection we could never meet. The precious "oneing" with our soul accomplished at creation is forgotten. The spectacular display of this oneing in the incarnation becomes for us not a sign of our solidarity but instead a bitter reminder of our sin, which required the death of Christ to atone. We are tempted to apply harsh remedies to cleanse away our pride. Cruel bodily practices, self-degradation, and acquiescence to unjust treatment seem to make sense when we have been made to believe we must tame the raging cesspools of lust and rage we humans have become. Cruel theologies do little to defang terror. And the beauty of the Holy Ones can be harder to discern when they are concealed behind a liturgy of judgment. It shows the incredible resilience of the human soul that it sometimes survives these poisonous cures.

To counterbalance some of these confusions, this analysis of particular passions will begin with terror. Like the other root passions, terror can be understood as operating at three levels (at least!). Terror can be a spiritual habit of which we are somewhat aware. That is, we are aware that fear and humility are more characteristic of us than are anger or licentiousness. At another level, terror lives in some persons and groups as a spiritual center of gravity yet remains below the level of explicit awareness. At a third level, terror intertwines with rage and addiction and with them shapes and distorts egocentric existence. The various passions might be emphasized differently, but in the deep recesses of the human spirit they form an interdependent knot. We rage and become addicted to distractions because we are terrified.

TERROR

It is appropriate that humans feel fear; much in our environment endangers us. But the passion cognate with fear is something else. Terror as a passion is a comprehensive and habituated pattern that organizes consciousness of self, other people, and the world we inhabit. Søren Kierkegaard, Martin Heidegger, Karl Rahner, Reinhold Niebuhr, Paul Tillich, Rudolf Bultmann, and others have argued that our precognitive awareness of death, indeterminacy, danger, and meaninglessness constitute a structural component of the human psyche. Structural anxiety accompanies psyches that live in a world in which emotional, spiritual, social, and physical well-being are never assured. As previous chapters argued, the ego stays busy obscuring and coping with this vulnerability. This pervasive, usually unconscious, awareness of vulnerability that others have analyzed as anxiety might be understood as a dimension of terror.[5]

But terror is also the soul gripped by a habituated fear that has morphed into a debilitating passion. There are creatures endowed with fear as a primary element of their survival. Those creatures that lack strong teeth and claws live off their ability to sense subtle changes in their environment and to stay very still when they perceive danger. A capacity for stillness can mean the difference between life and death for a camouflaged bird or fawn. Human beings are not distinguished from one another by the fangs they possess or lack, but for some humans stillness is a way of forestalling danger. It is an effort to defend oneself that is left to those who either do not have or do not believe they have access to overt forms of self-defense. Abused children may have few resources for self-defense. "Good girls" may not be aware of the resources they do have. Terror might be understood in part as the passion that shapes a soul habituated by an effort to forestall danger through stillness. Terror takes root as this stillness becomes a kind of second nature. It is characteristic not only of particular individuals but subsets of a society.

This general sense of passivity, paralysis, or attempted invisibility arises in part from the perception of the world as inordinately dangerous. Rage can be another response to the dangers of the world, but terror is a hypersensitivity to danger that results in stillness rather than violence. The expectation of harm, perhaps even only trivial harm (being embarrassed, evoking someone's ire), becomes so ingrained as a part of consciousness that we do not even notice it. Yet this grid of terror shapes the way we inhabit the world and effects a mutilation of the will. Terror is like gravity: you must accommodate movement to its pull, even though you are hardly aware of it. "The supreme violence is the supreme gentleness."[6] The terrorized not only respond to the threat of the blow-up, the violence, the humiliation, or the icy silence by remaining still. They respond to the world *as if* these threats were always imminent, whether there are symptoms of danger or not. Stillness is a way of life.

Through this stillness, terror freezes portions of life so that creativity, beauty, adventure, intensity, intimacy, novelty, and curiosity are numbed and shut down. This numbing affect may possess some parts of a person or community more than others. But all of life is diminished by terror, even if it is only certain chunks of us that are bound to it. Terror does not have to be accompanied by an explicit awareness of fear. The passions hide even as they install themselves throughout the chambers of the interior castle. But they leave traces. Someone gripped by this passion may appear calm, cheerful, even gregarious. But there may be hints of the terror these conceal: an inordinate fear of harm to oneself or others or a fear that pops up in odd places; a body that is held close in as if taking up as little space as possible, a body that minimizes movement or avoids things that might make it stand out (an open laugh, awkward efforts at a new activity), uncharacteristic passivity that suddenly appears from nowhere, passivity that unnecessarily chains someone to deadening patterns of work or relationship, or difficulty in doing certain simple things or completing a project. You may joke with a friend about his inability to buy new clothes. But this paralysis may be a trace of a terror that makes attractive clothes dangerous because they might call attention to him. A man may throw away his creativity and joy by succumbing to the family's insistence he take over its business. Although he is beloved by all, the terror that keeps him bound to a barren town and stultifying work retains the power to wrap his soul in a shroud long before his body is dead. Perhaps you are irritated with a friend who throws up all kinds of obstacles to a much-desired trip together. It may be terror that has constructed an impasse between the desire and the ability to pursue it. These are examples of vitality paralyzed by a stillness that the psyche insists is crucial to self-preservation.[7]

Terror can also be noticed when it is unexpectedly contrasted with a burst of vitality. Suddenly there is a vivid flash that escapes from some not-yet colonized region of the heart. In its light, the dullness of terror can be recognized more easily. In my neighborhood there was a woman whose husband did not let her leave the house for many years, but long after her death her exuberant garden refused to die. Cutting back weeds set free plants and flowers that she had planted a decade or more earlier. From the confines of her domestic prison she created astoundingly complex and vivid adventures in beauty.

Incongruities cut in both directions: vitality hits against an invisible wall or emerges from what seemed like hopeless passivity. In both instances, we may be witnessing the last traces terror has left before slipping under the surface of awareness. Terror shuts down the adventure of life, and it does so in part by deflating a healthy sense of self-worth and agency. The terrorized may be obviously among the afflicted, traumatized, or oppressed. Through affliction, one might inhale the loathing for oneself that has been inflicted. It may become part of one's own consciousness, so that one hates oneself even more than does one's victimizers. The afflicted embody a prolonged apology—for having suffered harm, for provoking the harm, for deserving the harm, for all of the imagined mistakes they make, for existence itself. But the deflation of self-worth accomplished by terror need not take the extreme forms of affliction and trauma. It might be a kind of distorted humility. The risk inherent in action makes quiet and stillness feel safer. But we exercise our spirits and manifest our distinctive embodiment of the divine image through action. The diminishment of action is itself a diminishment of self. Terror diminishes the self on a sliding scale from self-loathing to shyness. Passivity deprives us of the occasions for self-expression, action, creativity, zest, and active self-defense. This flattens out a capacity for initiation, even the initiative to exist more fully. The deflated self recites the familiar stanzas of impotence, reminding us of our awkwardness, inabilities, incompetence, and the dangers of visibility: "Who are you to try such a thing?" we ask ourselves.

Terror deflates the self and reduces its scope of action. Because of this passion we are tempted to perceive others as better, more important, more interesting than ourselves. Because of its false humility, terror is too often confused with virtues like patience and even agape. This confusion arises in part because the symptoms of terror can appear to be the very opposite of vanity or aggression. Yet it is in its own way a pernicious cancer of the ego. Hypersensitivity to danger, passivity, and diminishment of self-worth do not forget the ego; they simply worry it in a different way. The painfulness of anxiety and the preoccupation with one's unworthiness pin us to egocentrism as securely as does any other passion. But because the religions generally offer humility and patience as crucial antidotes for egocentrism and because they confuse the symptoms of terror with these very virtues, the toxicity of terror is often not only undiagnosed but valorized.[8]

RAGE

Anger is a natural emotion, appropriate to beings that need a capacity to protect themselves. Wrath is a spiritual power that energizes the contemplative path. The terrorized could often use a good dose of anger and wrath. But rage is a different phenomenon. The potency of rage is estimated by Evagrius in relation to what is required to counter it: "Anger [rage] stands more in need of remedies than concupiscence and for that reason the love that is charity is to be reckoned a great thing indeed in that it is able to bridle anger."[9] Love, the urge to care for and delight in oneself and in others, is one of the most beautiful names of Holy Power, and our capacity to love is a shining of the divine image in us. But rage is a will to harm, acted upon or not, and this makes it the passion most at odds with the impulses of the Divine Eros.

Rage, like all passions, eats into various depths of the soul. To some extent, most of us have some taste of this passion. Because of the vividness of our own experience, we tend to exaggerate harm done to us and to exaggerate the inhumanity of what thwarts or harms us. A canker of rage gnaws at us, even if it is disguised or overshadowed by other stronger or more acceptable feelings. While assent to a passion gives it greater power, when a passion is modified by other desires and interests it is less able to overpower impulses toward compassion and truthfulness. For example, one might agree with neighbors that Jews or Koreans, immigrants, lesbians, Catholics, or Republicans are a wretched nuisance. These people may receive our overt scorn or tacit blame. It feels good to translate inchoate fears and irritations into a directed, focused anger. Our small flame of rage comforts us; it gives us a place to dump our frustrations about the world. But to the extent that rage remains relatively weak in us, we are able to resist the consolations of violence or more overt oppression.

Bondage to rage is greatly intensified as a person or a community discovers the potency rage gives them. A display of anger can be an efficient way to get what we want. This useful stratagem takes deeper hold as we discover the pleasures of rage. Rage is not just useful; it is intoxicating. We seek this high in ever more varied situations. We loosen, bit by bit, the reins that hold it back so we can experience a greater intensity of the wild, freeing intoxication of rage. It is like a balm to our battered, frustrated, humiliated soul. It restores dignity and power to our community or nation. Like other intoxicants, rage is pleasant because it gives us a rush and makes us feel vital and powerful. It is pleasant also because it shuts out what we do not want to see and numbs us to what we do not want to feel. It replaces painful feelings with pleasant ones, and it eases the confusions of life.

Rage presents us with a hallucination of reality in which truth is simple and one-dimensional, emblazoned with stark reds and intense blacks. It is easy to know who we are, where we stand, and what is happening. In our intoxication, there is no need to investigate those shadowy forms on the edges of vision. If they begin to trouble us by moving into focus, a deep draught of rage confines them again to their place in that large, undifferentiated black hole that absorbs all ambiguity. The intense clarity of rage gives us power to act and act forcefully. Action makes us feel even more alive, alert. It seems that our power should extend over the entire world. It is incredible that anything could withstand us and the righteousness of our cause. But even very powerful hallucinations occasionally bump blindly into a real world. Rage cannot accept a world outside itself and rages at its own limit. Rage blocked in its expression ruptures; poisons seep through our whole system. We feel choked and nauseated, and our hangover is truly terrible. The hair of the dog is our only relief.

Rage, perhaps more than any other passion, closes the ego to everything it understands to be outside itself. This may be why monastics such as Dorotheus, Amma Syncletica, and Shantideva evaluated it as the most dangerous passion. Egocentrism is the illusion that we are the center of reality. Others are rather shadowy; they do not have the same hold on us as our own experiences. For rage the ego is, of course, the center of all things, but it is experienced as wrongly threatened. Others remain shadowy, but to the extent they exist they threaten us. It is not necessarily irrational to believe we are threatened. Individuals and communities are threatened and injured, even annihilated, all the time. Being angry at being hurt or insulted is natural. The possibility of rage is rooted in our vulnerability.

Pain degrades us because it carries with it, inexplicably, a feeling that the pain was somehow deserved. Terror accepts this and the implication that we are worthless. Rage offers the psyche another option. In contrast to terror, rage does not respond to danger by passivity and a sense of worthlessness but by inflating our importance beyond all bounds. Rather than trying to become smaller, more inconspicuous, more insignificant, we focus intently on ourselves, deepening and expanding the energy we dedicate to ourselves, worrying the wound we feel we have received. As we contemplate the injury we have suffered it appears more and more unjustified and outrageous. Not just the pain itself but the outrage over the pain takes up more and more psychic space until the pain becomes an epiphenomenon, a mythically revered basis for our outrage.

The degradation of pain is put out of commission as we consider the sheer outrage that we would be subject to such treatment. Rage aides the afflicted by reinforcing a sense of indignant suffering; rage is a faint trace of a memory that affliction is a violation of the divine image. But this memory is distorted by the invention of a persona that rage throws up to mask its humiliation. It is not just that rage conceives itself to be entirely innocent and the wrong entirely unjustified. This might be true. For some, recovering the feeling of being wronged would be very healthy. The distortion lies instead in the scope and the impenetrability of the enraged person or community. The persona of rage becomes an adamantine wall within which the ego is perfectly self-contained, good, reasonable, justified, innocent. On the other side of the sheer rock wall of the ego is the paradox of a world that is at the same time without reality yet possessing threatening power. When rage comes to the assistance of pain, the humiliation of pain is displaced by self-absorption; its anguish gives way to intoxication, and vulnerability is overcome by a mighty fortress and a potent power.

Our invulnerability is achieved more thoroughly as others recede from view. Rage achieves this by encountering others as obstacles rather than persons. The shift that makes one the only real center of experience defrauds others of personal existence. They are not persons, with their own center of experience and value, their own ambiguities and complexities, tragedies, desires, bondage, and craziness. They are one-dimensional things, offensively resistant to our understanding of the world. This objectification of others by rage can degenerate to the point that others are not only empty of humanity but actually evil. This follows from the metaphysics of rage. There is really only one precious, genuinely existing reality and that is me or my community. Whatever challenges or threatens this being is almost by definition evil because it threatens the one most precious thing in the world. Rage may do this in a more or less localized way. It may only be men or women, one's spouse, co-workers, the oppressors, or bad drivers that provoke rage and thus fall out of the world of living beings into the unreality of sheer obstacle. The more rage takes over, the more completely will the range of unreality extend. Rage can be like a black hole, sucking everything into it until very little except our own excruciating, magnificent self exists.

The tendency of rage is toward outrage that anything other than our self exists. News from the outside is threatening and enraging because it threatens the mode of our existence. This aspect of rage shows most clearly its contrast with normal or healthy anger. We are angry when we are hurt or insulted or frustrated. We might be angry with a person, a situation, a state of affairs: anything from a rained-out picnic to violence or war. Anger might be misguided or excessive, but it is contained. But the object that evokes rage is not something concrete; it is not something that defrauds us of our natural well-being. It is the very existence of others. Rage might attach itself to something concrete, but its apparent object is only a face for the outrageousness that other things exist at all. Even if we are not threatened in any obvious way, the kind of existence rage has procured for us is at risk. If it were true that others genuinely existed and existed as themselves valuable and mysterious, than we would cease to exist as the Essential Reality, the Really Real, the totality of Being. We might not literally disappear in a puff of smoke, but we would no longer be the kind of being that we cherish. We would no longer be invulnerable. The intoxication of perfect power and right would no longer be available to us. This would be a kind of death and therefore intolerable.

Many of us are not really in a position to act on our rage. It becomes the primary feeling tone of our spirit but is routed in more or less socially acceptable directions, even as it gnaws at us like a cancer that devours us alive. Or it hitches its wagon to some avatar of rage personified on the world stage: totalitarian dictators, terrorists, righteous warmongers, or ideologues. The passion of these people and movements to annihilate all opposition and their characterization of others as demonic enemies are horrific illustrations of the destructive energy of rage. Absolutely anything is justified in the work of eradicating resistance: deceit, torture, mutilations, war, poverty, genocide. The fantasy of invulnerability extends so far as to remain supernaturally ignorant of the laws of physics. For rage, it is reasonable to drop nuclear bombs on our enemies not only because "everything is justified" but because we are magically and morally exempted from the consequences of this ultimate violence.

ADDICTION

Desire occurs at so many levels and in so many forms it will be difficult to sort out even a few of its characteristics. These reflections started out identifying holy desire as that in us that most resembled the divine image and that was the pathway of our deepest joy. Christianity and Buddhism identify distorted desire as the power that binds us most pervasively. The Buddha's succinct wisdom expressed in the Four Noble Truths identifies attachment as the root cause of suffering. Augustine notices that only a stronger desire can cast out desire. Aquinas identifies concupiscence, that is, inordinate desire, as the form of original sin. Following these traditions, earlier chapters have described our painful preoccupation with our own experiences as the vulnerability that opens us to the predations of the passions. Addiction refers to this deep level of absorption into pain and pleasure that tethers us so mercilessly to our egocentrism. In this sense it may not be a distinct passion but the most basic and virtually universal distortion of holy desire. It is also a passion, however—that is, a distorted attempt to relieve the painfulness of existence.

Like all other sentient beings, we are drawn to those things that give us pleasure and nourish our existence. Addiction goes beyond this basic need by so strongly attaching itself to some ostensible or real good that it becomes harmful to us. It is rooted in the subconscious insistence that some good thing will be able to provide sufficient relief from pain, boredom, and anxiety. We may be more or less strongly addicted to some particular good: shopping, video games, TV, food, success, adventure, our religious denomination, physical pleasure, and so on. We are also likely to relate to everything addictively by entering into our experiences with the silent expectation that they will ease our pain and exhilarate our hearts. We do not become addicts because we are all libertines, shunning the rarefied satisfactions of the spirit in favor of the crude pleasures of the flesh. It is as spiritual beings that we are addicts. The flame and emptiness of holy desire calls us to happiness. The divine image will be satisfied with nothing less. But here in this "weary land" we must constantly cope with the frustration of happiness. It is this harsh paradox at the heart of our primordial experience that translates holy desire into addiction. To accommodate our omnipresent restlessness and suffering we cling to the comforts still available to us.

Like rage and terror, addiction diminishes our spiritual power and truncates our relationships. We want what we want, and our desires worry us and assault us like stinging flies. We experience a kind of desperation to ease the painfulness of desire. We become indifferent to the harm satisfaction will cause us, caring only for relief. We are stung by particular desires: more books, a hair ribbon, a new job. They assault us like bad insect bites that distract our attention from everything else. We are stung also by the restlessness of desire itself. If only I had . . . something. It seems there is something we lack, and if only we were able to get it or do it or arrive there this restlessness would cease. Responding to this harsh master, we form the habit of reaching for a drink, a credit card, or some physical exhilaration when our spirits sink.

Our psyches become sedimented around habits of relief that are difficult to break, even when we begin to understand that they are harmful to us. We cannot afford our purchases. Our relationships are threatened by alcohol, unfaithfulness, the ever-elusive high of physical adventure. Yet so often our endless titillations bore us to death. Like all passions, addiction is deceitful. There is an appearance of freedom in our licentiousness or extreme sports, just as there is an appearance of happiness in the abundance or novelty of something new. But it is also important to remember that the destructive power of addiction does not lie in wanting things or enjoying them. It is in allowing them to obfuscate the depths of our soul, blocking access to the spiral that carries consciousness through fire and emptiness to compassion, eros, and joy.

As we have seen with rage, the impoverishment of our own souls translates into an impoverishment of our relationships with others. Addiction induces us to objectify the things we desire; they become objects promising satisfaction and cease to have much existence in themselves. When we relate to the world as a depository of satisfying objects, we become less attentive to the complexities of beauty and wonder that rise up all around us all the time. It takes energy to attend to something in itself, free of the desire to possess it. Concentrated attention is required to enter into things for themselves. We must focus ourselves outside of our pleasure and pain; we must still our craving long enough to see and feel something else. The energy we need for this is dissipated by addiction. We cannot concentrate long enough or with enough energy to allow the vitality of a poem, an idea, meditative silence, or a simple ecosystem to appear to us. We are also cut off from the net of interdependencies that holds all phenomena together. We want a hamburger and do not want to see the burning rain forest that keeps fast foods in business. We want adventure and, because we are exceptions to rules, we despoil wilderness. We want what we want and deplore the thought that we inhabit webs that carry the consequences of our actions far beyond us. The natural tendency of holy desire is to live into more awareness of connection. The tendency of addiction is to become more isolated and ignorant of connection. Our inattention to connection destines us to be outsiders and strangers, aliens to the beautiful earth that is our home.

Addiction's preoccupation with satisfaction deadens its awareness of other people as living beings, irreducible to our satisfaction. There is an inherent violence in this blindness to others' personhood. There is a shock and violence in the perception, however indirect, that we are being perceived by someone else as a thing, as an instrument of their satisfaction. When we are on the receiving end of this objectification, we must perform the macabre task of being in relationship with someone who cannot or will not recognize us as a living person. Waiting tables, we become instruments of someone's dining pleasure, the more invisible the better. As secretaries we are extensions of the office equipment we run. As lovers we satisfy physical and, if we are lucky, emotional needs of someone else. At the same time, we respond to others as instruments of our own needs. The girl chatting with her coworker is a nuisance because her babbling delays my coffee. She is not being paid to chat! And as long as she is being paid, she is not a person but the mechanism of my satisfaction. It is a deadening thud to the human spirit to be treated as an instrument. But it is also deadening to lose the capacity for recognition. This loss is not only the absence of a particular experience, but the diminishment of a human power to enter into intimacy with others. Intimacy, which we seem to dread above all things, heals the wound of solitude and solipsism that causes us so much pain. It is dangerous, and it is no wonder we fear it. But when it occurs it foreshadows and enacts the "oneing" of the soul with mother and lover Christ.

Addiction follows the pattern of rage when objectification sanctions overt violence. Gradually the illusion takes over, and others really are nothing but utilities of my pleasure. Destroying environments and ravaging bodies makes perfect sense because there is nothing in them that could challenge the supremacy of my desires. There is nothing in them that could resist me, even ethically, because they do not really exist at all. They are phantasms of my pleasure. Rage and addiction can become allies when my desires are thwarted. The fulfillment of my own or my people's desires—for land, oil, honor, prestige, power, stuff to buy, cheap labor—is much more urgent and immediate than any counterclaim that might be posed. Nothing is real but my craving for relief and my rage that I am thwarted. When we come to this point we are capable of almost anything.

HATRED, CRUELTY, AND AFFLICTION

The root passions of terror, rage, and addiction intertwine in us, even though one may be more pronounced than another in various times, places, and peoples. They are the stuff of everyday life. These passions mix in us with eros, selfishness, self-contempt, freedom, love, and bondage, and they produce the constant spiritual ambiguity that most of us live. We act selfishly, repent, try to do good, succeed, then fail, succeed only awkwardly, bury our fears, act boldly, expect too much and also too little. But we can abandon this confusion if we choose. We make our pact to trade pain, ambiguity, terror, and humiliation for the intoxications of rage and addiction. The power and pleasure these passions lend us become more precious to us than anything else, and we become more devoted to them than to anything in real life. In this intensification of egocentrism, we are like houses with no windows; every opening is bricked up. It is almost impossible to get news from the outside, and we are locked in with our passions.

In this haunted solipsism we cling all the more ferociously to our power, agreeing to a dark bargain in which our erotic powers are exchanged for the devil's mimicry of power: hatred and cruelty. Through this alchemy we become like Amnon in whom addiction and rage flow as one and we "hate with a very great hatred so that the hatred with which we hate is greater than the love with which we had loved" (para. 2 Sam. 13:15). It is this disease of the soul that invites the speculation that the divine image can be defaced beyond recognition or recovery. But even while we humans engage in every atrocity, we cling to the belief we are right in our actions. As Benjamin Franklin noted, it is a wonderful thing to be a reasonable being because we can find reasons for everything we do. Solipsism makes this reasoning all the easier: nothing exists outside the black box of our own self. Nothing can testify against us.

Hatred and cruelty include an element of satisfaction or even pleasure in the pain they inflict. For hatred, this satisfaction comes from the righteousness of its cause. Since hatred arises in relation to someone that has thwarted some good, their suffering helps restore the metaphysical balance between good and evil. The object of hatred is so toxic that it is not enough to neutralize it. It must be purged. Hatred might wish to kill its opponents, but it might also wish even more to hurt them first. White supremacists do not wish only to annihilate other races. They wish also to subject them to maximum suffering: degradations of racism, torture, poverty, drawn-out violent death. An abusing husband wants least of all for his wife to leave or die. His assertion of power over his wife and his wife's suffering are necessary to atone for the injustices the husband has suffered.

Only suffering can atone for the injustices I have suffered. Restoration, reconciliation, and redemption do little for the heart enraged at its suffering. This is why Jonah was so outraged at having to prophecy to Nineveh. The children of Israel had suffered cruelly at the hands of the Assyrians. When the Ninevites repented, Jonah was furious. "O LORD! Is not this what I said when I was still in my own country? That is why I fled to Tarshish at the beginning; for I knew that you are a gracious God and merciful, slow to anger, and abounding in steadfast love, and ready to relent from punishing. And now, O LORD, please take my life from me, for it is better for me to die than to live" (Jonah 4:2–3). God gently chides him, "Is it right for you to be angry?" (v. 4), and Jonah later tells God, "Yes, angry enough to die" (Jonah 4:9). It is easy to sympathize with Jonah. Christianity has tended to be on his side in his feud with God. Christian history, theology, art, and liturgy are filled to overflowing with worship of cruelty as a display of the divine power and the divine way of restoring justice.[10]

But it is this aspect of hatred that is especially difficult for its victims to take in. It is terrible to suffer; it is even more terrible to realize that the reason we suffer is that our pain brought satisfaction to someone else. This is the extreme objectification. Cruelty does not make us only into a utility or pleasure for someone else. These might allow some scrap of personhood to survive. But suffering foreshadows death; it is the diminishment of life's power and the limit of our agency and desire. Hatred wills this attenuation of life; cruelty is its tool to find that delicious point where something can be held in existence when it has lost everything except the capacity to experience pain. This is the point when life and death are locked in their most intense conflict because they are in this utterly opposed.

For hatred, the infliction of pain and death are just not enough. It is necessary to make someone experience themselves as nothing but pain and the just desert of pain. Hatred and cruelty thrive on the suffering of spiritual beings. Having to embody this contradiction as an object of hatred and cruelty is intolerable to us. It is not that our spiritual suffering is worse than our bodily suffering. But it is the last place we exercise agency. We can fight this meaning hatred embroiders on our body even if we cannot protect ourselves from assault. To fight the meaning of hatred, we will believe anything as long as we did not have to take in this image of our suffering as nothing more than the play of cruelty. We believe ourselves guilty. We will bow down to the divine justice that persecutes our people, murders our children, and destroys civilizations rather than believe our suffering has no cause other than someone's cruelty. Somehow by fleeing the logic of hatred some shred of human dignity is sustained. If we are guilty at least we are not what hatred would make us: nothing but empty objects of pain. Spiritual beings can stand being guilty, but we cannot be stand being nothing.

Those who preserve themselves through the satisfactions of hatred flee direct knowledge of cruelty as energetically as do their victims. When faced dead on, there is nothing more horrifyingly ugly than cruelty. It is unbearable for us to see this ugliness inside ourselves, so we shield ourselves from knowledge of our cruelty by the righteousness of our cause. We are weakened by terror, empowered by rage, and distracted by addictions, and it can be hard to resist the pleasures of cruelty.

The passions seem beautiful and invite us to access the power within us. But they offer a kind of power that can do nothing but dominate or destroy. For those of us who sojourn here in this beautiful, terrifying world the temptation to use this kind of power is overwhelming. Once tasted, the power becomes our master, and its hold on us seems unbreakable. Like others of Christ's lovers, undutiful daughters of this hubristic and violent tradition, I testify to another power.

The Demons Hide Themselves

Temptation by the Good

Question: When sin is transformed into an angel of light and seemingly appears as grace, in what way can [one] recognize the deceits of the devil? And how can he [sic] receive and discern the ways of grace?

Answer: The signs accompanying grace are much joy, peace, love, and truth. . . . But the signs of sin are accompanied by turmoil, not joy and love toward God. Take the example of the plant endive. It looks like lettuce. But the latter is sweet, the former bitter. Also in the matter of grace, some things resemble truth. . . . So there are certain features related to grace that, when a person looks at them from a distance, as certain visions, delight him. But he is quite different when the power of God enters into him, takes over his members and his heart and captivates his mind by the love of God.

Pseudo-Macarius, The Fifty Spiritual Homilies

Folktales, Scripture, and theology agree that evil has a deceptive quality; it approaches us indirectly. We do not typically embrace evil straight on, for itself. We have to be seduced or deceived. "The devil was a liar from the beginning." In the fairy tale "The Girl without Hands" the miller does not knowingly agree to hand over his daughter to the devil in exchange for money.[1] He is tricked into it. Why did Eve accept the fruit? There is no indication in the biblical text that she was motivated by the perversities of pride or disobedience. She was not even present when the command was given, so it is not clear that it should count as disobedience at all. The whole conversation she has with the serpent is an odd combination of half-truths, second-hand information, and misquotations. In the end, she just looked at the fruit itself and "saw that the tree was good for food, that it was a delight to the eyes, and that the tree was to be desired to make one wise" (Gen. 3:6). She chose three good things: nourishment, beauty, and wisdom. Nonetheless, we are told that things went badly for her. It is not that she chose bad things, but something about the way they were presented to her by that cunning serpent made them harmful to her.

In both of these stories, temptation occurs in the context of deceit. Tales like these retain their vitality because they resonate with something in our experience. A deceptive quality in our environments and our psyches is concealed by the apparent clarity we experience as we navigate through our days. We have available to us so much news, so many photographs, so many up-to-the-minute reports, yet information distorted or left out of the news makes it hard to understand what is going on. The maddening absorption of religious holidays into consumer culture erodes even the memory of the sacred. Deep structures of every form of prejudice and domination belie rhetoric of equality. As individuals and communities we desire justice even as we embody self-hatred, suspicion, and fear of others. We believe we are powerless even as our bodies sicken with the effort to hold in the enormous power that has been given to us. In this quagmire of half-truths, absent teachers, and second-hand stories, even when we choose things that are good, somehow they end up hurting us. Temptation is one pathway for exploring this paradox.

Temptation can carry negative connotations, as if we were awash in illicit desires that we constantly labor to keep at bay—or at least *should* labor to keep at bay. But in this context temptation does not refer to a struggle against moral imperfections. Temptation is entanglement with *anything* that subdues, chokes, misfires, or distorts our holy desire. As we saw with the passions, this may be "virtue" as easily as "vice." And, as we see in the story of Eve, choosing good things does not protect us against harmful consequences. Temptation reflects the muddled context in which we act and the way in which in our everyday life our actual situation can be veiled from us.

The idea of temptation indicates a conflict within us between a desire for good things and the attractiveness of harmful things. "I can resist anything but temptation," Oscar Wilde quipped. How easy it would be to be good all day long if harmful things were not so mesmerizing, so inviting. But chocolate and useless plastic items are not the primary front on which our conflicts are fought. The older stories are right. It is our soul that is at stake in temptation. It is easy to understand why we succumb to various small pleasures even when we believe they are not very good for us. It is perhaps less obvious why we would barter away the good in us, our heart's desire, and our deepest happi-

ness in favor of harmful ways of life. The association of temptation with deception may be related to this counterintuitive preference. Who among us
directly, self-consciously prefers unhappiness to happiness? But who among us
is not entangled by things that bind us to unhappiness?

On the other hand, considering the omnipresence of cruelty and dishon-
esty in our world, we might think temptation is not necessary at all. We
humans seem to be in love with violence and everything destructive. Yet direct,
straight-up, unadulterated consent to evil is harder to get than one might
think. We humans usually need a veil of some sort between ourselves and the
destructive things we do. Our most hideous evils and worst self-mutilations
are accompanied by a propaganda machine inside our heads that describes the
good we are accomplishing. That we can be so easily deceived suggests a terrible fragility of our spirit.

This fragility is only worsened by the fact that very little is in itself good or
bad. Almost anything that exists can be helpful or harmful given different circumstances. Scripture is a divine reading (*lectio divina*) that takes us to the
womb of God or a forceful tool against injustice or the divine authorization of
slavery, war, and the degradation of women. Wine can become the blood of
Christ, lend a spirit of conviviality among friends, or destroy families and bodies. We cannot always simply look at something and see clearly and unequiv-
ocably whether it is helpful or harmful. This means that many things that
appear to be good are actually harmful, and many things that appear to be bad
are actually very good. What appears to us as good or as harmful are all mixed
up higgledy-piggledy. Given the deceptive qualities of our environments and
our spiritual fragility, this disorienting instability of good and bad makes us
easy targets of temptation.

It is anachronistic, to say the least, to appeal to the "demons" as the source
of our difficulties. But detached from literalism, they remain an evocative
metaphor for the patterns of illusion to which we are subject. Today psy-
chotherapists are aware of ways our minds become our enemies, inflicting us
with a kind of internal oppression that mirrors harm done to us in the external world.[2] The demons are personifications of some of these dynamics. They
do not refer to real personalities that exist over against us, trying to work our
defeat, but to the inner workings of mind that can sometime feel as if they were
alien forces. They symbolize the paradox of wishing for good but becoming
entangled in evil. The demons are famous for their talents at seduction and
deception. They seduce us with a promise for some sweet good: wealth, nourishment, beauty, wisdom, love. But the demons' promises conceal some nasty,
often fatal, surprise. In "The Girl without Hands" it turns out that it was the
miller's daughter, not an apple tree in the back yard. In Genesis, it turns out
that the fruit was actually the one that was forbidden. Seduction, the appeal of

something good as the bait for something harmful, is probably the strongest weapon of temptation. On the face of it, the offer seems wonderful. It is only after consenting to the deal that the hidden hook bites into us. Folktales can be structured around revealing the hidden price. But in real life, this price may become apparent to us late or not at all. Chancing upon some painting of rare beauty in an old trunk and suddenly recognizing that we ourselves had painted it, we may realize too late that "selling our soul" for artistic success was less of a bargain than it looked when we were twenty-one. Seduction works so well because it travels in the company of deceit. The real thing one is agreeing to is concealed. The actual situation one is in, the true identity of the other characters, and the nature of the transaction are all disguised. The seductive and deceptive qualities of harmful choices make it easier to understand why we are all so entangled in them.

The imagery of demonic temptation displays a deeper way in which our consent is extracted from us. At first, we consent in ignorance. We can insist we were misled, tricked, and swindled. "The woman—that *you* gave me, by the way—gave it to me!" "Well, the serpent beguiled me! (Maybe if you had mentioned the fruit thing to *me*, instead of my husband, things might have gone differently!)." It is in what happens next, when the scam is exposed, that our collusion is more evident. When the unfortunate miller is told by his wife that it was his daughter in the backyard, he is distraught. But when the devil comes to take her, he makes no objection. Unlike the miller's daughter in Rumplestiltzken, he makes no effort to strike a new bargain. There are no tears, no piteous pleading. In contrast to Psyche, he makes no effort to undo what he did. It is at this point that his assent to what he has done really takes hold of him. What he agreed to at first in ignorance, he now accepts as his own.

A story like this allows us to see some of the indirection of consent, but it also shows us that we do choose. In the beginning we must be beguiled, but having tasted the sweetness of the fruit, it is much harder to refuse it. It may be that it is only after tasting it that we can see we are eating poison, but at that point, addiction has already set in. Once we have tasted it, consolation is hard to give up. Yet we also hate to give up the remnants of our genuine desire for good. We hate, too, giving up our *idea* of ourselves as good people. The association of evil with deception in theology and folktales points to the psychic quagmire in which this assent occurs. We are not "rational economic men" choosing obvious goods. Our minds are crisscrossed with secret passages and rabbit holes we run down to avoid being presented with painful realities: betrayal by our ideals, the backfiring of our best intentions, the good and bad in us that are so painful to see. Obfuscation is essential in deferring knowledge of trivial misdemeanors and in concealing the large narratives we inhabit. We are often like *Bulstrode*, from George Eliot's *Middlemarch*. Course hypocrisy was not sufficient to bridge the gap between his vaunted piety and his crimes.

> He was simply a man whose desires had been stronger than his theoretic beliefs, and who had gradually explained the gratification of his desires into satisfactory agreement with those beliefs. . . . But a man who believes in something else than his own greed, has necessarily a conscience or standard to which he more or less adapts himself. *Bulstrode's* standard had been his serviceableness to God's cause: "I am sinful and nought—a vessel to be consecrated by use—but use me!" had been the mould into which he had constrained his immense need of being something important and predominating.[3]

Bulstrode displays remarkable psychic agility in preserving his self-image as a pious, God-fearing man, dedicated only to obedience to the divine will. He remains undaunted in this belief, even as he maneuvers to disinherit the beloved daughter of his widowed bride and to extend his fortune by marketing stolen goods, and ultimately murdering the man who could bring all of this to public knowledge. Bulstrode's interior machinations are psychologically essential self-deceptions rather than simple hypocrisy. Deception is potent not so much because we want to trick other people but because it is essential that we trick ourselves.

Bulstrode is an example of how we work harm while preserving our good opinion of ourselves. But similar convolutions occur that bind us to genuine goods in ways that are destructive. Understanding temptation as seduction and deception reminds us that the most dangerous temptations are present in the guise of something we think of as good. Stunned by endless permutations of pain and urged on by sincere delight in the good, we remain open to the classic devices of the demons: deception, illusion, and seduction. Operating in disguise and darkness, the demons hide themselves. They are hidden in the words of the authorities we love and in the social institutions we trust: "Women cannot be priests." "We are a peace-loving nation and abhor being forced to go to war."

The demons are disguised in our unperceived beliefs, forgotten traumas, and sacred images. Unbidden, they structure our minds and our societies, sustaining racism we despise, goading us with fruitless obligations, and conflating patriarchy with the holy. Because of their skillful hiding, the demons render our assent to temptation invisible to us. The deleterious affects of our acts remain difficult to recognize. There is now before the Georgia Legislature a bill to deny partner benefits to gay and lesbian people. This is presumably motivated by a kind of "moral clarity" that renounces sexual relations that are perceived to be contrary to Scripture. Supporting this bill means accepting the intense anguish and degradation it causes to couples and their families. It also means accepting that children and adults now covered by health insurance will become uninsured. The gap between "moral clarity" and the emotional, economic, and physical suffering it causes exemplifies the obfuscation to which temptation subjects us.

The variety of ways we are vulnerable to deception, seduction, and illusion are probably as numerous as the stars in the sky. Only two general styles of temptation will be explored here: the way genuinely good desires and impulses can be distorted and the narcissism that addiction to pain relief can accomplish. These two styles may reflect the two stages of temptation described above: assent in ignorance and then consent even after the true nature of the agreement has been revealed. Although they are described as if they were distinct from one another, they are actually closely woven together. In each person and community, they modify one another in complex ways. Teresa of Avila, like most spiritual directors, spends a great deal of time giving clues for discerning what is genuinely helpful and harmful. She allows that the devil can speak as clearly as the spirit of truth, "but he will not be able to counterfeit the effects which have been described, or to leave the soul this peace or light, but only restlessness and turmoil."[4] The discouraging wisdom Teresa offers us is to realize that temptation does not come to us as a choice between good and evil but as something good, and that the sign by which we discern one from the other is not freedom from pain but rather peace.

TEMPTATION BY THE GOOD

As hard as it is to discern what is helpful from what is harmful, human beings retain the capacity to truly *desire* good for one another. We can work for social justice and be moved by sympathy for people we know and for people we do not know. We can feel the violations of the earth as if they were in our own bodies. Intoxication with beauty in nature, in a concert hall, in a beer joint can relieve us, for a time, from our egocentrism. We can create great works of art or wisdom. We can yearn for God and love all of God's creatures. We can take the vows of the bodhisattva to express our desire to move forever toward increased skillfulness in alleviating suffering. We can sacrifice for our children, volunteer for the benefit of our neighborhood, teach Sunday school, water parched plants, save stray dogs and cats from the pound. We may do these things from mixed motives, but that does not mean that we have no genuine impulse to seek others' good or to delight in the beauties of the world. In this section, it is not the mixed motives that draw our attention, but ways in which *genuinely good desires* can be destructive to us. Even with all of our foibles we are able to do beautiful, healthy things. Because much of what we are drawn to is good and helpful, it can be hard to discern the harm that is concealed.

Our habituated passions make it difficult to identify what is healthy in a particular situation. But another dimension of our difficulty is that although the unity of the Divine Eros dwells in us, we perceive this unity in splintered and opposed capacities. We distinguish courage, wisdom, serenity, love, energy, patience, strength, anger, forgiveness, self-manifestation, humility, kenosis, mercy, forbearance, urgency, justice, and so on. These separated virtues are healthy when they are united and interdependent. When they are split apart, they can be distorted and damaging. But it is primarily through isolated virtues or ideals that our desire for good comes to us. The formation in us of desire for good happens in particular families, societies, and historical epochs. But particular communities tend to sever these erotic powers, exaggerating the importance of some, vilifying others. At the same time, each of us has a natural affinity for some powers for good more than others. We may be strong and energetic, aflame with anger over injustice, but, when severed from mercy or wisdom, these erotic powers can themselves become instruments of violence and humiliation. Our zeal for justice can wear us out, body and soul, in the absence of equanimity or nurturing companionship.

The wisdom that allows erotic power to shine forth in its natural harmony does not come to communities and individuals quickly or automatically. As this harmony is broken apart, its luminosity dissipates. Each splinter retains some of the gleam and efficacy of its original power, but it becomes distorted when split off from its erotic unity. The beauty of its divinity continues to draw us. But it sometimes happens that we understand whatever fragment we encounter as if it alone were the fullness of the divine: we devote ourselves to love or truth, to a sacred authority, to moral perfection and righteousness, as if each one of these contained by itself the full revelation of God. By making only one aspect of good stand in for the whole Good, even the good we honor becomes distorted and less good. This privileging of some shard of good has made us Christians hard-hearted to others. We have, for example, used the good of revelation as a source of domination and violence.

It can also happen that in developing and honoring one complex of goods we become like an athlete who overdevelops one set of muscles. The disharmony between muscles that are too strong and too weak results in injury. We might sprain our "compassion muscle" when it is left unsupported by anger or serenity. The fragmentation of our erotic power leaves us open to the relentless wiles of the demons. They do not have to appeal to anything harmful or illicit. They need only appeal to the goods we adore, goods that are divinely sanctioned by Scripture, church, and reason itself. The demons slip into our morality. Suddenly it makes sense to us that a young girl should be condemned to the Magdalene laundries in order to spend her life washing away the sin of her sexual impropriety. They sabotage the ideals of self-sacrifice, and we find ourselves crushed to death as, stone by stone, we attempt to carry everyone's burdens but our own. Even love, "the greatest of all," is no match for the demons. We burn people at the stake rather than let their souls burn in hell out of love. We destroy cultures and the ecosystems that sustained them to bring strangers the gospel of love. We look away from the domestic violence in our families and churches, lest anger overpower our love. We forgive too soon, even if it tears us to pieces, in devotion to love. The good we crave has become the instrument of our undoing.

We may do all of these things from much less noble motivations, too. But attributing everything that goes wrong to selfishness places yet another veil over the dangers to which our desire for good subjects us. Teresa of Avila is one who understood temptation by good. When we are self-consciously devoted to something good, we can fail to discern ways these good things themselves can become traps. Teresa identifies for her sisters ways they can be led astray by their zeal for God.

> "Dare I begin such and such a task?" "Is it pride that is impelling me to do so?" "Can anyone as wretched as I engage in so lofty an exercise as prayer?" . . . Oh God help me, daughters, how many souls the devil must have ruined in this way! They think that all these misgivings, and many more that I could describe, arise from humility, whereas they really come from our lack of self-knowledge.[5]

Teresa roots our vulnerabilities in our lack of self-knowledge. We do not realize who lives in the center of our being or how powerful and precious we are. Unable to embrace our power, we turn back from our vocations. Teresa's admonition to her sisters is as timely now as in the sixteenth century. For many of us, it is not pleasure or ambition that tempt us. It is our own reckless dutifulness, our inability to nourish ourselves, or our distorted humility. Perhaps following Teresa's lead we will better understand how vulnerable we remain to confusion even as our desire for good intensifies.

MORALITY

Morality is a good thing; it can contribute to the stability and order that are necessary to hold a society together over time. Honesty, loyalty, good manners, sanctions against harmful exercises of sexuality, hard work, and so on are socially stabilizing and provide a kind of foundational moral pedagogy. But when one with a desire for the good is tempted to think of morality as the absolute good, desire becomes an arrow that falls short of its mark. It can do so in a variety of ways.

A familiar distortion of morality is when it is confused with social structures that in themselves have no more to do with the good than the choice of forks with which one eats fish. This confusion tempts us to allow structures of domination and oppression to be obscured by good manners, propriety, and morality. One's table manners identify one as of a lower class, therefore less intelligent, honest, and dependable, unsuitable for certain professions and marriage partners. A culture that fails to cover appropriate parts of the human body with clothing is obviously savage and must be dominated or destroyed. These are not very subtle examples of the temptation to use morality for harmful purposes, since the self-interest in them lies so close to the surface.

One can also think of the ways moral values make us blind to human suffering. Our commitment to the value of work can make poverty seem like the just dessert to those who do not or cannot gain self-sufficiency through work. All over the world, "improper" sexual behavior calls for imprisonment, torture, murder, disenfranchisement, or humiliation. Victims of rape "deserve what they get." The scourge of AIDS is divine punishment of same-sex love. The satisfaction we experience when hard times fall on people with loose or otherwise offensive morals is a milder version of these temptations.

Another temptation by morality is that of self-righteousness. How satisfying it is to see the faults of those incapable of emulating our virtues. Perhaps we savor the knowledge that they will soon be rotting in hell. We may satisfy ourselves with a more temperate pity for the moral frailties of others: "How sad that people can be so hard-hearted and selfish, such moral imbeciles!" It is also pleasant to notice that other people succumb to this vice, when we, of course, do not.

Morality can also tempt us to divide virtues from vices. Love, patience, forbearance, and forgiveness are good while anger, pride, and pleasure are not. In another setting, bravado, courage, or impervious obedience may transpose pity and gentleness into moral pitfalls. Social settings will determine what counts as virtues and vices, and some will do this better than others. But the impulse to divide out spiritual energy into opposing camps is likely to disarm certain virtues while turning others toward violence.

In these examples, morality ends up being the occasion to think of some people as less worthy of love and care. Human history shows how easy it is to succumb to this temptation as well as the spiritual, physical, and cultural violence it produces. Morality can misfire in the opposite direction as well. It can demote the fire of goodness to an attractive but tepid niceness. In his one novel, *Pictures at an Institution*, the poet Randall Jarrell created two characters that are pure in heart but pinched and cropped like human bonsai trees. Morality has halted the adventure of goodness in them; first, in the perpetually innocent Miss Batterson and second, in Flo, the indefatigable mom, wife, and social activist.

Miss Batterson embodies an otherworldly sweetness that preserves itself by remaining adamantine against any disillusioning knowledge of evil. "There was almost nothing you could safely ask her advice about, except perhaps thank-you letters. *Safely* meant, without injuring Miss Batterson's understanding of the world."[6] This kind of goodness is warm and cozy and sweet-tempered. This stability comes from the choice (and luck) never to stretch beyond the confines of her known world. In this way she is protected from ever being broken open by the contradictions of life. For Miss Batterson, suffering is the subject matter of poignant, stirring poetry, not "real life." It is easy for her to be kind, and she feels no desire to judge others. Within the safety of this lovely, orderly universe, there is no temptation to be otherwise than benevolent. But

> when she died the Recording Angel would look at her accusingly and she would say defensively, "I haven't done anything," and he would close his book and sigh—she had not understood at all. . . . Yet perhaps the Recording Angel would reach out to Miss Batterson and touch her with the tip of his finger, and the poor dew would at last thaw, the seed in the tomb begin to sprout.[7]

Flo, Miss Batterson's best friend, also inhabits a kind of perpetual innocence, but of an activist, energetic variety. Flo, is honest and hard-working,

> public-spirited as the sun. She thought of others night and day, and never about herself—but if she had thought about herself, she would have done something about that too. She worked for causes; she really *worked*. Yet she did not neglect her family for them; she didn't neglect anything for anything. She treated you, no matter who you were, exactly as she treated everyone else, so that after she had talked to you a while you almost doubted that you existed, except in some statistical sense. . . . After a few minutes with Gertrude you wanted to be good all day every day; after you had been with Flo you didn't know what to do—honesty and sincerity began to seem to you a dreadful thing, and you even said to yourself, like a Greek philosopher having a nervous breakdown: "Is it right to be good?"[8]

Awareness of the massiveness of human suffering and the political causes of it almost requires this kind of shield. But it is not just the shield of the statistical that makes Flo's goodness seem "dreadful." For all of her genuine kindness and cheerfulness, she has "lacerated not simply the flesh but the heart, all the instincts and prejudices and fancies, base or bewitching of the human animal."[9] This laceration is the telltale footprint of the demons. Flo has not only translated compassion into statistics and causes, but in expunging selfishness she also had to lacerate her own heart so that the ridiculous and beautiful were also neutralized. The natural affections of the heart seemed to stand in the way of the ideal of disinterested justice for all.

> She was a kind and a selfless and a ludicrous woman. I used to look at her with wonder and exasperation. . . . I felt for her, sometimes, a despairing tenderness: I wanted to say "Don't you mind, Flo," to pat her poor bare bony shoulder. But it was a shoulder armored with something stronger than steel, more impervious than adamant: with righteousness; my hand fell away from what it could never touch.[10]

Flo's commitment and cheerfulness are achieved by the unconscious mutilation of the capacity to be *touched*. She has lost contact with the very world she cares for. Her advocacy and sense of equality are stronger than steal, but her kindness and joy are on automatic pilot. It is a Faustian bargain. The world may greatly benefit from her work. But, the Recording Angel will have to quicken her as well.

Miss Batterson and Flo are in solidarity with all of us who have been persuaded to allow the fiery divine image in us to shine only with as much brightness as morality permits. Their delight in good has remained relatively untainted by egocentrism, but the price for this purity is the absence of intensity and scope. Morality plays a critical role in stabilizing a society. But it can blind us to the vitality of life or shut down our awareness of suffering others. When morality is not balanced by other erotic powers, we are compelled to live in a tiny broom closet off the main hallway of our interior castle.

SACRIFICE

Societies value acts that put the well-being of others before oneself: military service, public service, motherhood, volunteer work, and so on. We tend to be egocentric beings, and this reversal is a "sacrifice" of ordinary impulses toward pain and pleasure. In sacrifice we give up something precious in order for some greater good to be accomplished. Self-sacrifice gives up more and more precious parts of oneself, and, finally, life itself for some good. The ideal of self-sacrifice is enshrined in religion: the "gift of the body" in Buddhism, martyrdom in Christianity and Islam, *sati* in India. Epic and folk heroes root the ideal of sacrifice not only in religion but in cultures all over the globe.

Much good is accomplished through ideals of self-sacrifice, but like all things human, it is easy to exploit these ideals. Patriarchy, militarism, and revolutionary zeal mask dynamics of domination by appeals to the virtues of self-sacrifice. But beyond noting that much good and bad is accomplished through ideals of self-sacrifice, it is not the purpose here to assess the ideal of self-sacrifice itself. Self-sacrifice is of interest here when it becomes a temptation, that is, when it *appeals to our genuine desire for good* but in fact *threatens to harm* the divine image in us. The ecstatic burning of egocentrism by eros is a grace and a miracle that releases the powers of soul and body rather than "sacrifices" them. Except for this kind of conflagration of egocentrism that arises out of intimacy with the Divine Eros, self-sacrifice does what it says: it sacrifices the self. It is a sacrifice that maims the soul without making it beautiful.

The temptation of self-sacrifice is as virulent as anywhere when it is disguised in its more mundane forms, as it is, for example, in motherhood. It is by looking at two examples of motherhood rather than by undertaking a more complete analysis that self-sacrifice will be reflected on here. Years ago, the scion of a wealthy and powerful family renounced these goods in favor of ordination as a Buddhist monk. In response to our fascination at this great "self-sacrifice," a woman of my acquaintance in her early sixties became increasingly irate. If you wanted to see genuine *self*-sacrifice, she said, look no further than motherhood: this was martyrdom. Compared to this, freedom to choose a noble discipline for the purpose of self-perfection is nothing but miserable self-indulgence. I looked at the signs of affluence all around her: magnificent house and car, fabulous vacations, four college-educated children. These did not appear to be the symptoms of self-sacrifice. Motherhood, of course, demands the daily sacrifice of one's needs and pleasures. But this woman's rage did not come from these minutia. Motherhood had demanded from her the sacrifice of that self she might have been if she had been allowed to use her intelligence, creativity, and energy for something larger than cleaning up after babies.

This woman, enraged amidst her wealth, and another, whose rage is known only to the angels, have been maimed by the ideal of self-sacrifice. One, daughter and wife of military officers, the other, daughter and wife of ministers, inhaled the tempting odor of self-sacrifice from their earliest years. For one, sacrifice was a duty above all others: sacrifice for the country and for the family. Domestic and military institutions required the daily martyrdom of her joy, freedom, education, friendships, and most horribly, her vocation. She believed that without these sacrifices, the protection of our nation and the continuation of the family would be severely threatened. As if she lived in ancient Sparta, she knew no other way to organize her moral life and her enormous intelligence outside the religion of duty. Even as an old woman, I believe she scorned every other religion as heresy.

The other woman was seduced by sweeter fare. Her parents loved her, and they loved each other, and they loved everyone else. Intoxication by love does not feel like martyrdom; it is pleasant and freeing. One's own will dissolves into the joyous good that nurtures all people. To love and be loved are so sweet, they disguise any bitterness left unconquered by love. Love put her in a kind of devoted stupor, so it was hard to notice that this religion of love was extracting the dignity of self-worth from her. Not from duty, but from love, she subjected her desires to those around her. She became the source of life while her own life energies and talents remained largely untapped. She was the smiling, kenotic facilitator who made her husband's career possible while satisfying her children's every need and whim. It did not occur to her until much later to resent this.

In the examples of these two women, significant goods commanded their allegiance. They were not simply being forced to submit to an irresistible authority. They more or less self-consciously chose the ideal of self-sacrifice because they perceived it as a genuine good. Each woman, in her way, loved the good and allied herself deeply with the face of the good that was shown to her. In the case of the one woman, the face appeared in the ideals of patriotic and maternal duty. In the case of the other, it appeared in an ideal of loving service. They did not have to be coerced; each willingly used the unique powers of her spirit to weave these goods into their own souls. Their efforts were not without fruit. Children were raised, meals cooked, laundry cleaned, civic and social work accomplished, officials elected, holidays celebrated, UNICEF boxes filled, virtues of self-discipline or gentleness inculcated—this list could extend indefinitely.

Families and communities are called into existence through the tiny and large acts performed by women (and men, too, of course) out of self-sacrificing devotion to these goods. But the women themselves appear stunted, like plants that have had to survive without adequate nourishment. They have had to accommodate themselves to a scope of spiritual expression that dulls rather than burnishes the divine light in them. Infinitely more horrifying examples of distorted self-sacrifice can be found. But if we thought of only the dramatic and horrible examples, we might overlook the temptation that haunts us in our ordinary, mediocre little lives to let the beauty of the divine in us drain away in useless deference to other's wishes.

We are beings that have the power to shine brighter than the sun. That is our nature. It is the divine image within us, and it cannot be destroyed. This shining, like the shining of the sun, generates incredible power. We encounter this power in Mother Teresa, who releases it to transform pockets of India, or in Nelson Mandela, who could help break the adamantine institutions of apartheid from his prison cell, or in a Tibetan lama whose teachings heal bodies and unblock souls. We encounter this power in a passing stranger whose smile at us mysteriously lifts us from doldrums, in tenacious teachers who open dammed up possibilities in their students, in those people who can listen invisible wounds into words and healing. Sacrifice is a temptation to violence against ourselves when it extracts good works from us without unleashing this power.

The women in our example wanted to do good works but were asked to do them by becoming small and quiet. "Clip this wing, stifle this desire; admit that your own will and intelligence are irrelevant to the goods you would accomplish." It is as if their personhood was understood to be more an obstacle than an instrument. We agree to this maiming of our erotic power out of our devotion to good. We thirst for good and are glad to martyr ourselves for it. The demons tell us, in the voices of our church, parents, workplace, nation, or the voice of our own psyche, that this "denial of self" is the meat and drink of the good. Who are you to have anything to give to God or the world? What can you contribute out of your puniness? But do not despair—even you can make a pleasing sacrifice to the Lord: amputate that hand, that ear, that foot; better yet, cut off your desire and allow yourself to become empty. An empty vessel can carry much good! Better to go to heaven with one hand than go to hell chock full of self-will!

When this deception is successful, a spiritual maiming occurs that cripples the good one would do. This maiming and crippling will take forms as various as the members of the human species. But in each case, the power to see, act, desire, and delight in the world will be compromised. One given the heart of a lion may find herself cloistered and hobbled—in the name of some good. Even if her mind believes in this good, her heart will rage at the useless sacrifice of her strength. Maybe she will master her rage, but the effort to do so shatters her. Therese of Lisieux, the chaste Little Flower of perfect obedience, tried to reconcile her ferocious heart with the limitations imposed on it:

> It should be enough for me, Jesus to be Your spouse, to be a Carmelite and, by union with you, be the mother of souls. Yet I long for other vocations: I want to be a warrior, a priest, an apostle, a doctor of the Church, a martyr. . . . I would like to perform the most heroic deeds. I feel I have the courage of a Crusader. I should like to die on the battlefield in defense of the Church. . . . How can I reconcile these desires?[11]

It would seem that she reconciled these desires by dying a horrific death of tuberculosis in her early twenties. But even on her deathbed she struggled with the gap between the intensity of her energies and the restriction of these by the church. Monica Furlong reports that as "she lay dying she confided to her sister that she was glad she would be dead before the age at which young men were admitted to the priesthood, that she felt this was a great kindness on God's part to save her from disappointment."[12]

Someone else may be at home with a smaller scope for her vocation. Rather than resist ideals of patience, smallness, and kindness, a person may splinter her energy in an embrace of these in all of their detail. She cannot admit to the infinite distance between these ideals and the emptiness of her sacrifice for them, but neither can she span the abyss that has sprung up between them. Distraction by the endless trivialities of small kindnesses consumes her. To someone else the good that gave him so much joy becomes more and more like a dead weight crushing his vitality. His compassionate nature remains, but he becomes stiffer and stiffer as if he were being slowly entombed from the inside out.

The divine image in us perfumes the world with its desire for good, but it requires a person to incarnate it. The temptation of self-sacrifice disguises the dissipation of our personhood by presenting it as an ideal of the highest religious or social virtue. But the crippling of personhood weakens the powers of the soul to shine with the divine image. The demons are pleased, but they never believed that maiming was a pleasing sacrifice in the first place.

LOVE

If I have prophetic powers, and understand all mysteries and all knowledge, and if I have all faith so as to remove mountains, but have not love, I am nothing. . . . If I hand over my body so that I may boast, but do not have love, I gain nothing.

Love is patient; love is kind; love is not envious or boastful or arrogant or rude. It does not insist on its own way; it is not irritable or resentful; it does not rejoice in wrongdoing, but rejoices in the truth. It bears all things, believes all things, hopes all things, endures all things.

Love never ends. But as for prophecies, they will come to an end; as for tongues, they will cease; as for knowledge, it will come to an end. For we know only in part, and we prophesy only in part; but when the complete comes, the partial will come to an end. And now faith, hope, and love abide, these three; and the greatest of these is love.

I Cor. 13: 1–13

In theory, at least, love holds pride of place in Christianity as that which most reveals the image of God within us and which imitates God's way with us. Traces of this idealizing of love continue in our culture: in popular songs, in advertisements depicting the joys of family love, in the apotheosis of romantic love as the highest human happiness, in movies that resolve even the most intransigent difficulties through the triumph of love. Like great compassion in Buddhism, agape displays the outrageous vitality released as we are rescued from egocentrism. But between the easy sentimentality of popular culture and the superhuman heroism of agape lie many dangers for the soul enchanted by this one of the good's faces. We can begin to explore some of these perils by dividing them into those that arise from within love itself and those that arise when this ideal is distorted by oppression.

Virtually all persons, societies, and cultures possess some sort of genius and lack others. For those that have a genius for love, it is no trial to be patient with others or rejoice in other people's good fortune or act out of steady kindness. Anger and arrogance have trouble finding a place in persons and communities deeply shaped by love. But a genius for love by itself cannot bear the weight of this great ideal. Like all of the soul's powers, it must be integrated with other powers: discernment, courage, equanimity, and frequent refreshment of our joy (to name only a few). Love requires the courage to move past sentimentality and pity. Love needs courage to face suffering's power to unravel those we love. In the mess of human affairs, it is often extremely difficult to discern what is actually going on, what might be useful to do, and what to leave alone. Wisdom and discernment are indispensable companions of love.

When our joy is depleted, we can mistake obligation and guilt feelings for love. The confluence of obligation and love is all the more troubling because the needs of all the beings and ecosystems of our planet are more countless than the sands of the seas. Each individual one calls out the impossible demand "Fix me! Protect me!" The boundlessness of suffering presents itself as one of the most severe temptations to love. The infinity of suffering and the paucity of our resources destines love to a kind of scorching few can bear. When love allows us to see the loveliness of all creation, there is no logical limit to the urge to respond to suffering, nothing to brake love's desire to empty itself in action. At the same time, the demons whisper that there is no time for prayer, for relaxation, for healthy food. There is so much to do, so much pain; even the smallest of our actions can relieve the suffering of some being or change the balance in a political struggle. Who are we to waste our resources on new clothes when so many are hungry and homeless? Even if we cannot do something in this particular instance, surely we can at least offer a prayer, offer the solidarity of our compassion as we meditate on others' difficulties. Surely our Holy Father in Heaven would despise our self-indulgence, even if He could forgive it? "Oh, God help me, daughters, how many souls the devil must have ruined in this way!"

Because of the outward-moving direction of love, the urgent necessity to care for oneself is not always obvious to those with a particular gift for love.

Unskillful agape may scorn the nurture it requires, but without the stability, peace, and delight that comes from the measurelessness of the Holy Eros, love can become brittle and fragile. Its unsteadiness makes it lean in the direction of self-righteousness or dull duty or tempts it to content itself with meretricious acts of kindness. The Divine Mystery resides outside of every logic of exchange, and without the nourishment of this foolish grace, love becomes a violent mangling of body, spirit, emotion, mind, and soul.

Love carries within itself temptations that can distort it and harm its emissaries. But these internal vulnerabilities are often combined with conflations of love with a logic of domination, and this wreaks enormous disaster. When we conjure embodiments of great compassion in people like Dorothy Day or the Dalai Lama, there is no mistaking them for passive, dutiful daughters who "endure all things" rather than resist what is harmful. St. Paul himself writes like someone completely intoxicated by love; his energy for Christ seems to burn off him and draw those he meets into his Christ ecstasy. But his much-quoted hymn to love is a kind of blank check in the hands of oppression and domination. The great NO that the kingdom of God sets against every cruelty becomes absorbed into the propaganda of regimes of power. The rhetoric of patience and endurance slides smoothly, seamlessly into a demand that the insulted and injured remain passive. Forgiveness is demanded of those who become angry or denounce injustice or talk about racism, economic injustice, or fiscal irresponsibility within the community. If some sharp stone of anger pricks someone's breast, the demons inside her head consort with the community's propaganda: "If you are only more patient, if you love a little longer, if you always forgive, if you quell your anger, you will save him. Love conquers all. By patient suffering, Christ saved all humanity, including your worthless hide. What if He asks of you a little forbearance? Besides, he cannot really hurt you; your soul is safe with Christ. And what about the children? Have you thought of them? Or are you so selfish you only consider your own happiness?"

Many women know these voices only too well, but the demons are glad to afflict anyone motivated by love and its evil twin, duty. Distortions of love crush those with a gift for love with a thousand reasons why they should never be angry, never live their own dreams, never leave an obligation unfulfilled. "It's a Wonderful Life" portrays the life of a man the demons tempt shamelessly in this way. We watch him give up chance after chance to get away from his suffocating town and find scope for his remarkable energies. We watch, too, his face get more shut down, his mood edgier. In the movie, he is shown all the good his sacrifices have accomplished and all ends well. But in life, such an angelic revelation is more often the propaganda of power. To anticipate later chapters, this does not mean that love is always a hoax or that "self-actualization" is the road to the highest happiness. But when the beauty of love disguises self-destructive ways of life, it is a temptation.

Love can be an instrument of control. It can also be limited so that its universal reach does not trouble a status quo. The rhetoric of love can be joined up with a rhetoric of morality to place whole groups of people beyond the pale of love: black people, white people, immoral people, savages, Jews, infidels, heretics, the non-elect, scriptural literalists, opponents in political struggles, and so on. In these ways love is rendered tame and manageable within the community.

The misappropriation of love not only tames and limits the meaning of love. The constant rerouting of love into harmless or self-destructive habits dissipates its power. The efficacy and energy love unleashes become less available, even to those who most admire it. At times, it has been considered "unladylike" to engage in any kind of sports, athleticism, or physical exercise. Physical strength was evidently not needed by women, whose main role was to be a loving presence in a family. Like the physical passivity imposed on ladies of previous generations, toxic love represses the development of strength to endure conflict or assert a position. The energy of the spirit remains as undeveloped as muscles that are never exercised. Emotional pathways become so calcified, it might take years for even a small trace of anger or indignation to find its way to consciousness. When love is not harmonized with other powers or when it is conflated with submissiveness, it is deprived of means to express itself. It is the soul of an athlete trying to make do with two broken legs.

But the demons hide themselves. We can remain satisfied with our patience, our relentless kindness, a habit of forgiveness so embedded in us we are not even aware of it. The diminishment of love's power may remain veiled or only dimly perceived, although the unconscious effort to contain love's intensity may be written on our bodies as heart disease, ulcers, migraines, depression, or breast cancer. Even if the desire to leap out of the prison of passivity arises, there is no habit of vitality or communal wisdom that would enable a person or community to live out a more active love. Damage to love may not be mortal, but love will have to go into remedial therapy: slowly, slowly restoring damaged nerve endings, building strength, and developing alien skills.

In these examples, genuine desire for good becomes itself an obstacle and temptation. Morality, self-sacrifice, and love are only illustrations. Every virtue and good could be explored for the demonic whispers they conceal. This is discouraging, to say the least. We want to complain, to point out how unfair it is. We want so much and we try so hard to "be good." And yet it remains insufficient. Should it not be enough to want so badly to "be good"?

To try so hard? Yet all our efforts go astray; they backfire, and we are accessories to the very harm we would avoid! Evagrius tells us, "It is proper that you be advised about another ruse. The demons divide up into two groups for a time, and when they see you calling out for help against the one group the others make their appearance under the form of angels who drive away the first group. They have in mind to deceive you into believing that they are holy angels in all truth."[13]

You see how tricky the demons can be. Wanting to be good, trying to be good—these are also temptations. There is a sense in which wanting and trying to be good can be good things, just as morality, self-sacrifice, and love can be good things. But all of these things are ways the demons try to get us to accept their bargain. They say, "In exchange for what is in your backyard, we will make you fabulously happy." We hear, "In exchange for a worthless apple tree, we will become perfect imitators of God: moral, self-sacrificing, perfectly loving." We do not see that the worthless apple tree was the delight of our hearts and the beloved of Christ. The demons have tricked us into trading away the powers of our soul by which the divine image shines in us. They have not done it by enticing us to debauchery. Instead, they first remind us of our worthlessness. We are slow to realize that, far from being worthless, we are most precious and beautiful. We are deceived into believing we must sacrifice ourselves, when in truth we must instead release our powers. Then the wily demons simply notice what fragment of Holy Mystery we have mistaken for the face of God. They offer us that fragment in exchange for ourselves. In our ignorance, we do not see that our cherished fragment has been torn away from the Holy Mystery. We are deceived into accepting a creation of our own minds as the Holy Eros.

We are like the foolish worshipers the prophet Isaiah scorns. They mistake their own wooden fabrication for God. "Half of it he burns . . . and says, 'Ah, I am warm, I can feel the fire!' The rest of it he makes into a god, his idol, bows down to it and worships it; he prays to it and says, 'Save me, for you are my god!" (Isa. 44:16–17). This may not be a good description of the other religions of the Near East, but it is not a bad description of our worship of the shards of holiness we cherish. We believe that morality or self-sacrifice or even love captures the essence of the Holy One, and we exchange the powers of our soul to worthily magnify that one holy name. We do not mangle our powers or worship idols because we are prideful or selfish or generally "bad." Desire burns in us unceasingly, but we are like the heroines of fairy tales who make mistakes and wander the wrong path and wear themselves out running in the wrong direction. After "many weary miles" seeking our lover east of the sun and west of the moon we end up in a troll castle. But that is not the end of their story, and it is not the end of ours, either.

CONSENT TO TEMPTATION

The miller in "The Girl without Hands" traded what he thought was an apple tree for wealth. But when he discovered that it was his daughter and not his apple tree, upset as he was, he made no move to undo what he had done. When the girl's innocence prevented the devil from taking her, he demanded her hands instead. The miller did not tell the devil it was his business to take the girl, and if he could not, the deal was off. He did not beg the devil to take him instead. He did not even tell the devil to do his own dirty work. The miller, too deep in by now to turn back, got out his ax and cut off his daughter's hands. We do foolish things in our ignorance and in our haste to satisfy our needs and desires. But the miller has gone beyond foolishness, ignorance, poor judgment, even selfish greed. He has become an active participant in carrying out a monstrous violation of an innocent girl, his own daughter. The bargain, made in ignorance, was fulfilled with full knowledge. In fact, the miller not only accepted the bargain but also the devil's extension of it to include the miller's own participation in the amputation of his daughter's hands. Once the miller agreed to a peculiar bargain with a stranger in the deep woods, he found nothing within himself to stop a free fall that transformed him from an impoverished but loving father into a cruel executioner for the devil.

We may not all become cruel executioners (or meet mysterious strangers in deep forests). But this slide from naïve entanglement to devoted allies of our tempters is something we probably all know about. We strenuously defend the harm we do and the harm that is done to us: "The really damned not only like Hell, they feel loyal to it."[14] Having spent an inordinate amount of time reflecting on ways in which our good desires tempt us, we will briefly consider our consent to temptation. To do this, we will return to the preeminence of pain.

Throughout our lives, our desires for good things and our subjection to pain provide the general underpinnings of consciousness. Neither our desires nor our pains are in themselves good or evil, helpful or harmful. But they are extremely potent forces in us. As long as we remain sentient beings, we are likely to experience a desire to relieve the discomforts of unmet desire and of unwanted pain. It is not this longing for relief itself that makes us allies of the demons. But as preoccupation with this longing intensifies, other things recede from our awareness. When we are tired, our patience wears thin. We long for rest, and this longing, recognized or not, intensifies our ego's awareness of itself and reduces our awareness of what is around us. The demands of students, children, partners, clients, and slow checkout clerks become irritating and unreasonable. Our awareness of them as tired, needy, deserving of help, amusing, charming, and interesting fades.

There is a strand of the human spirit that craves relief more than anything else. It waxes and wanes in us and in everyone else, taking a million different forms, wearing as many different disguises. But as it waxes, awareness of our own experience intensifies and awareness of others diminishes. This is what makes it so easy to become addicted to actions and beliefs that grant us some relief from the discomforts of desire and pain. Again, this seems a virtually inevitable dimension of consciousness. But it is a chink in our implacable eros for good.

Without desiring harm, we become absorbed in the painful experience of unrelieved needs and fear. We crave relief and everything else fades from our awareness. When we discover some relief, however small, we resist giving it up. This is perfectly reasonable and understandable, but it is the weakness in us that brings us into collusion with what is harmful. Because they bring us relief, we come to love pleasure or anger or guilt feelings, limitless responsibility, the adrenaline rush of making money, the dullness of endlessly deferred hopes; we love sustaining the appearance that everything is "fine" more than we love anything else. We do this as individuals, and we do this as communities. Generations of rural poverty can addict a community to lethargy that makes all change, even an influx of much-needed social resources, suspect. Generations of southern Presbyterian women can die, one by one, of heart failure rather than sacrifice their "niceness" to a flash of anger. These may not sound like enticing painkillers. But they are examples of things we hold to our breast to comfort ourselves, distract ourselves, or so enervate our desires and fears that we hardly feel them. Should we laugh at ourselves or cry that our painkillers cause us so much pain?

Our addiction to painkillers causes us harm. But it also causes others harm. Consent to temptation accepts not only the price *we* pay for pain relief; it accepts the price *others* pay for our relief as well. There is, deep within me, an awareness that my painkilling tactics exact a toll that others are forced to pay. My allegiances shift slightly when I consent to this toll. Perhaps I relieve my deep terror as well as my compassionate impulses by becoming universally responsible. My massive responsibility maintains others in dependence. It fixates me on impossibly controlling my environment, so that any small disorder enrages me—and this outrage pours out on everyone else. Even as I am crushed and my real powers are squandered, my control and my anger steal power from those around me. But my omnicompetence and my omniresponsibility really do keep my terror at bay. The demons might add, "Yes, and your good work helps so *many* other people!" I choose not to see the fear and the passivity in the faces of those I am helping.

Or I might find relief in the intoxication of pleasure. The strategies of seduction, the thrill of the hunt, the pleasant buzzing of alcohol that flows through my body during the hunt, the camaraderie with fellow hunters—all these release me from the tensions and humiliations of the week. A successful hunt brings my delectable prey to my bed. Perhaps she is too drunk to notice. Perhaps I have mesmerized her with my charm and false promises. Perhaps I am a more ambitious hunter, and I have convinced her over time of my love for her. In any case, at last she is mine. How delicious! It may have been that once, long ago, I was ashamed in the morning when I watched her face as she realized she was nothing to me—merely a toilet in which I relieved my pent-up desire. But if I ever was, I am not any more. I do not even see her; how could I care how she feels? She does not exist at all, really; but my pleasure does, and it brings me delight and relief.

The disintegration of our awareness of others can continue beyond an inability to remain conscious that we are harming other people or that this matters. We can harden our hearts, individually and as a society, and decide that giving up our pain relief is impossible, even if it causes other people difficulty. But we can go further still and incorporate the difficulty we cause others into the pleasure and relief we find. It is no longer simply that I do not see and do not care that I am harming others. It is now a positive pleasure to see the power I have over others. At one time, I might have been troubled when I saw that my need to be responsible for everything had the unfortunate side affect of squashing other people. But now I see it as part of my relief. My terror is assuaged; my pity, manifest—and, best of all, I realize that I enjoy seeing those flashes of fear on my coworkers' faces. How wonderful that I can keep my spouse and children as helpless as infants—they can hardly breathe without me! At one time, I might have been indifferent to the pain I caused my lovers. But now, seeing the misery I cause them becomes essential to my pleasure. Everything is my possession, and I can do what I like with it. I am no longer completely indifferent to others. I awake to the pleasure I take in their responses to me. Their pain has become delicious to me, the sweetest pain relief yet.

Little by little I accept the cost of my pain relief. It seemed a bargain at first: wealth in exchange for a worthless tree. Then I realized it was not a tree but my daughter. Then I found I had to amputate her hands myself. But the sweet relief that came when I accepted the bargain is stronger than anything else. If I am sometimes troubled by what has happened to me, a thousand rationalizations come to my aid, reminding me of the good I am doing. In any case, to the extent that I can no longer taste the living reality of other beings, no longer delight in their beauty or sorrow with their suffering, relief will remain more attractive to me, whatever its cost.

Through the mysteries of grace, circumstances, and desire, we might begin to feel that the cost to ourselves or to others is higher than we could possibly pay. This does not mean that temptation is an on-or-off switch, that we resist temptation or fail to do so. Desires to do good, deceptions, craving for relief, consent to the hardships of others, are all mixed up in us all the time. We tacitly agree to things that are destructive, yet we remain in living contact with beauty and suffering. These chapters have suggested ways of thinking about how we become entangled in harmful ways of life. The following chapters turn attention to powers that help extricate us from our bondage.

6

The Divine Eros

But from my sorrow you'll carry me not,
My heart is bound, my soul is chained to the rock.
Emmylou Harris

During Advent and Holy Week more than at any other time we are exposed to oxymoronic symbols of divine power that constitute a residue of Christianity's greatest wisdom:

Infant holy, infant lowly, for His bed a cattle stall;
Oxen lowing, little knowing Christ the babe is Lord of all.
Polish carol

What wondrous love is this that caused the Lord of bliss
To bear the heavy cross [or 'dreadful curse'] for my soul, for my soul.
American folk hymn

In these familiar hymns something of the absurdity of divine power is expressed. It is the task in these last chapters to reflect on this absurdity and to conceive how this power runs through us to "set at liberty" (Luke 4:18; Isa. 61:1) what the passions bind so tightly.

In Christianity, the Divine Eros is understood to be a trinity. It is impossible to say in any clear way what this means, but trinity is one of Christianity's primary symbols for the Holy Beauty that is beyond all words and concepts. The decisive icon of the Divine Eros, for Christians, is Christ. That is, Christ is the refraction of divine power that is available through Christianity. Christ has always been a terribly offensive icon of the Holy, not least because he is perhaps the poorest display of power one sees in any of the world's religions. In him, we see immortal, invisible God birthed into this world through an impoverished and nearly outcast young woman. We watch Jesus wander around a little rag-tag occupied country for a while and then leave it by one of Rome's most hideous methods of execution. Although we love these stories and tell them over and over again, they capture something about divine power that great theologians and pain-weary worshipers often find indigestible. Our love of power finds little satisfaction in Jesus.

We can ameliorate our discomfort with such a low-rent Savior by remembering God the Father, the unmoved mover and Master of the Universe. This "God of power and might" is very comforting. But when we imagine God in these ways, we move far away from the icon of the Holy that is offered in the Gospel narratives. As Whitehead puts it,

> When the Western world accepted Christianity, Caesar conquered; and the received text of Western theology was edited by his lawyers. . . . The brief Galilean vision of humility flickered throughout the ages, uncertainly. . . . The deeper idolatry, of fashioning God in the image of the Egyptian, Persian and Roman imperial rulers, was retained. The Church gave unto God the attributes which belonged exclusively to Caesar.[1]

But our attachment to images of divine omnipotence is the result of more than this political sleight of hand. In the midst of our suffering, imagining that God really does not control events can seem more terrifying than imagining that God uses violence, war, injustice, and disease "for our own good." Hebrew and Christian Scriptures do little to support our love for omnipotence, although it is true that virtually everything under the sun can be found in Scripture. Notwithstanding the occasional blaze of temper and destruction, for the most part Hebrew Scriptures offer quite different images of God than those of control. God creates an incredible world but things go awry almost immediately. The beloved Israelites languish in slavery, but God has to rely on a stuttering murderer who is hiding out as a shepherd to free them. When a king was called for, God again resorts to a shepherd, a youngest son who writes poetry rather than goes to war, except to bring his brothers food. But with the help of God, this nurturing act becomes the occasion for David to defeat the giant that has been terrorizing Israel.

When Elijah is on the run from King Ahab and Queen Jezebel, God comes to him not in the storm or in the great wind but in a "still, small voice" and sends the isolated prophet out to defeat the rulers (1 Kgs. 19). The prophet Hosea describes God's maternal nostalgia for the days when Israel let Her hold him by the hand and teach him to walk. But now Israel has grown and, like grown children everywhere, gotten into trouble from which even a doting and divine mother could not protect him (Hos. 11). Much later, God "ransoms" humanity from bondage, but, according to the symbolism of ransom, must resort to trickery, disguise, and a cruel death to nullify Satan's rights over us. Each image of God baffles us with absurd combinations of outrageous power and equally outrageous powerlessness. When we compare divine power to the power of judges, rulers, warriors, or even minor authorities, we see an energy that is both too much to be contained by these images and much less effective in shaping history in its image.

There is a third member of the Holy Trinity: Spirit. She is outrageous because of the kind of power that seems to spin off of Her. She is a trouble-maker, always stirring things up in crazy directions, and blowing wherever the hell She wants to: "The wind blows where it chooses, and you hear the sound of it, but you do not know where it comes from or where it goes" (John 3:8). Most denominations try to keep quiet about Her, remembering Her flame only on the Sunday of Pentecost.

The Holy Trinity disappoints when we look to it for reliable help against what hurts us most: pain, suffering, and injustice. The supremacy of might does not seem to have been even challenged, never mind defeated, by the "unending" reign of King David, a crucifixion in Jerusalem a couple of mil-lennia ago, or the Paraclete whom God sends when Jesus ascends to the heav-ens. We seem caught in a terrible Catch 22. We find ourselves in near despair over the abuses of the church's power and when we look at our history of war and terror, we adore our infant Savior, who abjures these means of control. If we have ever known crushing pain, or been on the wrong side of a twisted legal system, or felt defrauded of means of defense, then we know the cost of being without power. There is nothing romantic or pious about being subject to the traumas of might. But it is only with dismay that we look to the crucifixion as the prize for renouncing power.

Yet from Miriam and Mary Magdalene to martyrs like Perpetua and Felic-ity, and to Beguines, Celtic saints, civil rights workers, and singers of spiritu-als, the witness continues that in the Divine Eros we have to do with a power that is unleashed to weaken and dissolve the chains that bind us. When we pay attention to great theologians and contemplatives, we also find witnesses to this power. But when we turn to them to help us understand, they teach us that what we mostly know about divine power is that it is mind-bendingly strange and that as soon as we think we have hit on something that makes sense, it becomes straw.

Trying to remember that talk about God is nothing more than straw, this writing focuses primarily on the Christian icon of divine power, Christ, and in particular, on three dimensions of the story we have about Christ: Christ's temptation, incarnation, and ransom. These three images constitute a kind of triptych, a three-sided "icon of God."[2] In these narrative icons, there is a refraction of the strange efficacy that is released from the powerlessness of the Divine Eros.

THE TEMPTATIONS OF CHRIST

Luke begins the story of Jesus' ministry by describing his temptations by the devil (Luke 4). The kinds of temptation described and the consequences of Jesus' rejection of Satan provide glimpses of the power that is available and not available to Jesus as one welded to the Good Beyond Being. They are icons of the power that he refuses and the power that is infused into him in the aftermath of his refusal.

After his baptism, Jesus was "full of the Holy Spirit" (4:1) and was led by Her to the wilderness, where he fasted for nearly six weeks. It was there, where the wild things of the desert and of the spirit are found, that Satan came to him. At first it seems that there is something childishly obvious about Satan's first temptation. We are told that Jesus was hungry and the first thing the devil says to him is "If you are the Son of God, command this stone to become a loaf of bread" (4:3). It would appear that Satan is exploiting the vulnerability of one depleted by a long fast, but the particulars of the temptation point to a deeper conflict. He is not really offering Jesus bread or trying to get him to break his fast, but rather demanding a miracle and a proof. He is rebuffed.

Satan then shows Jesus all the kingdoms of the world, spread out over all time. This has all been "delivered" to Satan himself, and he offers "their glory and all this authority" in exchange for worship (4:6). What is startling about this temptation is not that Satan is trying to seduce Jesus with the glories of power, but that Satan possesses all of this in the first place. Again, Satan is rebuffed. Finally, he takes Jesus to the pinnacle of the temple of Jerusalem and again demands a proof. "If you are the Son of God throw yourself down because it says in the Scriptures that God will not let anything harm you" (para. Luke 4:9–10). Rebuffed a third time, he goes away "until an opportune time" (4:13).

This is a very odd story, and like most of Scripture, one could spiral through it for ages and not come to the end of it. The strangeness of the story begins when we ask, What could Satan possess that he could seriously offer Jesus, the Son of the Most High, already the maximum of cosmic power and dignity, entrained by the awesome magnificence of angels? The strangeness continues when we notice that each temptation exemplifies something Jesus ends up doing in more extravagant form: he feeds the five thousand from virtually nothing. Gabriel has already promised that "of his kingdom there will be no end" (Luke 1:33). Jesus comes to harm, but he also overcomes death more dramatically than through a death-defying stunt. But each of these parallels is also an inversion of the works demanded by Satan. Jesus does not feed himself but rather a hungry crowd. Whatever form his kingdom takes, it does not appear to have much to do with the authority and glory of all the political regimes of history. His defiance of death is not a stunt from the top of a temple but a "ransom for many." Each of these emblems of power are, in the hands of Satan, about authority and glory. But in Jesus they are erotic: they flow out from him and pour out like balm onto those he loves.

Satan tempts Jesus with particular things: bread, nations, and victory over death. In each case, Jesus refuses them in the form suggested by Satan but ends up fulfilling them according to some other logic. But in these particular offers, Satan is really attempting to seduce Jesus into accepting the dynamics of power as Satan understands it. In this sense, temptation is not so much about particular ends but the possession and display of power. "*Prove* to me you are the Son of God." "Take over all the *authority and glory* of empires throughout all time." This is not a discussion about good or evil goals. It is about an economy of power that is completely different from that available to Jesus as the Christ. Satan himself is the perennial image of a son of God enthroned in glory, possessing all the kingdoms of the world. Satan symbolizes exactly what that kind of power looks like. We who live on this earth know very well what his "authority and glory" look like: we see it every day on the news. "Proof" that Jesus is an embodiment of the Divine Eros is pure illusion, less substantial than a conjurer's trick. There is no such proof. There is no such thing as a Christ that could display such a proof. To draw Jesus into this economy of proof and power would be to negate the very nature of incarnate divinity.

The power of Christ is erotic; it is "divine yearning and zeal" as Pseudo-Dionysius put it. Compared to the power Satan possesses, it is practically nothing at all. Erotic power is an absurdity, an oxymoron. Its nothingness will be displayed in the death of Jesus, when he is again taunted by his inability to prove or even help himself. Yet this absurdity, this nothingness, worries Satan. It is a small hemorrhage in the midst of his authority and glory. It reverses the flow of energy in unsettling ways. He tries to seduce Jesus, to deceive him. He flings up illusions. He offers Jesus means to pursue his mission. Later we will see the grotesque revenge he exacts for Jesus' rejection of him. Jesus rejects him—to our great loss, as Dostoyevsky's Grand Inquisitor believes. And anyone who has loved another and wished with all his or her heart to save, relieve, or protect that beloved can understand why the Grand Inquisitor preferred power to impotence. Those who have known powerlessness know the crucial importance of power. But after reading the temptations of Christ, we realize that it is to a world dominated by might that the incarnate Eros abandons us.

But we are not left to utter powerlessness. What follows the story of Christ's temptation are sketches of the kind of efficacy that surges through him when the temptations of Satan are repudiated. "Then Jesus, filled with the power of the Spirit, returned to Galilee" (Luke 4:14). Jesus comes back from the wilderness, not only "full of the Spirit" but now, after the temptations, "in the power" of his outrageous and magnificent Sister, the Holy Spirit. The Gospel narratives give glimmers of what Jesus gains through his Holy Sister. He teaches familiar things as if no one had ever said anything like them before. He feeds people. He lets other people feed him. He seeks solitude for prayer. He heals incurable illnesses and injuries. He raises people from the dead, walks on water, calms storms, and throws out legions of demons.

He walks over every social boundary laid down by the various intersecting societies in which he lives as if they are completely invisible to him. We find him in the company of Pharisees, fishermen, and Zealots, as well as Roman commanders and soldiers and their lackeys, the tax collectors. He converses with pious Jews, educated Jews, disenfranchised Jews, and ethnic outsiders. He socializes with laborers, rich people, all sorts of unclean people, children, and the insane. Most indigestible of all for the church ever afterward is his particular intimacy with women. He counts as friends single women, mothers, and mothers-in-law; women who approach him with shocking intimacy and women who are, as my grandmother might put it, "no better than they ought to be"; unclean women and sick women; women who are, inexplicably, able to follow him around Galilee; and women who support him. Among those who first proclaim him to be the Christ are an adulterous Samaritan woman (John 4), his friend Martha (John 11:27), and a woman whose insanity he healed (John 20:17–18). His own power flows from the Holy Spirit: he is not afraid of the power of women.

At the significant moments of Jesus' life—his birth, his death, and his dealings with Satan—it is his powerlessness that is most obvious. Yet we can still be seared by the intensity of zeal that burns off of him through the Gospel stories about his wanderings and his dealings with people. Reading the Gospels is worse than playing with matches. But whatever it is that can still burn us, it is neither the "authority and glory" of Satan nor the choking despair of impotence: neither power nor powerlessness as we know these things. We turn to the second image of our triptych, incarnation, for more clues.

INCARNATION: WELDED TO HOLY MYSTERY

When Christians claim that Jesus is the "Christ," we mean that Jesus is an incarnation of God, an embodiment of the Good Beyond Being. Like trinity, incarnation is one of Christianity's great mysteries, equally impenetrable to discursive reasoning. But it seems to be an effort to say that Jesus manifests Holy Mystery with perfect intensity. Jesus embodies the Divine Eros as perfectly and completely as is possible by the human form. This means his efficacy and vulnerabilities are rooted in that Mystery. Pseudo-Dionysius gives us a picture of what this efficacy and vulnerability looks like:

> . . . and in truth, it must be said too that the very cause of the universe in the beautiful, good superabundance of his benign yearning for all is also carried outside of himself in the loving care he has for everything. He is, as it were, beguiled by goodness, by love, and by yearning and is enticed away from his transcendent dwelling place and comes to abide within all things, and he does so by virtue of his supernatural and ecstatic capacity to remain, nevertheless, within himself. That is why those possessed of spiritual insight describe him as 'zealous' because his good yearning for all things is so great and because he stirs in men a deep yearning desire for zeal . . . zeal is always felt for what is desired and because he is zealous for the creatures for whom he provides. [3]

It is to this kind of power that the incarnate Christ is welded. We will pause here to explore these words at greater length, before turning to what it might mean to "embody" this power.

Holy Mystery Is Erotic

Christ is a name given to this embodiment of the Divine Eros by her lovers. This Eros is a burning and an emptiness that dwells within each soul and within and beyond the cosmos. Hesiod foreshadows this naming of divinity when he names Eros as the power that lies at the beginning of creation. Centuries later, Jakob Boehme describes the divine emptiness whose eros for existence begins the conflagration that becomes the cosmos. Both of these poets of the divine reach into the logic of desire for images that display the efficacy and creativity of the divine emptiness.

Eros is the power of love in the form of desire. We experience "love" and think of it as an emotion. This power manifests in feeling, and we call it love, but more fundamentally love *is* power. This does not mean that there is an entity, Holy Mystery, who feels love. Rather, the efficacy of the most superabundantly real Holy Mystery is love. As desire it is movement toward the objects of its yearning. Poetically speaking, the movement of Eros is the efficacy by which cosmos and every individual entity comes into existence. Because it is the essential nature of this power to move, to yearn, to manifest itself not by wrapping itself in solitary potency but by desiring others, divinity can be said to be *ecstatic*. It is the mode of reality that most characteristically exists outside itself, always leaving itself. This ecstatic or kenotic quality differentiates the divine from finite forms of existing. Divine Eros is not a substance or an existing *thing*. If divinity were an entity that possessed attributes, it could not be "oned" with creation. It would be juxtaposed to beings as one being among others, but its solidity would preclude perfect intimacy. Eros names divinity because it is movement and yearning rather than substance. Its stability does not come from its solidity but from its perfectly realized and endlessly fecund "zeal." It is this stability of the divine zeal that Dionysius is referring to when he says that the Divine Eros comes to dwell with all things and yet does so "by virtue of his supernatural and ecstatic capacity to remain, nevertheless, within himself."[4] That is, the movement of Eros through which divine power creates and is oned with creation never wanders from love as its source.

The ecstasy of the Divine Eros is not only yearning but also union. It is because divine power is ecstatic that it can be "knit and oned" with creation.[5] It is empty and self-emptying and therefore capable of the deepest intimacy and most perfect union. At the same time, created by and through Eros, eros is the movement that characterizes the deep structures of the cosmos and of the soul. In the ecstasy of love the lover belongs not to himself or to herself but to the beloved.[6] This mutual, ecstatic emptying into the beloved is union, care, and desire.[7] It is the bond that holds creation in existence, stronger than the forces that hold neutrons and protons together in the microcosm of an atom. It is the also the luminous and "precious oneing" of the divine and human in each soul. Dionysius finds this ecstasy by which a lover gives herself to the beloved expressed in St. Paul's words, "It is no longer I who live, but it is Christ who lives in me" (Gal. 2:20). "Paul was truly a lover and, as he says, he was beside himself for God, possessing not his own life but the life of the One for whom he yearned, as exceptionally beloved."[8] This mutual ecstasy of yearning and union is not the abolition of particular beings but their foundation. It is precisely possessing "the life of the One for whom he yearned" in such full measure that Paul is most potently and joyfully himself. The Good Beyond Being can be perfectly intimate with creation because it is desire, lover, breath. The cosmos is held together and each soul is held together by these ecstasies of desire, ever self-emptying, ever uniting.

It is Eros that names the power that creates worlds, as Dionysius says: "In truth, it must be said too that the very cause of the universe is the beautiful, good superabundance of his benign yearning for all is carried outside of himself in the loving care he has for everything."[9] The power to create is nothing other than the divine yearning that carries the efficacy of that yearning toward everything as loving care. The structure of this care is beauty, and so it is that the structure of the world and everything in it is beauty. This power is erotic, that is, it is the flow of love toward the beloved: the Divine Eros is "as it were, beguiled by goodness, by love, and by yearning and is enticed away from his transcendent dwelling place."[10] The characteristic movement of the divine is ecstatic, self-transcending love that bestows beauty and therefore existence on a beloved cosmos. This cosmos is so beloved, it has "beguiled" Holy Trinity into the eternal ecstasy of creation. "That is why those possessed of spiritual insight describe him as 'zealous' because his good yearning for all things is so great and because he stirs in [humanity] a deep yearning desire for zeal . . . zeal is always felt for what is desired and because he is zealous for the creatures for whom he provides."[11] The burning of the Divine Eros is fundamentally power—not the efficient or formal causality of an artisan but the contagion of power that sets nothingness ablaze with being. Eros, intoxicated by beauty, creates by singeing nothingness with beauty and in this way drawing it into existence.

The burning of Eros is the burning of love, which purifies in the very act of loving. Everything exists through the power of this loving, so everything is purified by the very fact of its existence. There is therefore a dimension of each thing that is perfect and allows us to say with Augustine that "all that is, is good."

But the exuberant intensity of beauty that burns off of divinity can only be communicated imperfectly to existing things: it is not in the nature of created things to withstand existence unscathed. Our diamond beauty is fragile, subject to maiming and ending. The harmony of a cosmos is unspeakably beautiful, but in each particular thing this beauty is only a temporary triumph before it fades "like the flowers of the field" (Isa. 40:7).

This mystery of an efficacy that overpowers nothingness but endures the mortification of everything created seems impenetrable. We try to form an image of the immensity of power that could call beauty out of nothingness, but then we immediately bump into the awareness of its extreme limitation in the suffering and cruelty of this world. Divine power seems to be equally outrageous in what it can do and in what it cannot do.

Erotic Power in the Flesh

Roberta Bondi is known to remind her students of early Christological controversies that the word *incarnation* has the same root as *carne*—as in *chili con carne*: chili with *meat*. The immensity of energy that sets the morning stars to singing and shuts in the sea, that binds the Pleiades and provides food for young ravens (Job 38) becomes meat for us. Incarnation offers a sublimely literal enactment of the truth that we are "knit and oned" with God. This union, in Christ and in the divine image, speaks the blessedness of this form of existence, of human existence. It is what Hadewijch of Brabant calls "that fearful and marvelous countenance which is Love's revelation of herself."[12] The Mystery Beyond Being, uncaused cause of all, empty of attributes because intimate to every concreteness, fills out the human nature in the one we call the Christ.

The human form of existence always appears somewhere in particular: in a particular body, culture, place, historical time, religion, and personality. The making into meat of Mystery is likewise embodied in a particular culture, moment in history, religious tradition, place on the planet, and personality. There could hardly be a more extravagant display of the intimacy of the Divine Eros with humanity than this impossible "coincidence of opposites" (to borrow a phrase from Nicholas of Cusa). Yet it is an excruciating reality of Christian history that this extravagant unveiling of the availability of the human form to Good Beyond Being became yet another occasion for the triumph of patriarchy and its logic of violent exclusion. While certain aspects of the concreteness of incarnation could be recognized as inessential (being Jewish, illegitimate, raised in Palestine, working class, and peripatetic), being male became essential to full participation in the Christian church and being Christian (like Jesus??!) became essential to "salvation." Other possible meanings of incarnation will be explored here.

As we saw in the first chapters of this work, our precious and undefiled intimacy with Divine Eros is not readily available to our ordinary experience. In fact, we constantly defile ourselves, each other, and the world around us with cruelty, timidity, despair, oppression, and suffering of every kind. Yet the Divine Eros seems drawn to the hard places in creation that resist the full force of Her efficacy. The same movement that draws creation into existence continues to draw this creation toward ever-more intense perfections of beauty. Eros is ever present to draw our beauty back to itself when it is marred, defiled, or stunted. It is, in a sense, natural that this endless, ecstatic fecundity would burst forth in human form.

It is not the way of the Divine Eros to despise what She has made. Becoming enfleshed, Christ reveals the sanctity of our own flesh. This sanctity is not something that is accomplished by a way of perfection but is present precisely in the form of our existence: luminous, wounded, and infinitely diverse. Our bodies expose us to enormous suffering and temptation. Julian of Norwich reminds us that our bodies are reluctant to accept the suffering we must bear, and we flee from it wholeheartedly. But she also insists that "God imputes no blame" for the inability of our bodies to accept the vicissitudes of life.[13] That is, it is precisely *as* wounded and fragile beings, unable to bear the conditions of our lives that Christ comes to us to reveal the sanctity and preciousness of this life. Many Christians have understood these bodies as obstacles to the desire for good. But the incarnation stands as Eros's enduring witness against everything that defiles the body, showing it to be the place the divine image has chosen to dwell. Julian reminds us that Holy Mystery is not dismayed by even the earthiest dimensions of our embodiment:

> A [person] walks upright, and the food in his body is shut in as if in a well-made purse. When the time of his necessity comes, the purse is opened and then shut again in a most seemly fashion. And it is God who does this as it is shown when he says that he comes down to us in our humblest needs. For he does not despise what he has made, nor does he disdain to serve us in the simplest natural functions of our body, for love of the soul which he created in his own likeness.[14]

The Divine Eros clothed herself with flesh and a human form, revealing that there is no contradiction between bearing God and living in a body, in the world. In Christ, not only is the soul created in the likeness of the Divine, but the Divine is created in the likeness of the human form. The incarnation awakens us to the power of the human form to bear such intimate presence of Holy Mystery within its own body.

More particularly, the Divine Eros is made meat by and through woman. Hadewijch compares the work of Mary to that of all of the prophets.

For Hadewijch, it was Mary who first enabled us to understand the depth of the mystery of divine love because she was the first to receive the Love in such fullness.[15] Hadewijch is a poet of the divine and we do not need to understand her words so literally as to exclude intimacy with the divine elsewhere before Mary. She helps us to understand that the embodiment of the divine is made possible in Christ through the strength of Mary's longing.

This is a sign to us women that the shame of embodiment with which we are assaulted by patriarchy is to be burned away. The holy fire of creation and redemption entered into the world in a human body through the blood and pain and muck of childbirth. The birth of Christ to Mary did not sanctify her body. It reveals the sanctity that women's bodies have always had. It is the power of women's longing to draw the Divine Eros into such intimacy with us that the divine image becomes incarnate in us and through us. Mary displays the fullness of this power in the incarnation of Christ. Every woman witnesses to this power who births another spark of the divine into this world.[16]

Jesus' ministry continually draws forth witnesses to the sanctity of female embodiment. The unnamed woman whose tears cleaned Jesus' feet reveals the sanctity of all of our tears. The unnamed woman whose precious oil is poured out on Jesus' head reveals the sanctity of our extravagant, though maligned, devotion and our power to recognize the reality of a situation even when others want to deny it. Jesus demonstrates a sublime indifference to social codification of women's sexuality when he sends the woman at the well to bring her people to him and when he saves a woman from stoning. He allows himself to be corrected by the Syrophoenician woman and scolded by Martha to reveal the sanctity of women's wisdom. He is not afraid to be touched by a menstruating woman, but blesses her and, through her, blesses all women. The death of the Divine Eros on a cross does not sanctify suffering; it reveals the infinite intimacy of Christ with our suffering. That this was witnessed by women who watched to the last at Calvary and first found him risen in the garden displays the preciousness of women's witness.

The incarnation manifests the power of the human body to bear the divine. As Julian points out, our suffering makes it hard for us to live into our power, but to see it displayed so vividly reminds us of our deepest possibilities. In the stories of Jesus' relationships with others we see the contagion of power that could burn off of him. This power is available to women as readily as to men. Christ shows the sanctity of women as bearers and witnesses of the Divine Eros. This is an astonishing rending of the "authority and glory" of patriarchy. But we know how women fared in the church that arose in his name and how assiduously women's witness is erased from history and theology. We know, too, how the preciousness of the human body was forgotten, displaced by a theology of sacrifice that glorifies the suffering of our bodies. In these disparities, the incarnation is yet another example of the bizarre coincidence of efficacy and impotence in the Divine Eros.

RANSOM

When we are afflicted, rejected, degraded, and most of all powerless, it is power that we need. Ransom is one of the older symbols used to evoke something of the power unleashed when the Divine Eros became incarnate in this world and subject to its difficulties. Ransom is to gain someone's release by paying a price. It carries the connotation of freeing someone unfairly held: a king captured in war or children kidnapped and held for money. In earlier times it could particularly mean freeing someone who was legally but unfairly held, as when a slave was ransomed.

This is one of the earliest metaphors used to try to understand the crucifixion of the Messiah. "For the Son of Man came not to be served but to serve, and to give his life a ransom for many" (Mark 10:45). In the early church's attempt to interpret this metaphor, ransom describes the way God freed humanity from Satan, who rightfully owns the human race fair and square. Frustrated by the letter of the law, the Persons of the Trinity needed a way to circumvent the legal bondage of humanity without actually abolishing law altogether. They needed to find a way to trick Satan into nullifying the law. So

God disguised Godself as a human being, and as such, appears as Satan's chattel. Satan is delighted, believing that at long last soft-hearted God was stupid enough to become vulnerable to Satan. He takes the life of Jesus, which, as human, belonged to him. But in doing so Satan also took what did not belong to him: God. This voided the law, so humanity is freed from its bondage to Satan. As the Norwegian fairy tale puts it, "Evil by excess of evil is undone."[17]

Like other icons of divine power, ransom is a picture of power that is nothing at all. God chafes against a law that She cannot undo. All of the awesome power that flings creation out of darkness and sustains it with eons of tender mercies comes to nothing when faced with Satan's exploitation of the law that orders the cosmic harmonies. The power that does find a way beyond this impasse is itself the nadir of powerlessness: exposed to the "authority and glory" of Roman rule, the incarnate deity is reduced to death on one of their cruelest instruments of torture. Yet from this excess of impotence arises power that unlocks humanity's bondage. "Oh happy fault that calls forth such and so great a redeemer!" as the ancient Easter hymn sings.

Like temptation, creation, and incarnation, ransom is a picture of power that is nothing at all and at the same time the astounding power to liberate the entire human race after reason and law have been forced to despair. Over the centuries, Christ as "ransom" has been absorbed into much less helpful images of atonement, substitution, and sacrifice. But ransom has very different associations, and to pry these away from the history of church doctrine, we will explore it in light of a folktale that surfaces similar themes. "The Polar Bear King," a Nordic folktale, is strikingly similar to the myth of Psyche and Eros; to another Nordic fairy tale, "East of the Sun and West of the Moon"; and to the whole family of folktales that variously describe the problem of "Beauty and the Beast." This folktale and all of its cousins are not allegories of Christian redemption, but they offer intriguing parallels for how the weak and powerless gain victory over one who is powerful and who technically possesses the privilege of "right." Looking at these parallels may help us envision meanings of a divine ransom that are derailed by atonement and sacrifice.

In the version of the story available in the video *The Polar Bear King*, an evil witch has put a spell on a prince so that he will be in the form of a polar bear for seven years, except for a period at midnight when he will be a man again. If anyone looks at his face during the time he is a man, he will belong to her forever. Notwithstanding his fierce appearance, a young woman falls in love with him. They marry and have children. The evil witch returns each time to carry off the infants, but the kind mother-in-law, who has some magic of her own, cloaks herself in invisibility and takes the children into her own keeping. They are safe, but the queen has no way of knowing what became of them. In her despair, she longs to see her family again. The polar bear king encourages her to visit but makes her promise not to bring home a present from her sisters. Her sisters give her a tinder box and insist she get a quick look at her husband—he could be a monster for all she knows. She does look at him in the night, and wax drips on his face; he awakens and is immediately whisked off to the castle of the evil witch.

The queen's beloved is now captive, held by the irresistible force of the law that binds him. At first she despairs. She has lost her children and her husband to an evil witch; in her madness she runs through the forest into the wilds. But it is here in the wilderness that she finds the power she needs to at last break the spell of the witch. Like so many folk heroes, it is at this point of despair and madness that she meets the magical older woman who can help her. She at last encounters her mother-in-law and her children. They feed her and clothe her and love her. Fortified by the courage she will need, she is also given three magical objects that will make it possible for her to penetrate the witch's impenetrable stronghold. Disguised as a servant, she watches as the witch prepares a magical potion to bind the king to her heart and mind. The witch is reminded by her "lord and master" (the devil) not to use *too much* evil, because "by excess of evil, evil is undone." When the witch leaves, our heroine sneaks into her workshop and cooks up a potion with a great deal of evil. Still disguised as a servant, she pours her potent concoction into the wine glasses of the witch and her guests at the wedding, and they all disappear into nonbeing: by excess of evil their evil has been undone. The king is freed both from the spell that made him a polar bear and from the tyranny of law that would force a union between himself and the witch. The queen and her king are happily reunited with their children and everyone lives happily ever after.

The Divine Eros, like the queen in the folktale, cares only for Her beloved. The law by which Satan has right to the human race, wherever it came from and whatever its righteousness, has become simply an obstacle. These stories do not rely on law to restore happiness; neither do they rely on force of arms. In both stories, intimacy with the power that binds was accomplished through the disguise of a servant. It was not through might but in the guise of service that power was penetrated. It was not through the clear light of reason that humanity was unbound, but in the half-light of disguise and trickery. In the Gospels, Satan tries to draw Jesus out, display to him his power and grandeur, appeal to his most-favored-son status. He suspects there is more to this disguise than meets the eye. But he cannot tear off the mask. Disguise is the very essence of the Divine Eros. According to the symbolism of ransom, his human disguise made it possible for him to pay the price we all pay for living: he suffered and died. But his disguise cloaked a power not subject to this economy. Like the queen in the witch's castle, Christ, disguised as a servant, carried the Divine Eros into Satan's most powerful stronghold—death itself. Outside of law, contrary to reason, and bereft of a conqueror's sword, the Divine Eros nullifies our bondage. A wonderful story, almost as good as *The Polar Bear King*, but cold comfort for those of us still bound by our passions and still destined to suffer and die.

This family of folktales inhabits a world resistant to the reduction of our woes either to straightforward victimization or to moral guiltiness. The heroine ignores the rule about looking into her lover's face and brings down upon herself the consequences of this disobedience. Yet it is hardly a morally compelling rule that she never see her husband's face, particularly since it is given by a witch. This is the order of morality that restricts itself to obedience and that bridles curiosity and agency. Our heroine bursts through this order when she looks at her lover's face and faces consequences that seem inordinate to her crime. In these stories, there is a certain lack of sympathy with this order of morality, this simple obedience to law. The queen must suffer the consequences of the law, but she is also determined to overcome its power, to break through to another order of good, which is love itself. The Holy Trinity in the symbolism of ransom is likewise portrayed as disinterested in the legality of bondage. Love quests for her beloved, indifferent to the fine points of law. Love is ill-equipped and overmatched: in the folktales she is a hapless maiden who has been little more than a pawn. She is opposed to a power both ruthless and mighty who requires that she perform various impossible tasks. Like Jesus, she lacks warrior strength and every form of worldly power.

We do not like to think of Holy Trinity being overmatched by Satan, yet in the contest between love and might, Satan holds most of the cards. These folktales tell the improbable story of how Might is defeated by Love. In the story of our ransom, the Divine Eros has neither the potency nor the authority simply to declare us free. Through some combination of fault, stupidity, and victimization we are bound to destructive ways of life. We are separated from our Lover, and our Lover intends to do whatever is possible to reunite with us. Love is oblivious to morals. Ransom is an icon of this love operating at the level of cosmic drama.

THE LAW OF CONSEQUENCES

Trinity will do whatever is possible to quest for enslaved humanity, but whatever is possible is constrained by a mysterious law of consequences. The ordering of cause and effect is part of what holds the universe together. The beauty of cosmos is deeply indebted to this ordering. Chaos would consume cosmos if consequences were not ordered by the rule of gravity, Newton's laws of motion, or the thriving that follows rain and perishing that comes with winter.

The seed fertilizes an egg, and life begins—in trout, platypus, and young women. The law of consequences marches on as impervious as death, indifferent to intent or desire, ignorance or regret. It is deaf to excuses, extenuating circumstances, misunderstandings, or force. If we plant a seed and it dies for lack of water, the law of consequence does not care whether this lack was from carelessness, drought, or mortal illness that kept us in bed. Consequence knows only that acts have consequences, and it is the glory of this law to carry them out. Our craving for relief binds us to destructive ways of life. We traded away our heart's beloved for a worthless apple tree, but the law of consequences is indifferent to the veil of ignorance and pain that hid the true meaning of our bargain. The law of consequences binds us to the results of our actions.

The law of consequences is the order of nature, and without it chaos would subsume the cosmos and nothing could exist. Ideas of karma or of divine justice transpose the law of consequences into moral life, but this transposition is not very neat. Hecuba, Queen of Troy, appeals to the law of consequences to condemn the destruction of Troy:

> I am a slave, I know,
> and slaves are weak. But the gods are strong, and over them
> there stands some absolute, some moral order
> or principle of law more final still.
> Upon this moral law the world depends;
> through it the gods exist; by it we live,
> defining good and evil.[18]

But on the moral plain, the law of consequences is understood within the symbolism of ransom to have fallen into the hands of Satan. He is the "Adversary," that is, the prosecuting attorney who knows how to use the law of moral consequences against us. Hecuba appeals to moral order in vain. After all, she is herself held by one of the laws of consequences: to the victors go the spoils. For those of us caught on the other side of the law of consequences, suffering the effects of our own and all humanity's actions and ignorance, the relentlessness of this law can make us quail.

It is to this relentlessness that ransom speaks. The power that is refracted through this icon correlates to the power that binds us. The passions bind us in a vice-like hold. The misery of the human condition that unfolds from this bondage is fair, according to the law of consequences, yet heartbreaking. The power that loosens the hold of the passions is essentially indifferent to the law of consequences, to the particulars of fairness. It is directed only at blockages to the flow of erotic power. This reminds us that the power of the Divine Eros is universal in the scope of its actions; it pours out without measure. Ransom is outside the logic of exchange; it is not motivated by legalities or just deserts. It is the outflowing of the Divine Eros, "whose only gift is love without measure," to borrow Hadewijch's phrase. Christ is the icon through which the nature of Eros's liberating power can be seen, but what we see is the completely uncaused, unrestricted, antinomian surge of erotic power unleashed not, this time, on nonbeing, but on beings that have become thwarted, wounded, and bound. There could hardly be a greater violence to this revelation of divine love than to cast it back into the logic of law, righteousness, and exclusiveness.

Ransom is resonant with Buddhist "skillful means": motivated by compassion, it does whatever it takes to unlock sources of suffering. But the deepest sources of suffering are locked deep within humanity itself. Only by penetrating the stronghold of bondage can that bondage be released. The imagery of Satan possessing the world suggests, among its meanings, the ways our own minds are governed by destructive tendencies. We are egocentered and tyrannized by pain and pleasure. This persecuting structure is reproduced at the various levels of human existence: intrapsychically as well as domestically, and in our communities, religions, and political units. The imagery of ransom shows the Divine Eros disguising itself to effect perfect intimacy with us in our bondage. In this disguise, erotic power enters the place of our deepest bondage: affliction and death. From this place of perfect intimacy and perfect powerlessness, the efficacy that enables us to release from the tyranny of the ego finds its way into the human condition. Freedom is available microcosmically in the human soul and macrocosmically as "the kingdom of God."

WONDER-WORKING POWER IN THE BLOOD

It is a fabulous story, and we love to tell it. But we do not really believe it. Or rather it does not speak to our longing for release. We want to be free from suffering, and the divine power does not accomplish this. The terms of our bondage are such that we cannot even desire to be free from them. Our ego continues to crave pleasure and freedom from suffering, and this is the language in which we speak our religious longing. We long for a power that will make everything OK, but it does not seem that the Divine Eros is this kind of power. The Beauty Beyond Beauty sings cosmos from chaos. Eros becomes embodied and shows us our transfiguration. In a mystery impenetrable to understanding, Eros enters into our worst nightmares to enact the "oneing" of the Divine and Her image through death and beyond. These are such outrageous and impossible displays of power that the light of them sears our eyes. It is just that they are not the kind of power we fantasize about.

The nothingness of ransom's power—frustrated by law and subject to Rome's cruelty—is repeated in the impotence of erotic power to address meaningfully the painfulness of life. So we flee this revelation of the divine. We reroute it in more familiar, more bearable terms: we are sinners, slaves deserving punishment. The divine Caesar must be appeased. Our big brother steps in and takes our punishment, and we are eternally grateful. We flee the revelation also by taming it, localizing it. We go to church, do a few good deeds but assiduously keep real life free from religion. The divine image remains locked away in us, desperately thirsting. We hear the "good news" only after it has passed through the gates of egocentrism. Christ comes to us in disguise, speaking to us first in the only language the ego knows. But according to the symbolism of ransom, the difficulties that bind us are not moral offenses but simply obstacles. Whatever blocks the flow of erotic power is a call to the Holy Trinity to unleash itself, to pour itself out "without measure." Ransom exists outside the logic of exchange, moved by an offensively flagrant disregard for just deserts. In creation, the Divine Eros is unleashed on nonbeing. In the passion of Christ we witness this surge of erotic power unleashed on whatever thwarts, wounds, and incarcerates the divine image.

There is another aspect to the passion that is acutely disturbing to feminists, womanists, and others who are appalled by the effort to understand redemption through a bloody sacrifice. For everyone desperate to break away from the toxicity of self-sacrifice, for all those driven to despair by the addiction of religions to violence, this story of Christ's passion can be about as unedifying as can be imagined. But it is in this depth of disfiguring agony that our intimacy with the Beauty Beyond Being must be found, if it is to be significant to a humanity that remains on a cross throughout its history. If we meditate on the passion of the cross, we discover in every lash and the gash of every thorn our own wounds, the wounds of each of us and of the human species itself. We hide these wounds from ourselves, burying them in recesses of mind and hiding the mass graves of history where we have massacred and tortured each other. Because Christ shows us his wounds, we can begin to show him ours. Because this holy and divine blood flows and unites with our own blood, our wounds are washed by the Divine Eros. Whatever power for healing divinity offers is carried to our most intimate and desperate wounds by the wounds of Christ. According to the logic of ransom, this healing is not one by which individuals are saved or damned for the glory of God but a cosmic and universal healing. This does not mean all human salvation must be routed through Christ, regardless of one's religion, but that no one is excluded from the healing power Christians know through Christ. Julian of Norwich saw in the wounds of Jesus "there revealed a fair and delectable place, large enough for all [humanity]."[19] It is not a story about why everyone must become Christian but a display of the completely unrestrained character of love. According to Julian, we are Christ's bliss, and because we suffer, Christ enters into Her bliss by coming to us in our need—in the bloody, wounded, despairing, and cruel realities of our lives. Bringing the power of the Divine Eros to this place does not make our suffering disappear or abolish the conditions of earthly existence, but it opens a way of healing.

7

Contemplation

I send witness to Spirit,
Who will heal my wound,
Who will make me as white
As the cotton grass of the moor.
                    —*Trace Murphy, editor,* Celtic Prayers

There is no joy save that in paradise to be compared to the joy of
the souls in purgatory. This joy increases day by day because of the
way in which the love of God corresponds to that of the soul, since
the impediment to that love is worn away daily. . . . As it is consumed, the soul is more and more open to God's love . . . . The
more rust . . . is consumed by fire, the more the soul responds to
that love, and its joy increases.
                                        —*Catherine of Genoa*

The dramas of temptation, incarnation, and ransom capture something of the
intensity of Erotic power exercised on our behalf. It is the power by which the
astonishing beauty of existence happens. It is woven into us in the mere fact
that we exist at all. We are shards and fragments of this power, bearers of the
divine image. The unending tragedy of our existence is that this deepest core
of who we are is largely unavailable to our experience. Remembering ourselves
as God-bearers is a spiritual work. It is the creation and recreation of ourselves
as spiritual beings: radiant with the power to love and be loved, to desire and
pursue our desire, to discern paths of wisdom, to thirst for truth, to assent to
who we are. These are quintessential powers of spirit that manifest the divine

image in us, but it is these powers in particular that are choked and imprisoned by the passions. That is, the powers within us that most assist us on our path toward the Beloved are precisely the powers that are most difficult to recover. Contemplation can help us navigate this paradox.

Contemplation has a variety of meanings. In the Christian tradition, meditation is often understood as mental prayer, that is, focused training of the mind in silence and concentration. Contemplation can be understood as the unity with God that can occur through meditation. This more technical meaning is not what is intended here. Contemplation is used more broadly to indicate a conscious desire to enter more deeply into the divine Eros that flows through all things as delighting, compassionate love, together with processes and practices that nurture that desire. Through contemplation, shifts can gradually occur in the body, in the emotions and in understandings, beliefs, vocation, and relationships. Transformation of desire slowly manifests in every aspect of our being. Likewise, changes in bodily practices, in how we attend to our emotional life, and in our thoughts can all contribute to the transformation of desire. Contentment and peacefulness begin to take root in the soul. But the transformation of desire comes at the expense of the egocentric structures of consciousness. The basic structure of egocentrism places oneself at the center of experience and organizes everything else around this center. As we have seen in previous chapters, this is true not only of obviously selfish motivations but also of impulses toward morality, service, and self-sacrifice. Even "good" impulses remain rooted in the distortions of an ego wounded by passions and confused by temptations.

Contemplation does not renounce selfish desires in favor of "unselfish" ones nor does it seek morality's or religion's seal of approval. Contemplation dislocates the ego, rerouting the flow of energy from the pains and pleasures of the ego to the river of Eros that bathes all of reality. As sentient beings, we continue to experience pain and pleasure. But contemplation affords us some breathing room so that our energy is not completely absorbed in these. From the time we were infants we have been forced to cope with the fact that pain and fear of pain are all around us and that pleasure is often delayed or denied. But guided by the panic-stricken ego, our ways of coping are often damaging to us. By giving us space, contemplation eases the discomfort of pain and pleasure. As this discomfort eases, the urgency for pain relief likewise eases. There is an eye of calm in the midst of the hurricane of daily life that allows us to orient with greater freedom to the difficulties we encounter.

If, for example, we have been seduced by the pain-relieving benefits of rage, we find that this small eye of calm allows us to discern what is going on, to choose anger or to let anger go—or choose at least to *desire* to renounce our rage. As this calm becomes wider and more stable, the rage itself weakens and subsides. We can see and experience its destructive effects on ourselves and our relationships. More irritant is required to ignite our rage than before, and it is easier to let it go. The space and calm that is generating within us also allows us to notice our feelings of remorse, terror, and sorrow beneath the rage without being overwhelmed by them. When it becomes possible for these feelings to arise, they can do their work and then pass away. They no longer stay buried within us, pricking and tormenting us so mercilessly that we cannot allow them to arise to our direct awareness.

If we have been driven to debilitating self-sacrifice, contemplation creates space to draw this demon into light and expose its chicanery. Self-hatred, or the theft of our capacity for pleasure, or slavery to duty are drawn into the calm eye. As they are recognized, they can gradually be released. This release gives all the more potency to the erotic power that feels compassion and recognizes beauty. As our passions are weakened, the scope of contemplative calm increases. A broader range of awareness, deeper roots of our passions, and more hidden virtues and vices are slowly brought forward into this calm eye, just as objects in a stream become visible when silt and muck settle to the bottom. This process is interpreted, shaped, and described in a variety of ways in the various religious traditions and within any single tradition. But within this variety is a characteristic desire of contemplatives for deeper wisdom and love, which begins with the cleansing of the soul from everything that obscures this desire.

We saw in the first chapters that our basic dispositions toward ourselves and the world are rooted in pain and ignorance, tyrannized by egocentrism, and addicted to passions. We cannot alter these dispositions simply by wishing them away. Even if we become aware of our desire for good, we are not able simply to leap over years of negative, harmful, and self-destructive habituations. We may come to recognize that our timidity or anger has proven a detriment to our happiness. Recognizing that these are habits and that they are detrimental to us is itself quite difficult, but the recognition alone does not break the harmful patterns of behavior. Yet even this awareness, difficult as it is, remains close to the surface, relative to all of the layers of confusion and paralysis that cling to the soul like rust. As Teresa of Avila puts it, our soul is like an interior castle "made of a single diamond or of very clear crystal, in which there are many rooms."[1] "[T]his castle", she says, "contains many mansions, some above, others below, others at each side; and in the centre and midst of them all is the chiefest mansion where the most secret things pass between God and the soul."[2] She notes that many of us "remain in the outer court of the castle, which is the place occupied by the guards; they are not interested in entering it, and have no idea what there is in that wonderful place, or who dwells in it, or even how many rooms it has."[3] Some do eventually "enter the first rooms on the lowest floor, but so many reptiles get in with them that they are unable to appreciate the beauty of the castle or to find any peace within it."[4]

Teresa's "interior castle" gives us a metaphor for the diamond purity and beauty we possess, the great intimacy we enjoy with the Beloved, as well as the obstacles we encounter when we seek "one taste" between ourselves and the Divine Eros. Contemplation is a way of understanding these different dimensions of our spiritual life. In particular, it holds before us a constant reminder of the fantastic beauty and power with which we are created, the complexity and depth of our spirit, and the length of the journey to our Beloved, which is at the same time, the journey to ourselves.

Walking the contemplative path within a Christian context means that we have some trust or confidence in the power of the Holy Trinity to relieve us of the pain of our bondage. But this confidence does not mean that God magically removes every obstacle from our soul and from our world so that we live instantly in a paradise of holy love. Awareness that erotic power works with us and not upon us is characteristic of a contemplative approach to religious life. Confidence in a religious tradition is at the same time confidence in ourselves, faith that we can live ever more deeply out of the divine image within us. Spirit has the nature of self-initiation, agency, and freedom. We are not like clay, which passively takes on the shape the master bestows. Spirit is the energy of self-movement and novelty. The Holy Spirit is most associated with this freedom of movement: She blows where She lists. The spontaneity of spirit is not the arbitrary movement of an unconstrained, undisciplined will. Arbitrariness is the *ersatz* freedom of egocentrism.

Love is the fullest form of spiritual existence, the most perfect self-manifestation of spiritual beings. It arises from the erotic energy that is uniquely embodied in each person. To love and be loved, unencumbered by the terrors of the passions and the tyranny of the ego, is the spontaneity of spirit in its freest expression. We are rivers of erotic power that have become hopelessly clogged by the flotsam and jetsam of life. The infinitely tender work of the Divine Eros is to enable this river to flow clear and strong.

This power, however, is spiritual power exercised with spiritual beings. It cannot undermine the spontaneity of spirit, even though it is this very spontaneity that is deranged and impoverished. Any of us who have ever loved another know the frustration of this paradox. We wish we could simply tear a friend away from the cruelty of his interior secret police. We wish we could reach in and break the hold of an addiction we see destroying someone we care about or *make* an adolescent see the destructiveness of her behavior. It is not that it would be immoral to do so. It is simply not possible. Spirit cannot be freed by force. As spiritual beings, we must participate in our own liberation; but bound by passions, it is difficult for us to do so.

Contemplation is one dimension of how religions think about this paradox. It seems as if we are being more active the more completely passive to the workings of the Holy Spirit we become. It seems as if we exert enormous effort but, at the same time, it seems as if we are doing nothing at all. Is contemplation wholly grace or work? Is it a technique or a miraculous intervention? Is it Christ's desire for us or our desire for Christ? I am not sure it is helpful to linger over these conundrums very long. Desire pulls us toward the root of our longing and that is all we really need to know.[5]

There are of course many ways to consider liberation other than contemplation. There are also many ways of interpreting contemplation other than the way it is being used here. These reflections are not meant to overshadow other possibilities but to incorporate contemplation in our understanding of the human condition. We will consider contemplation in two stages, by looking first at dimensions of contemplation and second at the darkness that overshadows the soul when the ego is dislocated. The next chapter will reflect on some of the energies that can be freed as the contemplative process proceeds.

DIMENSIONS OF CONTEMPLATION

As contemplative desire is aroused, the desire for genuine freedom from the passions intensifies. Our longing to connect to the divine image in us, to live more completely out of the "oneing" of our soul with Holy Eros, and to radiate this love to other beings becomes increasingly, painfully urgent. Religious traditions offer one of the only places in culture that can interpret these longings, provide communities and wisdom to shape them, and practices that deepen them. Different traditions operate within somewhat distinct metaphysical universes and therefore interpret contemplative longing in a variety of ways. Christianity, Islam, and other theistic traditions conceive of this longing primarily as a longing for God. Buddhists interpret it more as a desire for the realization of emptiness and the fullness of compassion that is the fruit of contemplation. It is helpful to have some framework that makes our longing more intelligible, but the diversity of religious traditions shows us that the longing is deeper than any concept a religious tradition supplies.

Perhaps even more important than the metaphysics of religious traditions are the communities that are available to us through traditions. The journey inward and outward is painful, confusing, and disorienting. In the absence of a community and the guidance of wise and experienced teachers, the contemplative path can be dangerous for oneself and for others. Religious traditions preserve the wisdom of thousands of years of practice and training that can produce contemplative communities and teachers. This is not to say that religious institutions are infallible guides, or that stupidity, cruelty, ignorance, folly, and abuse do not reside in them. Nonetheless, both our essential inter-dependencies and the intrinsic difficulties of transformation make companionship a crucial part of contemplation.

Part of the guidance that religious traditions offer is the knowledge that desire for God (as Christians put it) has as its twin a desire for deeper compassion and love for other beings. Contemplative desire is reducible neither to a longing to be free from the pains of the ego nor to ethical commands. It is deeper than both of these. It is a longing for a truth more ultimate than what the world offers as well as a longing that one's fledgling compassion become steadier and more efficacious. Contemplative desire is inseparable from "love of God and neighbor." Some version of the twin love commandment present in the New Testament is found in virtually every religious tradition. The awareness that these desires are fundamentally intertwined is a deeply ground-ing wisdom that religious traditions have carried. When contemplative prac-tice tempts us to more refined forms of egocentrism or to obsessive pursuit of ascetic practices, we can be brought back to deeper freedom by the reminder that the principle fruit of contemplation is love.

Conversely, our dedication to justice or works of service can easily outstrip our capacities, and we are at risk for over-use injury, self-righteousness, and burnout. Deep compassion for all beings needs roots in something deeper than ethical principles. The twinning of contemplative desire provides our care for others with the nurture of the Divine Eros or, as Buddhists might put it, in the equanimity that arises with the realization of emptiness. Sometimes access to religious traditions is blocked by negative experiences with a religion or some other difficulty. But considerable stability can arise out of this balance between our desire for wisdom rooted in ultimate dimensions of reality and our desire to be more radiant with love.

Religious traditions also offer a wide range of practices that can come to our aid at this time: meditation, centering prayer, yoga, chanting, and many more. Contemplative practices are techniques or tools that assist us in calming the chatter of our consciousness so that silence, the first language of the divine, can speak. Practices are not like recipe books for the soul: a pinch of medita-tion, a cup of *lectio divina*, fast for twenty or thirty years and—voilá—enlight-enment! As the desert ascetics knew, we can heroically meditate with unfailing concentration for decades or fast until the flesh falls from our bones but find relief from not one iota of the rage that tortures us. The contrary is equally true. With little or no regular contemplative discipline, we might find the chambers of our heart opening like a flower as we become filled with coura-geous love. We might appeal to the vagaries of grace or the mysteries of karma to explain these discrepancies, but accounting for the mysteries of the soul's movements is beyond the power of any theory.

Religious traditions have carried the beliefs, communities, values, and practices through which contemplative desire is articulated. But contemplative desire digs into these traditions in a quest for the deepest possible healing. This means that contemplation moves through beliefs and practices of particular religious traditions to the source of wisdom and healing that animates every religious tradition. But what actually unfolds as contemplative desire is released is outside of our control. When a woman is pregnant she can do many things to contribute to the health of her unborn child. She can eat certain things, avoid others, exercise, listen to Mozart, train for a "natural" childbirth, try to avoid catastrophes. These things can be very important and useful. But in the end, she cannot control the place she gives birth, the kind of birth she experiences, or what child it is that is born to her. She can participate in what happens, but she cannot control the world around her, and when the pangs of labor are upon her, all she can do is ride out the storm any way it comes and love the child that is born to her as best she can.

Contemplation is the birth of ourselves. It asks us, "Do you want to be healed? Do you *really* want to be healed?" If we assent to the pathway of healing, even with only a little part of ourselves, we engage various practices and believe, expect, anticipate various things. We participate, but we cannot control or even fully understand what happens within us and in the world around us. Here, too, we ride the storm of birth and love the child that is born of us.

I have already used the word contemplation in several different ways in these few pages. I will sort some of this out by looking at different dimensions of contemplation: desire, path, and practices.

Contemplative Desire

The first chapter made the admittedly counterintuitive claim that we human beings are in truth flames of desire, aching for the Good Beyond Being. As evidence, I cited folk songs and an ancient philosopher or two. The other direction from which this point might be made is by appeal to the God-intoxicated lovers for whom desire is the medium through which the solidarity of humanity and intimacy with their Holy Lover is experienced. A contemplative dimension of ourselves awakens as awareness of this intoxicating, mortifying thirst. The painful, delightful goading of this desire is described by Beatrice of Nazareth:

> For the more the soul is given from above, the more she desires, and the more that is revealed to her, the more she is seized by a desire to

draw near to the light of truth, of purity, of sanctity, and of love's delight. And thus she is driven and goaded on more and more and knows no peace or satisfaction; for the very thing that tortures her and gives her the greatest suffering, makes her whole, and what wounds her most deeply is the source of her greatest relief."[6]

Mechthild of Magdeberg says, more simply, "For the deeper I sink, The sweeter I drink."[7]

Contemplative desire awakens us to the unity of the love of God and neighbor, but it does not accomplish the perfection of this love; it rather incites our thirst for it. When Helen Keller crouched by the water pump while Annie poured water over her hand and spelled the word for water over and over, in her blindness she experienced nothing but water and the strange movement of fingers on her palm. We are "commanded" to love. Love pours over us like water, and the meaning of love is spelled into our hand over and over. But, like Helen, we are blind and enraged by our blindness, and we cannot understand its meaning. But suddenly Helen grasped the connection between the fingers in her palm and the water pouring over her hand. Grasping this connection did not itself open all of the world of language and meaning and human relationship to her, but it fired her desire for these things. Over many years, her desire continued to burn. It took her from the solitary confinement of darkness and silence to friendship, Radcliff, social activism, and intimacy with God.

Contemplation is an analogous awakening of desire. With this awakening, awareness dawns of how little we are able to love, how bound we are to our fears. This is why the great saints describe themselves as such terrible "sinners." They become more and more aware of the awesome infinity of love open to them. Contemplative desire sparks our awareness of this infinity of love within us and available to us, just as the knowledge of that single word "water" made Helen know that a universe of connection was available to her. From one word, an infinity of meaning opened. From the tiniest taste of Holy Eros, the infinity of love manifest in every soul and spiraling through the endlessness of our own soul is apprehended. The thirst of contemplation lives in the gap between that single taste and the infinity of the cosmos.

Learning five words or one hundred or ten thousand does not assuage desire but fires it. With each word, with each taste, we can better imagine the distance between ourselves and the satisfaction of our knowing and loving. From one word, we may imagine that there is a word for every object we see. Our desire and our pain fuse as we think of the length of the journey to knowledge of all of those words. But then we encounter stories, philosophies, the deep symbols of the world's cultures, and we realize that the endless list of names for objects is nothing at all compared to the endless dimensions of meaning language begins to open for us. We could spend a lifetime learning the names of every object in the world and not come to the end of them. We could spend a lifetime reading a single page of Scripture or studying every detail of the life cycle of a gnat and not come to the end of these either. The smallest opening of our heart to adoration of our Holy Lover and erotic compassion for all beings shows us the endless beauty of beings—receding endlessly beyond our capacity to love them. And every time the floor opens beneath us and we realize the poverty of our imagination, our thirst and our anguish fuse in the paradoxical sweetness of contemplative desire.

The economy of desire is not toward possession. Certainty remains within the economy of possession, and the way of contemplation leads us in the opposite direction. Markers thin out. Beliefs, images of God, practices, goals, and moral commitments that seemed self-evident or essential lose their stability. We may wish to assuage the anguish of desire with clarity and certainty, but certainty is a pleasure one must learn to do without. In its place, it is only the more intense burning of desire that is our guide. Desire is like a magnet, weak at first and finding the object that pulls it only with difficulty. Naturally, we make mistakes and are tortured by doubt. We remain unclear about what to do, believe, and practice; whom to believe; and how to test the wandering insights of our hearts. We can be aided by all of the resources available to us, but it is desire itself that draws us implacably to our Beloved. Through all of our mistakes and lack of clarity, desire continues to seek out what draws it. The urgency of desire moves us through the difficulties we encounter and allows them to be purifying rather than overwhelming. The Beguines describe the suffering that accompanies contemplative desire, deeply aware of the painfulness of desire as well as its trustworthiness.

Desire itself is the surest road, but as we "flee from adversity," we become confused. This is inevitable, but even so, desire remains the holy road to the Divine Eros. Our desire is the abode of the Divine Eros. It is the place where we are conjoined with the power of Eros, and this power makes use of every difficulty. Love leads us, transfiguring obstacles into the path itself. For Love (God) "will repay all pain with love."[8] The purifying power of desire enables us to focus more intently on the source and object of desire, even in the absence of the comfort of certainty about where we are going or what we should be doing.

We can be mistaken in the way we pursue our desire or in the way we interpret its meaning or demands. Vulnerability to error does not decrease as we assent to a contemplative path; it may only increase. As Teresa of Avila admonishes, "Even with these desires to help others, sisters, we may make many mistakes and thus it is better to attempt to do what our Rule tells us—to try to live ever in silence and hope."[9] But desire is fire, and it purifies. It is the medium of intimacy with the Holy One, one of whose names is Desire. Through desire our own small powers leak into the great stream of power of the Divine Eros.

This is one reason the contemplative path is dangerous. But it is also why desire is purifying. Desire, in lieu of safety or certainty, allows all of our errors, mistakes, misunderstandings, wrong turns, harsh deeds, incapacitating weaknesses, and meretricious strengths to be integrated into the contemplative path. As we fumble along, witnessing the inadequacies of our efforts, the Divine Eros burns in us all the more deeply. Like pregnant women, we can participate in this process, but we also simply rest in it, allowing our desire to be purified, strengthened, satisfied, and intensified. Mechthild describes this dialogue of desire that occurs in the soul:

> Ah, Lord, love me passionately, love me often, and love me long. For the more passionately you love me, the purer I shall become. The more often you love me, the more beautiful I shall become. The longer you love me, the holier I shall become here on earth.[10]

God answers the soul:

> That I love you passionately comes from my nature, for I am love itself. That I love you often comes from my desire, for I desire to be loved passionately. That I love you long comes from my being eternal, for I am without an end and without a beginning.[11]

Through this dialogue of mutual desire, over time interior awareness of the faith we acquired but did not believe even as children is carried more deeply into us: the gracious adoration of Holy Mystery for us requires nothing at all of us. In whatever tiny measure we awaken to desire for the Beloved, we become aware that the infinite depths of the Beloved's desire for us preceded us: the eternity of divine love for us walks before us, follows after us, protects us from above, nourishes us from below, and burns within us. It can no more abandon us that it can abandon its own nature. The sublime indifference of our Beloved to our imperfections can be almost intolerable.[12] We crave this Love yet find it unbearable. Desire teaches us to detach from our certainties and our need to be perfect, releasing more and more fully into the flow of desire between Holy Eros and ourselves. In this way, the painfulness of desire, the anguish of uncertainty, and the inevitability of errors that harm ourselves and others become as nothing compared to the urgency of desire as it carries us to our Beloved. It is this loving and being loved that purifies us, removes the "rust" from our souls, and makes us "as white as the cotton grass of the moor."[13]

The Path of Contemplation

Because the desire of contemplation is directed toward the abyss of love, contemplation is not a final achievement or a finished work but a path. Buddhists seek enlightenment, and Christians long for union with God. These supply us with images of a contemplative path that has discernable stages and ends up someplace, a journey that concludes when we find ourselves snug in a castle, the strains of the journey safely behind us. But Buddhists and Christians also describe stages within the enlightened or united condition, and they tend to postpone the perfect realization of these states to another life or another mode of existence in "heaven." The idea of an ending or conclusion provides us with a more definite shape for our desire and criteria for our "advancement," such as it is, along the path. The fruits of contemplation are said to include equanimity, deep peace, joy, undisturbed compassion, and love. In the confusions of life and the disorientation of contemplation, these markers can be helpful. If we find ourselves hating ourselves or others more than ever, this is a signal that perfect possession of enlightenment continues to elude us. But even if there is a consummation of the contemplative path, it is the path itself that we walk, step by step. As we walk we should not expect that the dawning of contemplative desire transforms us into peaceful, loving, joyous, calm people. In fact, the opposite experience is more likely to arise at various moments (or years or decades) of the path.

It is crucial to remember that contemplation is a path because this allows us to attend to the place we are right now. We may deeply desire to be calm and loving people, but this ideal should not become a fantasy or condemnation of what we are experiencing right now. The Tibetan Buddhist nun, Pema Chodron, has particular wisdom about the difficulties that accompany contemplative practices:

> The essence of bravery is being without self-deception. However, it's not so easy to take a straight look at what we do. Seeing ourselves clearly is initially uncomfortable and embarrassing. As we train in clarity and steadfastness, we see things we'd prefer to deny—judgmentalness, pettiness, arrogance.[14]

Unhappily, desire does not give us seven-league boots that enable us to step over all of the difficulties that arise as we move through the chambers of our heart. But in her compassion Pema Chodron continues,

> These are not sins but temporary and workable habits of mind. The more we get to know them, the more they lose their power. This is how we come to trust that our basic nature is utterly simple, free of struggle between good and bad.[15]

Contemplation stills thoughts and emotions so that we can become more conscious of dimensions of mind beneath the grunge and distraction of everyday life. Even sitting still for thirty seconds and focusing awareness on our breath can clear out an excess of anxiety, restoring a level of calm and confidence that seems disproportionate to the simplicity of what we have done. Various contemplative practices assist us in deepening this calm. As stillness increases, mind is able to open onto its own depths. The underworld of mind is not for the fainthearted. In the silence of contemplation, intimacy with our Lover can be deepened and our own power tapped. But the underworld is also the wilderness where the passions reign, where our "demons" live, where our exiled experiences and disowned virtues have been banished. Mind protects us from the wild ones within us for good reasons. Passions have held us long and deeply and will not be transformed overnight. Unleashing intolerable awareness when we are not prepared for it is dangerous.

As long as they remain unintegrated, the inhabitants of our psychic underworld also sap our energy and block our capacities for love. Gradually, the contemplative path will pass through these regions and integrate every aspect of ourselves with our erotic desire. In this aspect, contemplation overlaps with therapy, where one is guided by a therapist who, if things go well, can help release psychic pain and obstacles slowly and carefully. We may believe desire for our Beloved should itself automatically clean us of all of our obscurations, but there is no direct route that bypasses the wounds of our psyches. Contemplative desire is like an athlete, intent on the Olympics. An athlete may wish an injury were gone or had never happened. Despair over the injury guarantees defeat, but to suppress knowledge of an injury can give it the power to become permanently debilitating. The only way to remain an athlete is to work with doctors and trainers carefully and skillfully, neither despairing over nor ignoring the injury. In this way, the injury will be transformed so that it does not exclude the athlete from the games. It can even happen that the courage to press one's limit in ways that risk injury, or something in the injury itself, or the process of healing, or the tenacity sustained throughout every aspect of practice, conspire to contribute even greater prowess than if no injury ever occurred.

The image of purification so common in writings about contemplation refers to this process of overcoming obstacles, what Catherine of Genoa refers to as "rust." Whatever anguish, traumas, errors, wrongdoing, bondage, passion, and terror lie within us must be carefully and skillfully healed. These must neither cause us to despair nor be ignored forever. Obstacles are simply a part of this path. If we imagine that obstacles are signs of our inadequacy, we are like athletes who believe a pulled muscle condemns us as unfit for our vocation. Just as athleticism invites injuries that the more sedentary are less likely to experience, the journey inward inevitably encounters the darkness of the soul that does not arise spontaneously to awareness. The image of path reminds us both that obstacles are essential components of the contemplative way and that we must attend to them as they arise. We need not anticipate difficulties that we have not yet encountered nor evade ones that do appear.

Mind is also the dungeon where our untamed power is held. We bear the Divine Eros within ourselves. This power is more a part of us than our memories or our personality. But it, too, is intolerable. Our power is splintered into more tame virtues, but the fuller intensity of our power is shackled more fiercely than Prometheus on his rock. Our power is the place of our union with Holy Trinity, but, like the demons that haunt our interior landscape, it cannot be released suddenly or carelessly. Learning to slowly release our powers might be like taming a wild horse. For some, power is seductive. A taste of the power released in contemplative practice can become intoxicating. Relishing our power, we find ourselves exploiting others. We allow our charisma or spiritual prowess to justify our vices, cruelties, and ignorance.

The desert fathers identified the temptation of "vainglory" as the most vicious and difficult of the passions. Religious leaders, gurus, and teachers who have been waylaid by this release of power, to the great harm of themselves and their followers, are only too common. For others, power is terrifying and the desire to avoid harm can make it seem preferable to keep our power bound, at whatever cost. For women in particular it can be difficult to imagine power that is not destructive or harmfully aggressive. We have too few models in our culture of powerful women. But the path of contemplation leads inexorably through this wilderness, too. The Lion of Judah does not wed kitty cats; our Beloved will not allow us to cling to our powerlessness indefinitely.

In leading us through the underworld of the psyche, the contemplative path rambles like that of a knight errant. Even if the goal burns always within, the journey can seem to be wayward and without any clear path. We are likely to wander in directions that we not only did not anticipate but that we would have thought abhorrent or terrifying if we had thought of them. A sensualist or scion of wealth may fall in love with "Lady Poverty" and turn his passions to asceticism and compassionate love. A monastic may find herself entering the world after decades joyfully dedicated to the divine office. One person who found the Christianity of her youth to be undiluted oppression may in her adulthood discover in it a backdoor to Holy Mystery. Another may find herself led to traditions that fill in gaps in her experience left by the formation in a Christian congregation she cherished. It may free up healthy sensuality and make possible the flow of physical pleasure. It may lead from the trenches of urban ministry to teaching or from teaching to the trenches. The demons that assaulted Anthony in the desert sometimes enticed him to more extreme fasting and sometimes enticed him away from fasting.[16]

We cannot necessarily discern from a particular way of life or practice that we are nearing our Beloved. A way that proved a high road for one person or community may be destructive and obscuring for another. Our beliefs about how a contemplative should live, our images of piety and morality, and our assumptions about what pleases God change over time. They can help us for a while, and then the path makes another turn and we have to leave them behind. Because they were helpful, they can be hard to leave behind. It is as if we are abandoning the path itself when we find we must leave the very things that have made it possible to walk it. But the path does not lead us to beliefs or practices. It leads us to our Beloved, and everything else, including those things that led us in the past toward our Beloved, fall away. It does not require that we reject or condemn anything; it simply means that we must try to recognize when the path is taking us in an unexpected direction and try to avoid clinging to one section of our journey. At the same time, discipline and fearlessness, or commitment to practices and companions, cannot simply be jettisoned in the name of spiritual freedom.

Guidance through these confusions can be available through religious communities, but there is no tradition or community that has been spared its own foolishness, violence, and ignorance. Reliable guidance from the spiritual friends we make with figures from history is likewise helpful and dangerous. The saints and contemplatives who become companions and guides can make dangerous examples. They may shine with the erotic power of their love and compassion, but the path they walked was the one laid down for them, given their time and possibilities, their talents and pathologies. That anorexia-like fasting or limitless service or intense visions were part of one person's path does not mean these are practices to be emulated. It may mean only that, like all of our mistakes and limitations, these particular pathologies and gifts were woven together with contemplative desire to lead a particular person to her Beloved. All of this makes *discernment* central to contemplative desire.

Contemplation is desire and a path, but it is not certainty. Nothing in particular guarantees that we are not being led astray by the self-deceptions, that we are truly being gentle with ourselves, or that what we believe to be the face of Christ is not really a destructive image projected by our ego, eager to avoid being displaced. No authority or practice or belief grants us unconditional security. Together with our companions, we have to make the best decisions we can. Each individual is unique and presented with unique challenges. Path is an image of journey, motion, and change. It undermines our dependence on certainty and stability.

We are led by the infinity of our desire for the Good Beyond Being through the wildernesses of our interior obstacles and untamed power. In this wilderness, where we need clarity more than ever, we cannot rely uncritically on our beliefs, traditional practices, or familiar models. In the absence of anything we can rely on absolutely, the role of community and companionship is greatly intensified. "There is safety in much counsel," as Dorotheus insisted.[17] Others can sometimes see ourselves better than we can and, if they are wise, be more gentle with us that we can be with ourselves. "Spiritual friends"; directors, sisters, and brothers along the way; small communities; and prayer or meditation groups provide crucial resources as we try to discern our path.

There is no antidote for uncertainty and the need for constant discernment. But what we lack in security can be made up for by ever-deepening trust in the path itself and in the tender mercies of our Beloved. As Teresa says, "provided we do not abandon our prayer, the Lord will turn everything we do to our profit."[18] Hadewijch, too, offers only love itself as an antidote for the confusions of the path:

> Nothing can dwell in Love, and nothing can touch her except desire. The most secret name of Love is this touch, and that is a mode of operation that takes its rise from Love herself. . . . No mercy can dwell in Love, no graciousness, humility, reason, fear; no parsimony, no measure, nothing. But Love dwells in all these, and they are all nourished on Love. Yet Love herself receives no nourishment except from her own integrity.[19]

Dedication to our desire does not free us from errors. But in it we grow to feel more strongly than ever that "my heart is bound, my soul is chained to the rock" (Emmy Lou Harris). That is the only security we are likely to know.

Practices

Desire carries our heart across the endless abyss between the love we are capable of now and the love we long to be able to give and receive. The path ties our desire to all of the concrete details of life, winding day by day through the murkiness of daily living. Contemplation is simultaneously a glorious winged creature, soaring above the dullness of the everyday, and a blind mole pushing its nose against dirt and rock. The pure luminescence of eros lives together with the trivia, rust, and refuse of life. Luminescence and rust are contained in all of the cells of our body; in the beating of our hearts; in the workings of our liver, intestines, kidneys; in the strength and weakness of our muscles; in the way our brains synapse and our hormones change. They flow through our blood and through the electrical currents of our bodies, which are not the mules that carry around our spirits but rather the spatial manifestation of our spirits.

Nothing happens to our spirit, good and bad, that is not written in the details of our body. Nothing happens to our body that is not at the same time a spiritual event. Whatever becomes of our particular incarnation of the divine image when death dismembers us, during our time here and now, spirit and body are "one taste." It is not most primordially what we think or believe or will but rather our bodies that carry our desire into the deepest intimacies of spiritual life. Our thinking can be extremely profound and our decisions can be wise and well intended. But thought and will can penetrate our spirits to only a limited degree. We may have written quite brilliant papers in college about Plato or Spinoza, without our brilliance affecting our desires and passions much at all. We can exercise our will power to perform rather amazing feats of self-control. We may stick with a decision to quit smoking cold turkey even after we discover our mother must undergo life-threatening surgery. But this enormous and admirable triumph of the will does not automatically translate into a more tender heart.

Because our erotic desire lives in our bodies, practices are important contributions to contemplative practice. From the perspective of Descartes or Calvin this may seem paradoxical, since they placed such great distance between mind and body. Following these harbingers of modernity, our world tends to overrate what thought and will can do. But if we do not integrate our body into our contemplative desire, we lose a crucial ally. Unlocking the bondage of the soul and enlivening our hearts for love is greatly assisted by practices that inhabit the places of intimacy between "spirit" and "body."

It is not that thinking and willing are irrelevant to the contemplative path. The great metaphysicians of the religions were also contemplatives, and contemplatives generally write and live out of rigorous and profound intellectual positions. It is not an accident that the women contemplatives whose writings survive the upheavals of history are brilliant and creative theologians. Systematically denied access to education, their incisive intelligence illuminates every genre in which they choose to write. The intellect and will are not left behind on the contemplative path. They are employed to their fullest capacity. But they do not by themselves penetrate to the places of spirit where egocentrism remains locked in combat against whatever would displace it. They cannot by themselves release us from the bondage of rage, terror, and addiction. These things are lodged in the body, and practices that engage the body are therefore helpful to contemplation.

In contemplative practice, the incarnate spirit itself is present to receive whatever benefits are to be had from the practice. It does not have to think through everything that happens or should happen and orchestrate the good effects of meditation or yoga or chanting. To a certain extent, contemplative practices are alike in seducing thinking and willing into relative stillness so that our deeper needs can be tended. Bodily practices like yoga or meditation, centering prayer, chanting the Psalms, gardening, or drawing relax the body so that the toxins of stress, fatigue, and tension can be released, allowing the body's energies to flow more freely. Practices also release discursive reasoning from the burden of micromanagement and in this way permit the body to accept a deeper restructuring. The body digests what has happened to it, loosening habitual attachments and passions, purifying the "rubbish" that accumulates within us and allowing consciousness to flow more easily. The opposite can also be said. Contemplative practices allow the stillness of the divine to work in us, less impeded by the mind. They remind us that we are not in charge of what happens but that when we relax into whatever practices are helpful to us, we give more space to the efficacy of grace.[20]

The aim of contemplative desire is the gradual recovery of freedom to love. Through the transformation of desire, we walk a path that integrates all of the parts of us and engage practices that energize our spirit. Our bodies burn off obstacles so the hold of passions can be weakened. We come nearer to our vocations, both the vocation of all beings to incarnate Divine Eros and our own unique form of that incarnation, whatever it is.

DARKNESS

Love breaks free in us as we disarm and dislocate egocentrism. The ego is not amused by this, for the egological structure of mind is intimately tied to the habit of egocentrism. This intimacy is so thorough that it feels as if there were no difference between mind and ego at all. We feel as if the dislocation of the habit of egocentricity would be tantamount to ceasing to be a person altogether. We rightly resist images of humiliation or annihilation that imply personal existence has no place in contemplative desire. The ego, a sort of organizing principle of personal existence, is not itself able to sort out the difference between egocentrism and egological life. The mind can conceive of this distinction, with the help of living teachers and the writing of sages from the various religious traditions. The heart can intuitively long for the deeper capacity to delight in others that undergirds all genuine compassion. But the ego is that part of the mind that is dedicated to survival, and it does not have easy access to the awareness that survival does not depend on egocentrism. This creates tension between contemplative desire and the ego that generates periods of difficulty and darkness.

The ego maintains its centrality by habituation, skepticism, and fear. The habit of egocentrism is so deeply ingrained that it seems to be existence itself. Buddhists and Christians alike note that all living beings are driven by the desire to live, and we do this by seeking pleasure and avoiding pain. In self-conscious beings like ourselves, it is largely the ego that orchestrates this work of survival. This includes physical as well as psychic survival, and the ego is very clever in its ability to carry out its job. But because pleasure and pain is the primary grammar that the ego understands, it is convinced that to abandon egocentrism would be suicide. The ego is not a moralist; it is in the business of survival. If we do not look after ourselves, who will? The ego has worked out a dependable mode of operation. It is familiar, even trustworthy. Even if the ego could be convinced that this mode of operation is actually producing more harm than good, it cannot give it up.

The habits of the ego are deep, and the habit of egocentrism, the deepest habit of all. Consider how hard it is to give up a simple habit like nail biting because we have decided it makes us look stupid or eating salt because we have high blood pressure. Spiritual habits—terror, guilt, ennui, hedonism—are even more difficult to break. They are the shape of our bodies and souls as we muddle through every minute of every day. But the habit of egocentrism is almost identical with consciousness itself. We are the center of all of our experiences, even experiences of compassion and empathy: it is *my* compassion or empathy, even if it is for other people. This centeredness in my experience structures consciousness and determines emotional habits and beliefs; it conditions my most intimate relationships; and it tyrannizes my desires. It does not go peacefully to any sweet, good night.

The habit of egocentrism is supported by the ego's distinctive mode of awareness. The ego is acutely aware of what it directly experiences, but it is a skeptic and tends to be dismissive of what it does not experience. Pain and pleasure completely dominate the ego's awareness of itself and of the world. Pain is pain. It is completely real. Pleasure is also completely real. Pleasure, because it is so pleasant, is to be sought. Pain, because it is so painful, is to be shunned, avoided, and feared. Generally speaking, pain and pleasure are good guides for survival. Food and sex are pleasant and help us survive; injury and danger are painful and threaten our lives. But the mind and the heart can move far ahead of us and bring back news of distant joys and sublime risks that awareness of pain and pleasure cannot envision. We have the power within us to overcome our fear of pain and our excessive attachment to momentary pleasure. We can be aware of goods that are infinitely more satisfying, delicious, sustaining, and delightful.

Still, the ego is a pragmatist and a skeptic: "'Unless I see the mark of the nails in his hands, and put my finger in the mark of the nails and my hand in his side, I will not believe'" (John 20:25). It is not that the ego is wrong about pain and pleasure in themselves. It is just that the ego has a limited perspective. The ego is deprived of almost all knowledge of what heart and mind desire. Regardless of what evidence heart and reason deliver, the ego does not believe them and can envision the transformation of desire only as suicide. Terrified of its own demise, it is like a stubby little creature, stamping its feet and shouting that it does not care about these ridiculous stories and idle dreams. The ego wants to exist. It loves its miserable, debilitated, tormented existence and is not going to risk a single hair on its stubby little head.

The Divine Eros, however, does not require the death of personal existence. To the contrary, when Eros breaths on the ego, it is filled with power: its capacities become like the mustard seed. From tiny, inconsequential beginnings grows the greatest of shrubs, and it becomes a tree, large enough for birds to come and make nests in its branches (see Matt. 13:12). But it is the ego's *way* of experiencing the world that is transformed by desire. This is a subtle distinction, and the ego has enormous difficulty believing in it.

A third reason the ego resists is that whatever awareness of desire it has seems terrifying. The small taste, the rare whiff, of desire that it does experience is completely overwhelming. Being so consumed with pain and pleasure, we might think that the ego would be delighted by joy, but this is not the case. Pleasure is easy. We do not have to dedicate much energy to the capacity for pleasure. We do not have to do anything special to taste the deliciousness of chocolate cake. We have only to put it in our mouth. But joy moves into the deepest parts of us. It is like a ferocious, tender lover who adores us so intensely that it will be not be satisfied until every corner of our body and soul has been drenched in delight. Joy requires the strength to receive joy. It is the same with beauty. Great spiritual energy is necessary for the soul to be able to receive beauty. It is so intense that we can accept it only in small doses. We do not have enough energy to take it in deeply or long.

We can stand aesthetic pleasures, but beauty is too strong for us. It is the same with compassion, love, sorrow, the light of truth, great peace. The intensity of the good and sorrowful things beyond pleasure and pain are too much for the ego. When the ego catches a glimpse of joy or compassion or beauty or sorrow or even peace, it is overwhelmed. "No, no, no, thank you very much. These are all too fine for me. I will just stay here and tend my own miserable, weed-choked garden. Actually, I'm feeling a little tired today. Maybe tomorrow. Thanks all the same."

Notwithstanding its lack of enthusiasm, the ego is our companion on the contemplative path, like the jabbering, cowardly, irritating mule that accompanies Shrek on his quest. On this path of contemplation we must not despise our companion. Its drive to exist is given to it by the Divine Eros. But the contemplative path does reorient the ego's preoccupation with pain and pleasure, and there are moments of this reorientation that are excruciatingly difficult. The anguish and confusion of these times can cover us with deep darkness. Although it can feel unbearably bleak, it is not the darkness of destruction but the painful release of the tyranny of the passions and ultimately, the great contemplatives tell us, of egocentrism itself.

Two kinds of darkness will be discussed here: the first is the "dark night of the soul," so brilliantly and tenderly described by St. John of the Cross. St. John writes to the Carmelite sisters and brothers under his spiritual guidance and describes the nuances of the dark night of the soul in detail so they would not despair during the periods of darkness that one inevitably passes through on the contemplative path.[21] The second is the darkness of extreme suffering that can also dislodge the normal functioning of the ego. The first darkness is a natural dimension of contemplative practice. It is a part of the process by which we are able to deepen our awareness of our unity with the divine image that dwells within us. The second darkness is neither natural nor inevitable, though it is commonplace enough. It is the affliction to which we are vulnerable because there is violence and difficulty in the world. These two are completely different, yet they are similar in structure and often occur simultaneously.

The Dark Night of the Soul

St. John of the Cross was the protégé and spiritual director of his mentor, St. Teresa of Avila. St. John and St. Teresa wrote for their own communities of monks and nuns engaged in a rigorous and dedicated life of prayer. My reflections on darkness here are much influenced by these writings, but they are written by a layperson for laypeople, so this description is also a work of translation. Even though laypeople do not engage the contemplative path with the single-mindedness that a monastic can, features of the dark night are likely to become familiar to anyone experiencing the transformation of desire.

St. John describes two stages of darkness: first, the dark night of sense releases us from ordinary attachments and effects a cleansing of the soul from the tyranny of the passions. Second, the dark night of soul cleanses us from egocentrism itself. This perfect freedom is what allows the soul perfect union with the Beloved. St. John provides a great deal of detail in his descriptions of what these periods of darkness feel like, how they differ from depression, and what their fruits are. He is painstakingly systematic. Teresa of Avila describes something more like a journey through an interior castle. She tends toward more ecstatic mysticism; he is the more detailed psychologist. For everyone who walks this way, the path will be unique. But these two theologians of the contemplative life help us to understand the strange suffering that accompanies the transformation of desire. They know only too well how counterintuitive it feels to run into these periods of darkness when the joy of contemplation has burned so brightly. They know, too, how easy it is to despair, how common is the belief that darkness means we are unfit for this path, how easy it is to believe that there is something wrong with us. They know that during times of darkness it is even more crucial than ever to find guidance and encouragement.

Most of all, it is necessary to understand that the darkness has nothing whatsoever to do with God's disapproval of us. Darkness does not arise because we are terrible sinners or because God has abandoned us. Darkness is the dismantling of the habits of egocentrism that have been so destructive to us. It seems dark and painful not because we must be punished or we must suffer to be worthy of God. St. John writes,

> There is nothing in contemplation or the divine inflow which of itself can give pain; contemplation rather bestows sweetness and delight. The cause for not experiencing these agreeable effects is the soul's weakness and imperfections at the time, its inadequate preparation, and the qualities it possesses which are contrary to this light. Because of these the soul has to suffer when the divine light shines upon it.[22]

Suffering and confusion are intrinsic to the process of transformation. The tenderness of the Divine Eros never leaves us and wishes us only good and joy. But the passions that bind us do not loose their hold easily. We experience the weakening of the hold of the passions as suffering. We experience the weakening of egocentrism as suffering. God does not "will" this suffering. It is simply the nature of the passions and of the ego to resist their transformation.

Given certain kinds of religious upbringing, the suffering of change is often interpreted as a sign of God's anger and our own sinfulness. This is itself the work of the ego, which has few resources to understand the mysteries of spirit beyond pain and pleasure, reward and punishment. When the infinite tenderness of the divine Eros is forced within this paradigm, whatever we suffer is understood to be punishment. To understand why suffering occurs during the process of transformation we would do better to look to the healing of the body. Physical healing almost inevitably entails suffering. The healing itself can be painful as cells knit back together bone or tendon, as fever awakens the body to the need to drive out disease, as convalescence restores vigor to a haggard frame. Healing may also require painful measures—surgery, bad-tasting medicine, a regimen of diet and exercise. The body sometimes must be cut open in order to restore a beating heart or remove a poisoned organ. A bone badly broken may need to be reset.

We do not conceive of doctors as disciplinarians or of the painfulness of healing as part of an order of reward and punishment. It is the same with the healing of our hearts and our spirits. The healing itself is painful, and healing can require remedies that are, in the moment, suffering. The association of suffering with punishment exists only within the order governed by the ego as this is extended from our own psyches through society, church, and theology.

But on the contemplative path, it is necessary to understand that suffering is part of healing and not punishment.

When darkness descends on us, we lose the joy we had in contemplation. We may have been experiencing something of the increase of love Catherine of Genoa describes. As the rust of confusion and passions is cleaned off, we know this love more and more deeply, completely, and confidently. But this awareness is weakened during times of darkness. It may be that we started with great energy and joy. We engaged in new practices. Our faith was deepened. We found community we never knew existed. But then darkness overcame us. Everything becomes like dust. It seems our joy was a fantasy. Our faith was nothing but an influx of good-feeling hormones. Our companions are just as selfish and foolish as our old ones.

Or perhaps we are afflicted more violently than ever with ugly upsurges of selfishness, cruelty, or self-destructive indulgences. Father Thomas Keating speaks of the anguish of sexual energy that can assault a monk of twenty or thirty years, decades after he thought he was finished with that struggle. He becomes like an adolescent boy in the strength of his desire.[23] Pettiness, rage, pride, unkindness, terror, lack of confidence—vices we finished with years ago, or perhaps ones that never tempted us in the first place, assault us full strength. A devoted mother is suddenly bereft of the tenderness and dedication that has guided her life for years. A social worker suddenly feels he cannot bear to hear about the disasters that have befallen even one more person. All of the love and responsibility he has felt for his clients over the years disappears, and he feels only frustration, contempt, and deep exhaustion. During periods of darkness, the virtues that were easy for us become impossible; the vocations that we loved are now confusing, dull, even a kind of torment.

The darkness of these assaults is only intensified by the desire to be good, loving, faithful people. We have tried to live well, care for others, attend mass. In large or small ways we have been dedicated to a contemplative life, even if we did not put it that way to ourselves. Now, after our years of effort to live faithfully or justly, the only fruit we have is to be mercilessly tormented by doubt, vice, confusion, ennui. We have hit a dead end in the path we were walking, and it seems as if our hearts will break from the pain of this, and, even more, the betrayal: "I have been faithful. I have walked a path of genuine care and faith. I have cared for others. And the only reward I have is dust in my mouth and a stone where my heart used to be. God has abandoned me without cause," we say. Or, we might join with Teresa of Avila in her complaint to Christ: "If this is how you treat your friends, it's no wonder you don't have very many."

It is the wisdom of Teresa, of St. John, and of others who have continued through this darkness to understand that this is suffering and not betrayal. There is not much that can be said in general about how one perseveres through darkness because each of our stories and our resources are different. But *that one can* persevere is what these teachers offer us. Part of what makes perseverance possible is the ability to interpret the various forms of our own darkness in the context of contemplation. If we understand darkness only in the terms in which it presents itself, it seems that our path has come to an end. But if we lean on the wisdom of those who have gone before, we can believe that this impenetrable wall will give way to something we could neither hope for nor imagine. In the darkness we cannot know what will happen next, and our heart itself is darkened. We may not directly experience the confidence that darkness will end. We may not believe that darkness will break open fantastic possibilities. At this time, it is the communion of saints that carries the faith we ourselves lack. All of those, living and dead, in every religious tradition, who have passed through darkness hold the certainty that darkness ends in dawn. During darkness, we must learn to lean on this communion. If we can no longer pray, we let them pray for us. If we can no longer read, we can yet know of the witness their writings bear. If we can no longer hope or trust, we have to let the communion hope for us. Contemplative desire has knit us to this communion, and it carries us even when we do not believe in it.

Perseverance is strengthened when any part of us assents to the belief that darkness conceals a broader meaning. But this understanding does not evacuate darkness of its more obvious meanings and difficulties. Family conflicts, a change in vocation, emotional tumult, feelings of despair or depression, and illnesses are part of the contemplative path. But they are still conflicts, change, tumult, and illness, and these things cause us terrible suffering. It is a good idea to find every resource and aid possible—not only prayer and the communion of saints but therapy, medicine, massage, friends, vacations, sleep, tears, anger, exercise, and everything else that comforts, sustains, and heals us in small and large ways. Darkness is a time for supreme gentleness because what is happening to us feels very harsh.

Darkness comes upon us because we can bear the divine image even more brightly and strongly than we could before, even if we do not realize it. Darkness is not a repudiation of what has come before but a strengthening of our powers and intensification of our capacity for erotic desire. It is a movement from genuine but dissipated goods to clearer focus and fuller embrace of our vocation as incarnations of the divine image. We humans are rife with muck, "rust," and confusion that weakens us and separates us from our power. St. John likens the process by which this muck and confusion is reduced to the burning of a log in the fire. We are fire, and the darkness is the process by which we are restored to our true nature. Fire is love, and it enkindles us to love, "just as the wood becomes hotter as the fire prepares it. A person, however, does not always feel this enkindling of love."[24] We are aware of our suffering and often feel as if we are terrible people, even though "the soul is no worse than before, neither in itself nor in its relationship to God."[25] But we are not so easily aware of the increase in our capacities that is being accomplished.

St. John notes that this process can let up sometimes and "we can observe and rejoice over the work being achieved . . . thus the soul is able to perceive the good of which it was unaware while the work was proceeding."[26] This is another cause of the painfulness of darkness. We experience only the darkness and for the most part are not able to experience either any good being accomplished or even the presence of the Divine Eros, tenderly, intimately present throughout our difficulties. In fact, it can feel as if our Beloved were more distant than ever or that our delight in the presence of our Holy Lover was only a self-aggrandizing illusion. It seems to be a common effect of darkness that we feel as if it is all a fruitless scam just when we are coming through to greater freedom and deeper intimacy with Christ:

> If there is no one to understand these persons, they either turn back and abandon the road or lose courage, or at least they hinder their own progress because of their excessive diligence in threading the path of discursive meditation. They fatigue and overwork themselves, thinking that they are failing because of their negligences or sins.[27]

In times of darkness our interior and our exterior lives fall into disarray. We are troubled, discombobulated, confused. We experience spiritual anguish because the way we had known to practice faith is now worse than useless. We are likely also to experience the anguish of life undergoing more or less severe dislocations. It is the very nature of darkness that we cannot see in the midst of it, so comfort seems impossible, and we are without any idea what we should do or should have done or might do in the future to ease ourselves or to live well. It is for times like these that St. John saves unexpected and delightful advice. He says that those in this state should simply "allow the soul to remain in rest and quietude, even though it may seem very obvious to them that they are doing nothing and wasting time."[28]

St. John encourages us to do nothing, to relax, to be still and stop making so many demands on ourselves. All of our fretting serves only to "distract [the soul] from the peaceful quiet and sweet idleness of the contemplation which is being communicated to it."[29] We are used to being busy, doing good deeds, caring for others, and it is very difficult to conceive of rest as a way of acceding to the desires of our Beloved. We are derided by all of our unmet obligations. We are acutely aware of our deficiencies. It seems to us that far from being a time for idleness, it is the time to override our fatigue and redouble our efforts, fulfill at least a small handful of our obligations, improve our concentration, extend our practices. St. John's advice is gentle but, it also seems completely impossible during times of darkness. If we could simply rest in sweet idleness, we would not be in darkness.

This state of tension is difficult to endure. Our spirit is undergoing a sea change. Our Beloved is calling us to rest, but our busy ego is demanding more and more from us. It is at this point that the body often steps in to take things in her own hands. We become sick. Meister Eckhart draws the conclusion that it is God, in Her tender love for us, that makes it impossible for us to work, if we cannot let it go on our own:

> The good God often lets his friends fall sick so that every prop they lean on or might cling to may give way. Loving souls find so much joy in doing many and great feats . . . and it is precisely this that our God would knock away so that he himself may be their only prop and stay, and he does it out of kindness and compassion, for God wants nothing for his works except his own goodness. Our acts in no way help to make God give or do to us anything whatever. It is this idea our Lord would have his friends get rid of, so he undermines their faith in it to make them trust in him alone who intends to bestow kindness on them not for any reason but for love.[30]

The fruit of contemplation is this and perhaps only this—the deepening experiential awareness of this love. As we know ourselves as lovers of Christ, this same love radiates through us to the world. This love is like water that moves from the Divine Eros to us and back and at the same time through everything created, bathing everything in this one love. But it is so hard to take it in. As Meister Eckhart says, it is sometimes only when we are deprived of the capacity to do good works—or perhaps even work of any kind—that the radicality of Christ's love for us can become apparent. The economy of exchange, of reward and punishment, of pain and pleasure, does not let go of us easily. Sometimes the economy of Eros has to be written on our bodies, in hopes that it will penetrate to our hearts, minds, and spirits. When our bodies are incapacitated and yet we feel the rush of Erotic love more than ever, we may begin to understand that it is nothing we do that makes the Divine Eros flow through us and among us. Our "work" is to learn to rest in this river. It is from this rest that whatever good we can do will flow.

Darkness incorporates many dimensions of our complex and contradictory lives. St. John advises us to rest in idleness. Meister Eckhart describes the loving tenderness of God knocking away all of our busyness so we can rest only in God. But we are busy people, and it is hard to know how to understand these words. It may be that rest is not possible for every part of ourselves, but we might think of ourselves as a house in which different things are going on in different rooms at the same time. In the kitchen, where we spend most of our time, we are working away, banging pots, being impatient with our children. We are cooking, cleaning, folding laundry, answering the phone, writing out checks: we are working hard because there is a lot to do. In the kitchen we are distracted from our confusion, but sometimes at night in the bedroom, when everyone is asleep, we have a chance to feel the heartache that dogs us throughout the day. The pain of our life hits us with great force, and we have a chance to cry out our misery. In the living room and the dining room we meet with people, seek their advice, their comfort, feed them and feed ourselves. We consider where we are and what we should do, both "practically" and "spiritually."

I am not sure St. John is suggesting that these things are not all going on and many more besides these. Perhaps he is reminding us of another room in our house that we rarely visit. In a small corner of our home is a nook, a small sun room where we can be alone. He is encouraging us to find our way to this room as often as we can, or, better, to send some part of ourselves there to stay, while other parts of us are "busy with many things." While darkness storms around us, this part of ourselves curls up like Jesus in the boat and goes to sleep, as safe in the fiercest storm as we were when we were held to our mother's breast. In this room, deeper within us than choice or decision, we find the courage to trust. In one sense, we do nothing at all. We rest, we sleep, we stop fretting about what will be or what was or what we should do. In another sense, we exercise the power of our spirit to the fullest extent possible because it is only when we do so that we find it possible to rest in "sweet idleness." In this room we are more passive and still than we are in sleep, and we are more energized than we are in all of our busyness. We are like Jesus asleep in the boat, both deep in rest and at the same time filled with power.

Finding this room does not mean we are not at the same time hard at work in the kitchen, figuring things out in the living room, crying out our grief and rage in our beds. But when we find this room we release a perfume of peace that circulates throughout the house. In this way darkness is integrated with our contemplation. We may have lost the ability to meditate. We may be unable even to pray in any way we recognize as prayer. We may find church intolerable. We may feel as if the pain of our lives is going to tear our body into pieces. We may envy martyrs. When they were burned at the stake, the fire lasted only until their bodies were consumed. But our soul is bound to a stake, and there seems no limit to its pain.

Life can overtake us, and our despair, destroy us. People do not always survive the tumults of life or the challenges of faith. But in this room where we rest in sweet idleness is the power to endure darkness and find that night does not last forever. The psalmist knows this deep night and knows, too, that "joy comes in the morning." This seems unbelievable in the night, not only unbelievable but offensive, facile, manipulative, saccharine. But John and Teresa are among those who know darkness intimately and can "send witness" that night ends and the morning is clearer, stronger, more beautiful for rising out of darkness.

Affliction

We humans suffer another kind of darkness than the spiritual darkness that St. John describes. The world can come at us with a ferocity that makes it impossible to survive intact. Violence, illness, poverty, abuse, war, terror, and grief are only a few of the ways that our souls and bodies can be taken up in a tempest too strong for us. Affliction can dismantle our egos whether we are interested in contemplation or not. Affliction can be a pure defeat. As Simone Weil says, affliction makes one a slave and like slavery steals half of our soul.[31] The dissolution of egocentrism is the goal of contemplation while the maiming of the ego is the horrific consequence of affliction. In the biographies of contemplatives, affliction often preceded their own conversion to a deeper contemplative path.[32] These resonances between affliction and the dark night of the soul are dangerous and disturbing. They can feed into impulses we have for self-sacrifice. Confusing affliction and the dark night can make us accept the bitterness of suffering as somehow "good for us." Christianity has muddied this all the more by its pathological valorization of suffering as an expression of the will of God and intrinsic to religious life. Because of these confluences and confusions, it is pressing to consider the relationship between these two forms of darkness.

The dark night that comes through contemplation occurs in the context of prayer, intimacy with the Beloved, and companionship that sustains and interprets practices. However harrowing it is, it can be understood as part of the process that unleashes our spiritual power. Affliction does not arise in this context. It arises out of the accidents and irrationalities of human history. Affliction is, in its nature, both violent and meaningless. It assaults the human spirit with no direction toward deeper healing, understanding, or love. The afflicted or traumatized person or community is one that has endured difficulties that paralyze basic and essential human capacities: memory, pleasure, relationship, concentration, hope. It renames us as less than human. Our egocentrism is distorted not because it is taught ways to release from its preoccupation with pain and pleasure but because affliction condemns us to passivity and suffering that is unbearable. Affliction bears down not only on our exterior circumstances but on our soul itself with such force that we are without recourse. This passivity, this inability to defend oneself even in interior recesses of the heart, effects great damage upon us. This extremity of defenselessness and suffering should not be understood within the context of some broader meaning: penance for sins, part of a larger aesthetic in which everything makes sense, necessary for a greater good. Since it is the nature of affliction to steal crucial spiritual capacities from us, it is in itself sheer destruction and absolute defeat.

Contemplation carries us in a different direction. Contemplation restores us to power. It may be hard to discern this right away. But even as one is undergoing the dark night, power is exerted that uses darkness to purify obstacles and to intensify the deepest levels of desire. This can happen even if we are aware only that the desires we are conscious of have become dry and fruitless. As darkness gives way to the gray, then the pinks and purples of dawn, and finally the clear light of day, one may be more aware of the release of energies that have been made available and to deeper capacities for joy, sorrow, compassion, and delight in the Beloved.

Affliction is the opposite. Affliction maims our power. We are hesitant, paralyzed, or terrorized by affliction. We are all the more likely in a traumatized state to be seduced by the comfort of the passions. Terror is a natural habit that arises out of affliction. The world is overwhelmingly dangerous, and shutting down contact with it seems the only possibility. Affliction can also take a form that looks like power. A soldier coming home from war who murders his wife is in one sense a display of power; certainly it displays a kind of absolute physical power over another person. But this is how a maimed and powerless soul often looks: incapable of bearing life, comforting itself with rage, condemning itself to a recital of further trauma in the courthouse and prison cell. Affliction dissolves the ego by defrauding it of a basic function: the capacity and desire to protect itself. This dissolution should be recognized for what it is: blasphemy against the Holy Spirit. Whether it is ourselves or another that is dunked in the poisoned stream of affliction, it should arouse our deepest compassion. In all of these ways, it is as far from the purifying "dark night of the soul" as east is far from west.

THE HARROWING OF HELL

When the ego begins to be cured of its egocentrism, power flows more fully. When the ego is assaulted beyond measure, it is defrauded of what power it had. Noticing this difference, we can discern whether suffering is a dark night or an affliction. But this simple, clear demarcation becomes confused in the actual living of life. These two kinds of darkness can be neatly distinguished in thought, but we who live do not fall neatly into the categories of contemplative or afflicted. We may be neither, or both, or move from one to the other or back again. There are many examples of contemplatives who do not seem to have suffered calamity at the hands of the world. But there are many in whom the mixture of affliction or trauma and contemplation is volatile.

The young girl who became St. Catherine of Genoa was a pious child. She wanted to enter a convent but was not allowed. Instead she was married off to a heavy-drinking, unfaithful rake who liked to party and whose family was the ardent foe of Catherine's own family. She spent several years in what we might call a depression. She made an effort to live the life her marriage fated her. But her efforts at partying did not seem to satisfy her. In her desperation she prayed to her patron saint, "Pray to God for me, oh, St. Benedict, that for three months He may keep me sick in bed."[33] After three months, her heart opened and everything changed for her. This depressed, impotent young woman who was more or less handed around by men is filled with power. She begins caring for the sick of Genoa. She becomes an incandescent embodiment of the active and contemplative life woven together.

Julian of Norwich also prayed for illness, a mortal illness so severe everyone would think her dead and she would receive last rites. It was during this illness that she experiences her "showings" that fed her, and those who have read them, ever after. Teresa also experienced a severe illness before her conversion to contemplative life. St. John was arrested by fellow Carmelites who opposed reform. He was kept in a prison for months, taken out only to be scourged once a week by his brothers in Christ. It was during this period that he wrote some of his incomparable poems of mystical devotion. Therese of Lisieux had tuberculosis and a maniacal mother superior. Simone Weil had her illnesses and the decimating effect on her of factory work. These are all famous people whose lives weave affliction and contemplation into a terrifying unity. But this weaving occurs all around us and within us as well. We see the sheer destruction affliction can bring, but we also see the strength and beauty that shines from those who have passed through the dark night of affliction and found Christ there.

It does not seem to be the case that affliction has any essential benefits. It is too easy to find examples of its sheer destructiveness and horror. Neither does it seem to be the case that the path of contemplation necessarily leads to affliction. There are many who have endured a contemplative dark night and enjoyed the fruits of its purification without the additional difficulties the world bestows so freely. It is necessary to understand that these two kinds of dark nights are quite different in their causes, in the experience of them, and in their consequences. It is virtually impossible to nurture the power of compassion if we are at the same time romanticizing suffering or imagining that God wills it "for our own good." But we see that many of our teachers have endured the darkness not only of the soul but of affliction. As we ourselves are constantly threatened with affliction, we may need to consider how what is in itself so wholly destructive can be woven into the contemplative path.

Affliction is not sought, but it can befall us. The terror of our suffering can make it impossible to imagine how God is present in such a situation, and our sense of betrayal may be even more intense than during the soul's dark night. But there is nothing in God but love; the Divine Eros is simple and unmixed, unchanging and good beyond being. The world is filled with things that can hurt us. The existence of the world flows from divine love. It is not in the nature of love to desire suffering, yet our world is filled with suffering. Christ is for Christians the great enactment of how the Divine Eros responds to suffering. In creation we see the power of Eros to overflow nonbeing; in Christ we see the power of Eros to overflow affliction. Merciless nails and sword pierced the body of Christ *so that when the merciless sword of affliction pierces us, the Divine Eros would be carried on the point of that sword.* The Divine Eros does not wield the sword of affliction, but that sword can carry Eros into the most shattered, maimed, and destroyed parts of us.

Affliction shatters us and disintegrates the power of the ego. It can go more deeply into us than anything else. Affliction is not only pain or suffering or even misery or illusion, deception, confusion. Affliction is the power of suffering to go to the heart of us and wreck us at our very core. We may feel many things very deeply. We love our children, parents, spouses, partners, friends, prayer, vocation, nation, faith. We may delight in many things or fear many things. We may be changed by any of these and act with heroism because of them. But these things almost always remain exterior to our deep heart's core. These very rarely have the power to break up the hold of the ego on us. Affliction alone reveals the shocking vulnerability of our ego. It can do so in an instant, or it can do so over a period of time. Affliction dissolves the power of the spirit and dislocates the ego from its appropriate function of living and wanting to live. It is extremely dangerous, and its victories are like the sands of the sea. But because Christ has put Herself on the tip of the sword of affliction, affliction itself can carry Christ into our deepest heart.

Affliction is the place farthest removed from the Divine Eros. It is destructive and ugly; in it we are not in misery; we are in hell. We are at the farthest reach from heaven. But the passion and death of Christ enacts for us the entrance of Christ into hell. Christ brings all the power of the Divine Eros to us in hell. This does not mean affliction ceases to be suffering or destruction. But the passion shows us that it is not one force but two that are present in hell. One disintegrates the ego and steals its power; the other is the infinitely fresh efficacy of love. That efficacy makes it possible to escape from hell. We are complex beings, and the journey from hell may take a long time. But the sword that pierced the side of Christ robbed hell of its absolute power over us;

that sword carries Christ into our hell. Even in hell, Christ is sweet, and that sweetness and tenderness transform hell into paradise and give us the power to depart from hell.

In one of his novels, Charles Williams describes the descent into hell of one of Christ's lovers, Pauline: "That adoring centre dominated her, and flashes of its great capacity passed through her."[34] She laughs at Illusion, who tempts her with a thousand promises "of health, of money, of life, or their appearances, of good looks and good luck, or a belief in them, of peace and content, or a substitute for them."[35] Her laughter exposed the sterility of hell, "as if the very air emanated power, the stillness became warm; a haze of infinite specks of gold filled the darkness, as if the laughter had for a moment made its joy, and more than its joy, visible. The sombre air of the chill city of the plain was pierced by the joy of the sons of God which exists even there."[36]

The harrowing of hell is not only for saints or heroines of novels; it is for us as well. I have known women filled at the same time with the impotence of affliction and the "great capacity" of love. One woman I met on retreat was known to the world as a reasonably successful professional. She knew herself as weak and terrorized, debilitated by years of abuse; as the mother of a very ill child. But from this wreckage came power that she herself could hardly discern. Destitute in body and soul, power flowed through her to bring her child back from the brink of darkness and to move into a future unconstrained by her past. Not only did her nadir of impotence coincide with the flow of power; her anguish was perfumed by Christ's presence. Heaven came into her hell and led her out of it. She is an ordinary person, like you or me, and she "sends witness" that the harrowing of hell is not reserved for saints or theology or medieval poetry or modern fiction but can be found in the substance of our lives.

Stories have a beginning and an end. The story of Christ's passion or of the conversion of a saint has a narrative structure. But life goes on in cycles, not in straight lines. The wounds of Christ did not change the structures of cosmos or of history. Everything is always happening at the same time: creation and death, affliction and conversion, imprisonment and the release from prison. Christ's wounds show us what is going on all the time. Governments are murdering and torturing their people. There is affliction and despair. Illness and accident wrack our bodies; drought and pollution wrack the earth. Christ's wounds do not make these things go away. They show us where the Divine Eros is in all of these things. Christ is there in the world, in hell, at the point of affliction's sword all the time, regardless of what anyone does, whether we pray or not, whether we hope or not. In prayer, in sickness, in death, Christ is "walking around our bedside." Christ shows us Erotic power as the power that keeps the story moving toward freedom at every point: at every creation, in beauty, in the dawning of understanding, in love between lovers, in the endless wanderings of the stars, in the first seed of erotic desire, in the dark night of souls, in death and in affliction, in the harrowing, in the release of captives. Contemplation is the desire to rest in that power.

8

"Christ Stripped Me of My Virtues"

Ecstatic Power

And so you must cast off from you
Both fear and shame and all external virtues.
Mechthild of Magdeburg, The Flowing Light of the Godhead

Our deepest fear is not that we are inadequate. Our deepest fear is
that we are powerful beyond measure. It is our light, not our darkness, that frightens us. We ask ourselves, who am I to be brilliant,
gorgeous, talented and fabulous? Actually, who are you not to be?
You are a child of God. Your playing small doesn't serve the world.
There is nothing enlightened about shrinking so that other people
won't feel insecure around you. We were born to make manifest
the Glory of God that is within us. It's not just in some of us; it's in
everyone. And when we let our own light shine, we unconsciously
give other people permission to do the same. As we are liberated
from our own fear, our presence automatically liberates others.
Marianne Williamson, A Return to Love, *as quoted in*
Nelson Mandela's 1994 Inaugural Speech

"We were born to make manifest the Glory of God that is within us." The contemplative path is the desire to live more completely into our birthright. Most
of these reflections have been dedicated to understanding what blocks us from
this birthright. This chapter will sketch a picture of what can happen when the
obstacles within us begin to weaken.

The temptations of Christ showed us two directions power can flow. In the
biblical story, Satan makes every effort to entangle Christ in the power that

147

flows from egocentrism: power to feed oneself, to capture the authority and glory of all the kingdoms of the world, to perform miracles of self-preservation. Like any decent temptation, this one offers things that are not entirely evil. Yet Christ rejects them. We who follow him receive the bad news that we, too, must not feed ourselves, accept authority, or care to preserve ourselves. But if we think of Christ's temptations only as renunciation, it is because we have not observed the conclusion of the Gospel story. In rejecting the power of egocentrism, Christ was not left impotent but was instead filled with the power of the Holy Spirit, the Wild Woman par excellence.

Renunciation of egocentrism does not leave us impotent; it fills us with power. But because most of us are babies in this work and have few guides to help us to maturity, the work of releasing from the passions and egocentrism is slow, and it is easy to err in one direction or another. On the contemplative path we are encouraged not to be impatient with ourselves because of our slowness or our mistakes but to understand that all of this is part of the gradual release. We should understand that we are leaning into *power*, not impotence, passivity, neurotic patience, self-sacrifice, or the evacuation of our personhood.

VIRTUE

The divine image that is shared among beings establishes us in the deepest possible intimacy with one another. This essential intimacy draws erotic desire. Desire yearns to reestablish the connections that undergird our existence; it moves toward others, delighted by their beauty and moved by their suffering. Desire and delight carry us toward intimacy with others rather than promote clinging, addiction, or self-possession. They are quintessentially relational, moving always toward particular others and the infinite variety of beings. Our image of ourselves as isolated beings that may chance to be in relationship with others and may choose to make those relationships more positive is misleading. Christ tells us that whatever we have done to "the least of these" we have done to Christ himself (Matt. 25:40). Gerard Manley Hopkins sees Christ in every being, "lovely in limbs not his, playing to the Father through the features of men's faces."[1] Christ's saying and Hopkins's poetry remind us that the deep vocation of Christians is to recognize Christ in all people. This is the basis (for Christians) of the radical solidarity and intimacy of humanity. We might be moved by the high rhetoric of these words, but it is hard to believe and harder yet to feel that these words are literally true. It is difficult to accept the intimacy of beings, intimacy arising out of the "oneing" of God with all of us. The ego's preoccupation with pain and pleasure conceals the fundamental intimacy we share with every being. In our ignorance, we act like little children who squabble and fight as if their lives depended on possessing some shard of meaningless plastic junk that they did not know existed seconds before and that they forget seconds later. Children can disappear into blissful play when the boundaries between them temporarily dissolve and they are intent only on the unfolding of their mutually evolving imaginations. "The play is the thing": their grasping egos are temporarily lulled into contented sleep as long as they remain focused on the play itself.

Inevitably, however, the energy for playful, intimate concentration fades. An idiotic plastic toy appears as if from nowhere, no doubt tossed into the children's midst by a bored little demon. Each child is now mad with the urgent need to possess it. Happiness, security, and life itself depend on claiming ownership of the molded plastic. Hard words are spoken. Hitting, kicking, and hair pulling displace the play of imagination. Bitter tears flow. Exasperated parents scold. The dreaded "time-out" is decreed. The idyll of intimate play is as forgotten as if it never existed.

Because it is so difficult to realize our deep intimacy with beings even for a few seconds, morality is necessary to hold us in place. Morality rewards "good" behavior and punishes "bad" behavior because we find it difficult to feel the intrinsic joy intimacy provides or the pain that isolation brings. But as contemplative desire quickens in us, this joy and sorrow become more accessible to us. We begin to glimpse the deeper joy that arises as we feel the connections to others moving through us. We are like the blind creature at the dawn of evolution who yearns to see, though it has never seen or even heard of this thing called sight.[2] We believe—or wish to believe—that Christ is in each of us. Though we remain blind and inert to the intimacy this forges, we experience a foretaste of joy. Christianity and Buddhism describe virtues that can come to our aid at this time. The virtues do not effect external rewards and punishments but are powers of our soul. They enable us to do things that we find difficult at first. Under the tutelage of the virtues, we begin to loosen our grip on those little plastic toys and return to the ecstasy of intimate play with the beings around us.

Virtues are habits.[3] They do not spring up overnight. They are more like muscles. One can decide to exercise and become stronger, but this decision only begins the work of actually becoming stronger. Strength comes slowly, bit by bit, as this decision is reaffirmed every time one returns to the exercises. One might get sick or experience a failure of nerve. In the absence of a good teacher, we might injure ourselves. The rehabituation toward strength is temporarily derailed. But over and over again, we begin again. We find that, against all odds, we are getting stronger and healthier. This motivates us to continue the effort. Things that were difficult become a little easier. It is easier to do things that require physical strength and to imagine ourselves as physically strong and, perhaps, by way of inference, strong in spirit as well. It is easier to overcome the inertia and distraction that interfere with our commitment.

Similarly, virtues begin when we desire to be stronger: to love harder, to become more courageous and less distracted. The powers of the soul are unleashed bit by bit as we practice them. The unwillingness of our old habits to let go makes it difficult to overcome our passions and egocentrism. Also, as long as we remain partly governed by our old habits, it is difficult to discern what would actually constitute a positive change. Tibetan Buddhists recognize what they call "near enemies" of a virtue. "The near enemy is something that's similar to these four qualities. Rather than setting us free, however, it burdens us."[4] Patience disguises neurotic passivity; compassion degenerates into pity or despair; love approximates clinging and addiction; courage is foolhardiness; and so on. The virtues that assist us in contemplative desire do not arise in their most helpful form automatically. But through all of our mistakes, our desire can burn all the brighter, and it will be the silver thread that pulls us home.

The cardinal virtues in the Western tradition are temperance, justice, courage, and prudence (practical wisdom). These are "cardinal" virtues because they challenge the supremacy of egocentrism. Temperance weakens our addictions to pleasure as courage weakens our fear of pain. As addiction and fear weaken, we act out of greater freedom to discern what is going on, to move toward more genuine goods and avoid things that are more deeply harmful to us. For some, temperance might help dismantle their anxious workaholic tendencies so they can begin to live a more balanced life. Courage might sow seeds of a capacity to enter more deeply into the work for social justice. Justice refers us to a broader universe than our own pleasures and pains and asks that we locate our own good within a harmony of goods that ultimately includes all beings. Practical wisdom is necessary because virtues do not arise as laws or rules but are habituated by concrete actions in the midst of the confusions of everyday life. The virtues are developed through the constant discernment of what is happening and what we might do in this actual situation. "Prudence" is this ability to discern well; it is the wisdom that enables us to know how and when to behave temperately, courageously, and justly. It is also the increased clarity that arises as we begin to be more temperate, courageous, and just.

Christianity adds to these virtues faith, hope, and charity, which root the work of virtue into spiritual desire. For Christianity, virtue is ultimately able to break the hold of egocentrism because it lives into our desire for the Good Beyond Being. Faith is the power to trust that the Divine Eros is intimately bound to us even when we are in trouble and doubt. Hope is the power to live in and toward deeper goods than our addictions and terrors show us. Charity, *caritas*, is the most fantastic power of our soul: the ability to love others with the same urgency and delight with which we care for our own pains, pleasures, goods, and sorrows. *Caritas* is the power toward which all virtues strive and the power that guides them on the path of true virtue.

Tibetan Buddhists identify the four limitless qualities: loving-kindness, compassion, joy, and equanimity.[5] Each of these quickens our connections with others. We feel moved by kindness toward others, feel sorrow with their suffering, and feel delight in their joy. Equanimity is the balance that helps us follow more genuine expressions of virtues, so that our love is not merely attachment, our compassion does not degenerate into mere pity, or our joy return to egocentric addiction.

However they are specified in various traditions, virtues are dispositions that both reflect and contribute to the process by which our passions are weakened. They help form us in ways that allow erotic power to flow through us more smoothly. In contrast to morality, they are not so much external curbs on our selfish impulses as ways to release us from the tyranny of pain and pleasure. Pain and pleasure inhibit our connections to others. They chain us to our experience so that others are obscured. We are only barely aware that others experience the same intensity of suffering, desire, pain, and pleasure that we do. The virtues ease the hold of this illusion of egocentrism and allow others to begin to take on more solid appearance. Gradually, we become able not only to see them but to feel them. We become more immediately aware of their sufferings and hopes. This more immediate awareness impinges itself upon us with a force more like the immediacy of our own experience.

A paradigmatic image of this greater awareness is the mother of an infant. Her concern for the baby's welfare is not intellectual or moral but visceral. However exhausted or pained, mothers want to care for their babies, to relieve their pain, to delight in their beauty. The deep impulse of maternity is loving-kindness. Love of this kind is not a sacrifice of self but its full expression. Mothers delight in their babies, and this delight is the source of their capacity to do rather amazing things on behalf of their children.

When mother-love becomes self-sacrifice it is because some imbalance has occurred. A healthy maternal relationship is most fundamentally delight in another's existence, just as it is, with all of its strange peculiarities and inconveniences. This delight is the basis of the intimacy between mothers and children that makes pain and pleasure, delight and suffering, flow back and forth between them with little regard for the normal boundaries that separate persons. Intimacy arising out of delight allows the infant's pain to impress itself on the mother as if it were her own pain. Mothers do not feed babies because they have a duty to do so but because the desire to ease the infant's suffering springs as spontaneously as the desire to ease the mothers's own suffering. This is not the secondary experience of morality or belief or desire to love, but the immediacy of deep intimacy. Of course, actual mothers do not always experience this or live it out. But everywhere in the world there are mothers who do love their babies.

This common, heroic intimacy of love reveals the possibility present in normal human beings to love so fully that they experience someone else's suffering and pleasure as even more compelling than their own. It is, however, a love that even devoted mothers have enormous difficulty maintaining. Mothers have to care for themselves, too, if they are going to care for an infant. It is hard to maintain balance. Mothers too often can become possessive, overly anxious, or self-sacrificing. Difficulties in their lives may be too potent altogether, and mothers end up abusing or neglecting their children. When we consider what mothers can be capable of, we realize that erotic desire is not only for saints and bodhisattvas but that it is a normal human capacity.

When we think of the difficulty of mother-love, we realize all the more forcefully how painful and demanding it is to remain so vulnerable to another's sufferings and joys. If it seems impossible to find a healthy and balanced love of even one person, how much more impossible it seems to love every being. Here again the virtues come to our aid. Love may be the most opulent expression of our power, but it requires the virtues to keep it balanced. We need courage and lots of it to love well. The vulnerability of loving intimacy is excruciating. Temperance and equanimity undermine our tendencies to transmute love into addictive pleasure. As our addiction to pleasure weakens, our heart is freer to open to others, and we become more susceptible to the joyous abandon of intimacy and tenderness. Practical wisdom gives us eyes to discern what of our difficulties arise from the intrinsic painfulness of loving and what arise from our lack of balance.

Immediate awareness of others is the great freedom contemplative traditions promise. But this loving intimacy is difficult for beings like ourselves, habituated so deeply to the experiences of our own pain and pleasure. Because of this difficulty it is important to remember another virtue, patience.

PATIENCE

In both Christianity and Tibetan Buddhism patience is offered as a practice particularly adept at unlocking our capacity to love. It is natural for us to respond with anger and frustration to what hurts us, thwarts us, or embarrasses us. Patience is the virtue that begins to dismantle our immediate impulse to feel hostility toward those things that impinge on our desire or elicit our fear.

In so much of the monastic writings, patience is given pride of place because it weakens the link between being thwarted and being angry and is a way to reorient our ego from its self-preoccupation.[6] Most of us can appreciate the emphasis these traditions place on patience when we consider how easily we are frustrated by a computer that is slow to react, children that whine while we are on the phone, or drivers that dawdle through a green light just slowly enough to make us sit through another cycle. And these are nothing compared to people whose political or religious views we consider dangerous, colleagues who dismiss what we say because we are women, lovers who mistreat us, or parents who were alcoholic, crazy, or unkind. At the same time, when we consider how often we endure persecution without knowing how to defend ourselves, we might be more aware of how dangerous the valorization of patience can be. But because patience can be a power in the face of difficulty, it may be worth trying to perform a feminist reconstruction of the term.

The practice of patience helps to expose how raw and tender we are against everything that thwarts us. But if patience is to be a virtue, a power, it must not be confused with self-deception or passivity. It is not the repression of anger or bitterness:

> We must deal with the cause of our anger: acknowledge the gift and message and respond to what our anger is calling forth in us. If we do not actively attend to our anger, it comes out in ugliness such as bitterness, whining, rage, and depression. . . . If we are willing to actively listen to what our anger would tell us, we can then act on what we must do: seek reconciliation, speak the truth, and/or make necessary changes in our lives.[7]

Patience, perhaps even more than other virtues, is extremely vulnerable to confusion with its "near enemies." We try to practice patience by repressing our anger and frustration. We enervate the power of patience by allowing ourselves to be passive, silent, and innocuous. We let our endurance of irritation run too long and allow others to harm us and in the long run themselves as well. We are all bound together in perfect intimacy, so when we are harmed, so are the ones that harm us. Even if we believe that patience should enable us to endure mistreatment, our compassion for those who would be destructive moves us to defend ourselves. Patience as a virtue is a power. A guide for us in this difficult and dangerous practice is to understand that things that make us powerless are distortions of genuine patience. Stability that is not thrown off balance by trouble is a kind of power, not pointless endurance or impotence. To identify deceptive masks of patience, it is necessary to focus not only on external frustrations but on our irritation with ourselves. The first exercise of patience must therefore be within ourselves.

Particularly if we are motivated to practice patience in the first place, we are likely to feel least patient with ourselves. This distorts our ability to practice patience with others. Amma Syncletica reminds us that we must not only attend to "attacks from people that come from outside us"; it is even more important to "repel the interior onslaughts of our thoughts."[8] A contemporary interpreter of Amma Syncletica identifies these interior onslaughts as "the messages we have internalized that tell us of our unworthiness, of our lack, of all that we are not and yet 'should' be."[9] When these interior vulnerabilities are allowed to assault us, we are more vulnerable to the assaults of others. The outer frustrations take on such painful force because they resonate with our deeper sense of inadequacy, imperfection, and self-hatred. Or to put this another way, if patience is not rooted in a healthy self-respect and gentleness, it will easily be distorted. For some, generating this self-respect will be a crucial preliminary practice before patience is possible. If we do not first practice patience with ourselves, we leave the seeds of hostility in place and are slower to generate the spontaneous compassion that establishes intimacy between ourselves and others. The courage that allows us to be gentle enough with ourselves that we can see our foibles without condemnation is the same courage that opens us to the beauty of others—complete with their foibles and difficulties.

As Pema Chodron puts it, when "we feel distress, embarrassment, or anger, we think we've really blown it. Yet feeling emotional upheaval is not a spiritual faux pas; it's the place where the warrior learns compassion. It's where we learn to stop struggling with ourselves. It's only when we can dwell in these places that scare us that equanimity becomes unshakable."[10] It is inevitable that we will struggle with our jealousy, resentment, terror, addictions, self-inflation, and self-hatred throughout our lives. Patience helps to remove the additional burden of self-condemnation that gives our interior obstacles their fuller potency. Chodron continues, "These enemies are good teachers that show us that we can accept ourselves and others complete with imperfections. We develop trust in our open and forgiving mind. In doing so, we discover the strength that allows us to enter into the suffering of the world."[11]

If we begin to practice patience with ourselves, we are better able to distinguish patience from its "near enemies": self-sacrifice, passivity, pathological endurance. We develop a stability that makes it possible to practice patience in situations that come to us from outside. In the writings of Christian and Buddhist monastics, the main emphasis of patience is to train in the discipline of putting the perspective of others before ourselves, even when they are unreasonable or harmful. When someone annoys us, for example, we consider the poisonous passions that provoke them. However we respond concretely, we remain moved by compassion for them. "Why hate the one who has grieved you? It is not this person who has done you wrong, but the evil one. Hate the sickness but not the sick person."[12] When we find room to disengage from the immediacy of anger, we realize that the annoying situation or person has its own story. That story may not excuse the action and does not mean we do not respond to harm. But we see the situation from the perspective of the other's story and this allows compassion to find a home, however modest, in us.

The need for patience arises in situations where we feel thwarted. It is easiest to practice on inanimate objects, like computers, traffic, lost shoes, and long lines at the airport. But because other people can harm us in ways that are potentially extremely destructive and because patience can bear the connotation of passive endurance, the need to discern how exactly one should respond to a difficult situation is urgent. The potency of patience lies in its ability to reveal the other side of the story to us. It calms the outrage of our egocentrism, opening a chink in the darkness when egocentrism would permit us to see only our own pain. The movement of erotic desire is outward, toward others. Patience calms us enough to follow its movement and see what else is happening besides our injury. In opening us more deeply to others, even difficult others, patience protects us from being completely thrown off balance when someone embarrasses us or harms us or makes us feel jealous.

Christianity and Buddhism both advocate patience toward those we perceive as our enemies. Christ gives us the impossible advice that we love our enemy. Buddhists characterize the irritating person or the enemy as our most helpful teacher. Rage is a kind of purgatory where we remain trapped with those we most despise until patience can begin to do its work in us. When we have been harmed, there is psychological as well as spiritual work to do. Patience does not bypass the work of seeking psychological and physical health. But if a time comes when we can practice patience with those who have really harmed us in ways that do not undercut our psychological healing, patience can move into other parts of our soul as this other work is also being done. As an example, one person asked a friend to pray for a man who had hurt her because she was too angry and humiliated to do so herself. It can be harmful to mask appropriate pain and anger with unskillful patience. This woman was able to sit with her pain without repressing it yet also acknowledge that the harm done to her was not the man's entire future.

Pema Chodron tells the story of a woman who had suffered sexual abuse from her father. She felt like a caged bird, so during a meditation retreat she would breathe into her feeling of being small and caged and on her exhale visualize letting the birds out of a cage. One day

> she experienced one of the birds flying out and landing on a man's shoulder. Then the man turned around and she saw it was her father. For the first time in her life she was able to forgive him. . . .

> Forgiveness . . . cannot be forced. When we are brave enough to open
> our hearts to ourselves, however, forgiveness will emerge.[13]

Working with the anger and hatred that is generated in us by those that
have harmed us is a powerful method for revealing and ultimately dislocating
egocentrism. This work enables us to find small spaces between harm, our
ego's natural and appropriate anger at being hurt, and the ones who have hurt
us. Over time, we can breathe into these small spaces and allow them slowly
to grow larger. The divine image shines brilliantly in these spaces between
harm and anger, however large or small they are in us. When these spaces have
been allowed to develop as strength and self-love rather than as repressed grief
and rage, they become openings for the power of Holy Eros to flow freely. But
patience in these dangerous places is difficult to distinguish from its "near enemies." It requires the nourishment of time, the aid of other virtues, and the
guidance of our spiritual companions so that this powerful but dangerous
virtue arises in its own time and in a genuine form, rather than as a mask for
the things that continue to hurt us.

Not all of our difficulties are caused by people working us harm. Patience
also refers to the psychological discipline of working with everything that
discomforts us. Patience in this sense is often advocated by contemplatives
who perceive the power to accept suffering as intrinsic to the path of erotic
desire. Hadewijch advises us to try to avoid "fearing pain" or "fleeing sorrow." She advises that we find contentment in all things: "For that is the sign
of love's presence and that you are so easily oppressed denies you many a
beautiful gift."[14] There are the pathological who seek out suffering as if suffering were an intrinsic good or because they believe God approves of our
suffering. These voices make it more difficult to sort out what someone like
Hadewijch means when she advises us to "be content with all things." The
patience that can sit with sorrow or endure pain is not a celebration of these
things in themselves but a freedom from their tyranny. Difficulties are
bound to come to us, and we will resist them, heal them, and respond to them
with whatever wisdom we can muster. But we cannot prevent difficulties
from assaulting us. Patience is not passive endurance but the energy to move
through difficulty without letting it claim our whole selves. In this sense
patience is a sublime power to encounter difficulty and extract from it what
it would teach us.

Difficulty, frustration, harm, anxiety, and affliction undermine our well-
being. Because of them our beauty and power and happiness deteriorate.
Patience is a counterbalance, an antidote. It is the miraculous power of Eros
to pass through suffering not unscathed but more powerful and beautiful than
before. Patience, far from being passivity, makes us more brilliant, shining like

the sun. Teresa of Avila appeals to patience as that which, as we sit with it, gradually allows intimacy with God to displace fear and anxiety:

> Let nothing disturb thee,
> Nothing affright thee;
> All things are passing;
> God never changeth;
> Patient endurance
> Attaineth to all things;
> Who God possesseth
> In nothing is wanting;
> Alone God sufficeth.[15]

It is this *power* to which Teresa attests in making the absurd claim that everything that threatens us is ultimately impotent. "Alone God sufficeth." To make sense of this we might remember that we inhabit any number of dimensions of reality at the same time. Patience is not ignorance of the ability of sickness, accident, oppression, cruelty, and random violence to effect physical and emotional destruction. In their realm, these things are quite powerful and must be taken seriously. Patience does not entail ignoring the things that are harmful. It addresses another dimension of our experience. Knowing only pain and pleasure, the habit of egocentrism is trapped by difficulty into paralysis, impotent rage, and despair. Patience opens up a part of our soul not governed by pain and pleasure.[16] Here the Beloved remains with us no matter what. Here our capacity for compassion survives every frustration and assault. In the midst of defeat and sorrow, a deeper joy sustains us here.

Patience is not passivity but the discovery of our spiritual power. This power is greater than anything or anyone that can harm us. Egocentrism is like a light skiff, attractive enough, easy to navigate in good weather. But when the storms come, as they inevitably do, this light skiff has little at its disposal to help it stay afloat. In its desperation, the ego calls on the quickest and surest help: the passions. Rage, terror, and addiction disguise the urgency of the situation. But this does not stop the storm. The ego battens down the hatches: it cuts itself off from the water, the storm, the world, seeking safety in isolation. It crouches down in a corner and makes itself as small as possible so it won't be swept away. It deadens emotions so it will not feel its suffering. Patience does not go to sea in a light skiff. Those parts of us that feel the anguish of pain and pleasure may be swamped by storm. But patience is that part of us that blows with the storm. It does not hide; it swims in the raging water, completely secure. It is more like a seal than a skiff. We are made in the image of God in a world created by God. The power of the Divine Eros flows through us. We are made for life: abundant, full, flowing, dangerous, beautiful, intense life. Patience is the power in us that sustains our connection to the Divine Eros even in the midst of difficulties and suffering.

VAJRA PRIDE

The virtues name powers that unfold as the energy of Erotic desire begins to displace, however incompletely, our domination by the passions and egocentrism. Much of the Christian tradition emphasizes humility as the root virtue that allows other virtues to flourish. Dorotheus, quoting "one of the Fathers," teaches his monks that "before anything else, we need humility . . . because through humility every device of the enemy, every kind of obstacle, is destroyed."[17] Teresa recommends humility to her sisters as the crucial antidote to distraction: "I am sure that if any of us achieve true humility and detachment . . . the Lord will not fail to grant us this favour, and many others which we shall not even know how to desire."[18] In these monastic writings, humility seems to refer to the decisive dissipation of egocentrism that clears the way for compassion and love. Monastic life is full of practices designed to further humility and the clarity and freedom of soul that humility makes possible.

Egocentrism has been presented here as the deepest structural obstacle to Erotic desire, and it might seem logical that humility would be offered as its chief antidote. This connection is offered to us all the time, by both third-rate preachers and writers of great wisdom. It is well enough known that I do not need to defend it here. But humility sounds very close to one of its "near enemies": humiliation. This proximity obscures another obstacle to love, one with which many women and others habituated to care for others are more familiar: the fragmentation or disempowerment of a self. For those who have been shaped by humiliation or affliction, those who have learned the art of self-sacrifice but not self-love, or those whose arrogance conceals deep wounds, language, images, and practices that seem to celebrate the disappearance of a self can themselves be obstacles to Erotic desire. Another name for the key that unlocks freedom from egocentrism is courage, the daring that embraces our own power.

Christianity and Tibetan Buddhism share the view that egocentrism is the core illusion that binds us to painful and destructive ways of life. Christianity has tended to use the language of humility and even practices of humiliation to enable the power of love to break out of the restrictions of egocentrism. But this approach has not been without problems. Tibetan Buddhism couches its admonitions to patience and compassion in practices that appeal to the energy of enlightenment that is within us. The Tibetan approach no doubt has difficulties as well, but it is a helpful antidote to a tradition that has sometimes been caught in a polarity between self-effacement and excessive inflation of its power. Because in the Tibetan Buddhist tradition the aspiration to compassion is framed by practices that connect us to the power and joy of enlightened being, the distortions of self-effacement, self-destruction, and self-hatred are less likely to find a foothold. To put this another way, every aspect of contemplative life and desire is fraught with danger and difficulty. It is easy to try to avoid one pitfall, passion, or difficulty by running in the opposite direction: we exercise temperance but become addicted to joy-crushing asceticism; we flee from our egocentrism but fall into a quagmire of despair and self-negation.

The virtues are powers that help ease the hold of egocentrism and the passions that bind us, but each carries the possibility of its own distortion. The protean resources of our wounded ego can infect and distort even the practices, virtues, and ideals of contemplative desire. It is dangerous even to conceive of the desire to overcome the passions and egocentrism that organize our psyches. Humiliation makes this desire more dangerous by depriving us of the stability of self-love and the strength of our personhood. The symbolism of Tibetan Buddhism places much more emphasis on the power of enlightenment that is within us. It nurtures the confidence that we, too, can aspire to great compassion. Practices that reinforce our connection to power can provide an antidote to the inevitable instability of Erotic desire and its attendant virtues. To emphasize that the unbinding of egocentrism is liberation and power, this process will be presented here not under the rubric of humility but rather as *vajra* pride.

Vajra Pride in Tibetan Buddhism

The term "*vajra* pride" has an oxymoronic quality to it. It juxtaposes two terms that are normally in complete opposition to one another. Pride, especially in religious circles, tends to connote the self-inflation that places ourselves above all others. It is the epitome of our fallen, egocentric existence. But in the context of the ideal of the bodhisattva and the iconography of deity yoga, *vajra* pride describes a confidence and trust that we are truly capable of making "manifest the Glory of God that is within us," as Mandela puts it.

The *vajra* is a knife-like weapon that symbolizes in Tibetan Buddhism the power to completely sever egocentrism so that every obstacle to perfect wisdom and compassion is destroyed. It can mean also the diamond purity and the adamantine strength of enlightenment. This symbol of brilliance, spotlessness, and indestructible power resonates with the pure luminosity that is the basis of all reality and is the true nature of mind. Tibetan Buddhism has developed a series of practices designed to effect this severing of egocentrism as efficiently as possible.

Two aspects of Tibetan Buddhist practice are a commitment to altruism and deity yoga. Altruism is understood to be an essential component to the mind of enlightenment; it is a commitment to radical compassion, that is, compassion for all beings and all forms of suffering. Deity yoga is a form of meditation that includes visualizing a unity between oneself and an enlightened being, such as Tara (a female embodiment of compassion), Vajrasattva (who embodies the principle of purity and purification), or Manjushri (the bodhisattva of wisdom). Central to the theories and practices of Tibetan Buddhism is the ideal of the bodhisattva, that is, compassion so moved by the suffering of beings that one vows to achieve enlightenment in order to relieve suffering as long as suffering endures. What is significant about this combination of practices for non-Buddhists is the emphasis it places on compassion and the intimacy with enlightened power that it envisions as possible for human beings. It is a quite different symbolic universe than one that emphasizes self-sacrifice as the pathway to agapaic love, although this *vajra* pride and intimacy with enlightened power are present in Paul's words "it is no longer I who live, but it is Christ who lives in me" (Gal. 2:20).

Shantideva provides a particularly eloquent description of the pathway to enlightenment that is motivated by compassion. His primary work *The Way of the Bodhisattva* describes with unparalleled eloquence the awesome power of *bodhicitta* (the aspiration to become a bodhisattva) as that which alone can withstand interior and exterior evil. Shantideva's writings are an important part of the Tibetan Buddhist canon. He is quoted by the Dalai Lama in the films *Kundun* and *Seven Years in Tibet*. He lived during the eighth century in India as a monk and a scholar at Nalanda, the Indian Buddhist parallel to Harvard or Oxford. The way of the bodhisattva that Shantideva describes is "the pain-dispelling draft" that alone is "cause of joy for those who wander through the world."[19] It is the "only remedy for suffering, the source of every bliss and happiness."[20] The bodhisattva urgently wishes to relieve every being from suffering and the causes of suffering. Ultimately, the bodhisattva wishes to bring every being to the state of stainless bliss. Aware of the difficulties of this, the way of the bodhisattva begins with desire and commitment:

> With joy I celebrate
> The virtue that relieves all beings
> From the sorrows of the states of loss,
> And places those who languish in the realms of bliss
> And I rejoice in virtue that creates the cause
> Of gaining the enlightened state,
> And celebrate the freedom won
> By living beings from the round of pain. [21]

But the great compassion of the bodhisattva is not limited to what might be considered an excessively otherworldly goal. Shantideva catalogs some of the powers he desires in wishing to become a bodhisattva.

> May I be a guard for those who are protectorless
> A guide for those who journey on the road.
> For those who wish to go across the water,
> May I be a boat, a raft, a bridge.
> May I be an isle for those who yearn for landfall,
> And a lamp for those who long for light;
> For those who need a resting place, a bed;
> For all who need a servant, may I be their slave.
> May I be the wishing jewel, the vase of plenty,
> A word of power and the supreme healing . . .
> Thus for every thing that lives,
> As far as are the limits of the sky,
> May I provide their livelihood and nourishment
> Until they pass beyond the bonds of suffering.[22]

For Shantideva, enlightenment is the necessary precondition of these powers. The would-be bodhisattva's way of life is dedicated to seeking the means to sever egocentrism and break the hold of illusion. The ideal laid out by Shantideva seems absurd in its scope. It includes all beings and every form of suffering, and it demands a cessation of egocentrism, a perfection of wisdom, and a renunciation of hatred and lust to accomplish this desire. Like the story of Christ's temptation, it describes the power that arises when we interrupt our clinging to our own egos. Following in the tradition of Shantideva, the Dalai Lama describes this great compassion (*maha karuna*) as "the inability to bear sentient beings' suffering without acting to relieve it."[23] Most of us can bear other beings' suffering fairly well. The inversion of psychic energy that makes us *unable to bear* the suffering of others reflects an unleashing of power that has been pent up by the tyranny of pain and pleasure. Few of us, even when compassion begins to stir in us, have the capacity or wisdom to relieve much suffering, let alone to cut it off at its roots. A bodhisattva must therefore aspire to become liberated from the domination of egocentrism, from ignorance, and from addictive desire, anger, and hatred that prevent us from being able to dedicate ourselves to a compassionate way of life.

The Tibetans offer an extraordinarily rich literature describing the ideals of the bodhisattva way of life and the metaphysical universe that provides its underpinning. But in contrast to Western religion, they have also developed a virtual science of spiritual transformation and practices that facilitate transformation.[24] Deity yoga is an example of a practice developed in Tibet to accomplish this severing of egocentrism as quickly and thoroughly as possible.

It includes a number of practices surrounding a period of meditation in which one focuses on the visual details of one of the pantheon of deities, each of which embodies a particular form of enlightened wisdom and power. Put most simplistically, deity yoga is meditation in which one visualizes oneself arising in the form of the deity. The "yogi's body appears to his own mind in the aspect of a Tathagata's [Buddha's] body, and at the same time his mind becomes the wisdom apprehending suchness."[25] That is, during the meditation, one visualizes oneself *as if* one were a fully enlightened Buddha. The practice of deity yoga includes meditation in which the distance between one's own imperfections and the perfection of the deity is temporarily dissolved. One visualizes oneself to be what one truly is: the perfect power of enlightened being. For the duration of the practice, one engages in an act of "creative imagination" in which ideal identity is substituted for actual experience.[26] One visualizes everything that appears from the perspective of Buddhahood and in particular visualizes oneself in the form of one of Tibetan Buddhism's deities, that is, in the form of a particular enlightened being.

The actual practice of this form of meditation traditionally includes extensive preconditions, including ethical integrity, stability in meditation, wisdom, and altruistic motivation.[27] Many, perhaps even most, Tibetan Buddhist practices begin with a commitment to the bodhisattva ideal. But deity yoga is preceded by a rededication to the *vow* of the bodhisattva. That is, one vows to continue to practice toward enlightenment for the sake of all beings not only in this life but throughout all time. Because deity yoga is "impelled by the precious aspiration to enlightenment for the sake of all sentient beings," *vajra* pride is purified of the taint of egocentrism.[28] The pride that enables us to visualize ourselves as a manifestation of perfect enlightenment arises from the reversal of energy that makes us "unable to bear sentient beings' suffering without acting to relieve it."[29] In the context of deity yoga, one begins to possess the pride or dignity of enlightened existence, but the source and goal of this pride is compassion that is alive to the joys and sufferings of all beings. Rooted in this reversal of psychic energy and desire, "'the pride of being a Buddha' . . . [is] free from the pride of ordinariness."[30] *Vajra* pride might be understood as confidence that pure luminosity of mind is our fundamental reality, and the way of the bodhisattva is one we can accomplish. Deity yoga is designed to assist us in taking this confidence more deeply into our lived experience. It is a good thing to aspire to great compassion and to believe that our deepest reality is pure luminosity, but to unleash the power within us to live out of these realities is difficult. This power emerges as our psychic energy is rerouted from egocentrism to compassionate and wise movement toward others. Deity yoga is a specific practice that integrates our aspirations and beliefs with our spontaneous and genuine experience so that we are better able to feel these realities and act out of them. It is designed to reroute our psychic energy by anchoring us more radically in the source of our power. By enacting our identity as enlightened being in a meditative state the roots of egocentrism are weakened. As we move into the post-meditation phase, the greatness of compassion is better able to move through us.

Vajra Pride for Laypeople

Very few of us, even if we were so inclined, are in a situation where we could study and practice deity yoga. This long aside into an admittedly esoteric tradition is intended to provide an image for power and joy that emerges from a place our culture has little use for. By contrast to the bodhisattva ideal of wisdom and compassion, we are constantly encouraged to find our happiness by remembering that it is "all about me," and this happiness is no farther away than a local BMW dealership. For those poor saps that can't afford a BMW, it can still be all about "me" by buying other things. Our own culture actively destroys ideals of compassion, service, and awareness of interconnection. We retain vestiges of ideals beyond consumerism and domination in our religious traditions, but the religion most often seen in the media is a conservatism that is almost insane with rage and anxious to cut itself off from everything that threatens its orthodoxy.

Women have been so burned by unskillful interpretations of love, patience, and self-sacrifice that we are more likely to be trying to learn how to engage "the dance of anger" or find a good day care while we develop careers. Those who do continue in traditional works of love—as "stay-at-home" mothers or social workers or teachers or activists or organic gardeners or devoted (if "working") parents—find little to teach us how to nourish ourselves. We may be encouraged to develop "better boundaries" or find stress relievers or learn to say no. But we remain locked in a zero-sum game in which it is hard to envision how to love others in a way that is not costly to our own physical and psychic health. We can learn the satisfactions egocentrism brings or the morality of service. We can make ourselves very big or very small, but finding a way beyond these two poles that tie us to the anguish of the passions is difficult. It is all the more difficult because of the scarcity of images we have for some way to freedom other than ego inflation or ego destruction.

Vajra pride is an image, borrowed from another language and culture, for an order of existence that is not governed by the duality of selfishness and humiliation. It is an image for the joy that comes as we find ways to unhook ourselves from the pathologies of egocentrism, the distorted pain relief the passions bring, and our preoccupation with pain and pleasure. It reminds us of the excessive modesty of our self-understanding. "Who am I to be compassionate or wise?

Who am I to shine like the sun?" Who are you that you do not recognize who you are? Who are you that you defraud yourself of your intimacy with Christ, with nature, with beauty, with other people? Who are you that you are sick and exhausted from holding back your stupendous power to love and feel and live?

For that part of us that is so anxious that we must erect strong walls between ourselves and everything else, *vajra* pride reminds us that connection and intimacy is our deepest reality and sweetest joy. For that part of us that is addicted to self-sacrifice and incapable of self-love, *vajra* pride reminds us that it is not by destroying ourselves that we become free. It is by expanding ourselves so we feel what we must feel, face what we must face. We become familiar and friendly with those parts of us that bind us and, in this way, help them ease their grip on us. We breathe into the places that hurt us; we allow Christ our mother and lover to breathe into these places.

We are God-bearers. As our trust in this reality becomes more stable, we will need to be less afraid. As we discover practices that help us live into this reality, we dismantle the polarity that bounces us between our self-inflation and self-hatred, our addictions and our terror. We tenderly embrace all the parts of ourselves, our virtues and vices, our compassion and our rage, our wisdom and our immaturity, so that we find that it is Christ in us. Mechthild seems to tell us that as we do this, we will become more naked to our desire and this desire will be lavishly satisfied.

BEYOND THE FANGS OF AFFLICTION

I don't know how far beyond the "fangs of affliction" we really get as long as we are "wayfaring strangers, traveling through this world of woe." Our deep wounds, which shape us body and soul, may not become completely healed. The ability to bear other people's suffering better than our own may remain fairly robust in us. But as we are broken open, bit by bit, by darkness and affliction, by prayer and anger and patience, the light within us shines through the cracks, through the bars. *Frango ut patefaciam*: "I break in order to reveal." We get glimmers of what we look like when terror, rage, and addiction begin to arise in us as freedom, compassionate wrath, and eros. These are energies that are liberated by the Divine Eros so that this same Eros flows within us and through us and to the world all around us. This power dissolves the dualities that hamper us, between egocentrism and Eros, between justice and compassion, divisions among the religions, and the separation of heaven from earth. The brutalities of our history make it easy to imagine that our "real" home is elsewhere, that there is a perfect home that awaits us, but that that home is not here on earth. Whatever home we might find in heaven, the earth is where Christ has chosen to dwell, not only long ago in Palestine but always and everywhere. Christ is incognito in every one of us, and the power of transformation Christians identify with Christ is incognito in every religion, in every act of compassion, in every movement toward justice.[31] It is our vocation as Christians to enter into this reality, by faith and by experience. The veil is thin. "Every moment is chalice and panem. In every moment, in every person, God is offering the fullness of the God-head to you. Practice. Practice. Practice."[32]

Notes

Preface

1. Bonaventure, *The Mind's Road to God*, 5.

Chapter 1: Wounded by True Love

1. Books 7 and 8 of the *Confessions* are particularly interesting examples among the countless places Augustine wrestles with issues of will and desire.
2. This is the theme of "On the Happy Life" and the last book of "On Music."
3. Augustine, *Confessions*, book 1.1.
4. Keats, "Ode on a Grecian Urn."
5. This image of being "oned" with God, a "precious oneing" established at creation is drawn from Julian of Norwich's *Showing*.
6. This phrase is from Ron Block's song, "There is a Reason," sung by Alison Kraus and Union Station on *So Long So Wrong*.
7. When I first conceived of this writing project I asked my friends Liz McGeachy and Tim Merrima if they could put together a musical accompaniment. They had several other CDs they had produced and were much more knowledgeable than myself about folk music. The CD they created is *Weaving Heaven and Earth*. It is available at their Web site: www.lizandtim.com.
8. "Magdalene Laundries," sung by Joni Mitchell, on the Chiefton's *Tears of Stone*.
9. This is a traditional Scottish song introduced to me through the recordings of Silly Wizard, but sung by Liz McGeachy and Tim Merrima on *Weaving Heaven and Earth*.
10. See Williams, *Recognition*.
11. As far as I can discover, this song is traditional. I found it on Ginny Hawker and Kay Justice's CD, *Come All You Tenderhearted*.
12. "If I Live," sung by Liz McGeachy and Tim Merrima, *Weaving Heaven and Earth*.
13. Diotima describes Eros this way in Socrates' speech in Plato's *Symposium*, 203C–204C.
14. This theme is eloquently developed in Welch's *A Feminist Ethic of Risk*.

15. "Sweet Sunny South," sung by Liz McGeachy and Tim Merrima, *Weaving Heaven and Earth*.
16. One source attributes this old song, "Oh Death," to Ralph Stanley, and another source identifies it as "traditional." It has been recently recorded on *Oh Brother Where Art Thou?* and as "Conversation with Death" on *Songcatcher*.
17. This song was found in an old Baptist hymnal (!) and was sung by Ginny Hawker and Kay Justice on their CD *Come All Ye Tenderhearted*.
18. "Talk about Suffering," sung by Liz McGreachy and Tim Merrima, *Weaving Heaven and Earth*.
19. Augustine, *Confessions*, book 9.12–13.
20. This paraphrases Augustine, *Confessions*, 10.6.
21. Charles Tazewell, *The Littlest Angel*.
22. The story of Psyche and Eros is told in various ways in various places. A good starting place is Bulfinch's *Mythology*.
23. Therese of Lisieux, *Daily Readings*, 41.

Chapter 2: "Knit and Oned to God"

1. Le Guin, *A Wizard of Earthsea*, 173
2. Weil, "Personality," in *Simone Weil Reader*, 315: "At the bottom of the heart of every human being, from earliest infancy until the tomb, there is something that goes on indomitably expecting, in the teeth of all experience of crimes committed, suffered, and witnessed, that good and not evil will be done to him. It is this above all that is sacred in every human being."
3. Introduction to these themes is available through *Christian Theology: An Introduction to its Traditions and Tasks* and its companion volume, *Readings in Christian Theology*, both edited by Peter C. Hodgson and Robert H. King. Comparing Origin, Irenaeus, and Augustine on the fall and the bondage of the will gives a preliminary sense of the range of options in classical theology. Hick's *Evil and the God of Love* clearly sets out some basic alternatives. Erasmus, Luther, Zwingli, Calvin, Barth, Karl Rahner, Tillich, and Rosemary Ruether as well as recent womanist, black, and liberation theologies provide a sense of modern and contemporary possibilities.
4. Important examples would include Gutiérrez, *A Theology of Liberation*; Ruether, *Sexism and God-talk: Toward A Feminist Theology*; Townes, ed., *A Troubling in My Soul: Womanist Perspectives on Evil and Suffering*; and Cone, *God of the Oppressed*.
5. Julian of Norwich, *Showings*, 262, 263.
6. Teresa of Avila, *Interior Castle*, 29.
7. Julian of Norwich, *Showings*, 267.
8. Chapter 3 will provide a brief catalog of some of this literature.
9. I would again recommend the Hodgson and King volumes to the reader for an introduction to the variety of ways some of these issues have been sorted out over the last two thousand years. But the emphasis here on the unstained luminosity of humanity, the radicality of divine love, and the intimacy with Christ in suffering represents a distinction between approaches characteristic of doctrinal Christianity, particularly of a Reformation variety, and the contemplative tradition. This latter literature has not been incorporated in the study of theology and will not be represented in volumes such as those edited by Peter Hodgson and Robert King. One must turn to the literature itself to encounter this option: Julian of Norwich, Teresa of Avila, Gertrude of Helfta, the Beguines, and Meister Eckhart are only a few examples.

10. The concept of *vajra* pride is explicated in chap. 7.
11. Augustine, *The City of God*, 2.11.11.

Chapter 3: The Passions

1. Evagrius Ponticus, *The Praktikos and Chapters on Prayer*, "Praktikos," 10, 12. See also Roberta Bondi's *To Love as God Loves*, 73–75.
2. Vajrayogini is a female embodiment of the wrathful energy of Enlightenment in tantric Buddhism. "Wrathful tantric deities are said to be 'fearful to fear itself'—or 'dangerous to danger itself' . . . and thus their wrath is understood to be an expression of their great compassion. Vajravarahi [a form of Vajrayogini], in common with other tantric deities, is described as 'terrifying. . . . With anger (which is in fact displayed out of) compassion." English, *Vajrayogini: Her Visualizations, Rituals, and Forms*, 48.
3. Dorotheus of Gaza, *Discourses and Sayings*, 138–9.
4. Ibid., 137
5. Ibid., 137.
6. Pseudo-Macarius, *Fifty Spiritual Homilies*, 154.
7. Ibid., 153–4.
8. Ibid., 154.
9. Dorotheus of Gaza, *Discourses and Sayings*, 85.
10. Pseudo-Macarius, *Fifty Spiritual Homilies*, 120.
11. Dorotheus of Gaza, *Discourses and Sayings*, 187.
12. Pseudo-Macarius, *Fifty Spiritual Homilies*, 154–5.
13. Evagrius Ponticos, *The Praktikos*, 50–51.
14. Ibid., 30.
15. Dorotheus of Gaza, *Discourses and Sayings*, 122.
16. Evagrius Ponticus, *The Praktikos*, 30.
17. Pseudo-Macarius, *Fifty Spiritual Homilies*, 155.
18. Evagrius Ponticus, *The Praktikos*, 38.
19. There is an enormous literature on the habits, of course. My own analysis is shaped by my readings of St. Thomas Aquinas, *Summa theologica*, first part of the second part, questions 49–67. These are nicely excerpted in *Treatise on the Virtues*.
20. Dorotheus of Gaza, *Discourses and Sayings*, 151.
21. Ibid., 183–4.
22. There are many versions of this folktale. It is included in some of the collections of Grimm's fairy tales and is sometimes retold as "The Silver-Handed Maiden." Both Gertrud Mueller Nelson (*All Who Live Here Dwell Free*) and Clarissa Pinkola Estes (*Women Who Run With the Wolves: Myths and Stories of the Wild Woman Archetype*) provide a feminist retelling and Jungian interpretation of the story.

Chapter 4: "Caught on the Fangs of Affliction"

1. The Dalai Lama summarizes this idea as an introduction to most of his teachings: "We all seek happiness and do not want suffering" (*How To Practice*, 1). Thomas Aquinas says, somewhat less succinctly, "Because in man there is first of all an inclination to good in accordance with the nature which he has in common with all substances: inasmuch as every substance seeks the preservation of its own being, according to its nature: and by reason of this inclination, whatever is a means of preserving human life, and

of warding off its obstacles, belongs to the natural law." *Summa theologica*, first part of the second part, question 94, second article.

2. See for example, Dorotheus of Gaza, "On Rancor or Animosity," in *Discourses and Sayings;* Amma Syncletica in *Forgotten Desert Mothers*, 53; and Shantideva, "Patience," in *Way of the Bodhisattva.*

3. One of the root texts in this feminist tradition is Judith Plaskow's *Sex, Sin and Grace: Women's Experience and the Theologies of Reinhold Neibuhr and Paul Tillich.* One of many other more recent examples would be M. Shawn Copeland's essay, "Wading Through Many Sorrow," in Townes, ed., *A Troubling in My Soul.*

4. Tillich, *The Courage to Be;* the cardinal virtues are set out and interpreted in many places. See Thomas Aquinas, *Treatise on the Virtues*, question 61. Note especially the second article in which he explains why fortitude (courage) is one of the cardinal virtues: "Second by the passions withdrawing us from what reason dictates—for example, the fear of dangers or of hardships—and then man has to be strengthened in regard to what reason requires, so that he will not turn back and fortitude is denominated from this."

5. This idea implies that our awareness of finitude was a kind of unbearable knowledge that translated into the distortions of a passion. It is suggested by Augustine when he argues that the fallen angels were denied the assurance that they would remain in a state of grace. Even in Paradise, the absence of assurance of unending happiness was sufficient to bring about the fall of angels (*City of God*, part 2, book 11.11–13). Tillich's description of courage as the crucial power that makes faith possible also carries this suggestion that apprehension of finitude is, in itself, unbearable: "The divine self-affirmation is the power that makes the self-affirmation of the finite being, the courage to be, possible. Only because being-itself has the character of self-affirmation in spite of non-being is courage possible. . . . He who receives this power in an act of mystical or personal or absolute faith is aware of the source of his courage to be" (*The Courage to Be*, 180–81).

6. Levinas, "Freedom and Command," in *Collected Philosophical Papers*, 16.

7. See Kalsched, *The Inner World of Trauma* for a description of some of the ways the psyche becomes bound to self-destructive means of self-defense.

8. M. Shawn Copeland is one of many womanists and feminists who are critical of the idealization of Christian virtues: "Because of the lives and suffering of Black women held in chattel slavery—the meanings of forebearance, long-suffering, patience, love, hope and faith can never again be ideologized" ("Wading Through Many Sorrow," in Townes, ed., *A Troubling in My Soul*, 124).

9. Evagrius Ponticus, *The Praktikos*, 26.

10. For a particularly unedifying example of this, I recommend book 21 of Augustine's *City of God*, in which Augustine exercises his astonishing intellect to describe how the divine could hold the contradiction of unending physical torture in place throughout eternity.

Chapter 5: The Demons Hide Themselves

1. See note 22 in chap. 3 for references to this story.

2. Kalsched's *The Inner World of Trauma* is one example of this literature from a Jungian perspective.

3. Eliot, *Middlemarch*, 428.
4. Teresa of Avila, *Interior Castle*, 146.
5. Ibid., 39.
6. Randall Jarrell, *Pictures from an Institution*, 90.
7. Ibid., 91–92.
8. Ibid., 44, 45.
9. Ibid., 59.
10. Ibid.
11. Therese of Lisieux, *The Story of a Soul*, 153.
12. Furlong, *Therese of Lisieux*, 5.
13. Evagrius Ponticus, *The Praktikos*, 71.
14. Jarrell, *Portraits from an Institution*, 28.

Chapter 6: The Divine Eros

1. Whitehead, *Process and Reality*, 342.
2. This image of an icon for God comes to me through Nicholas of Cusa, who begins his magnificent "On the Vision of God" by sending his brothers an icon and asking them to perform a practice with it before they read his text. See Nicholas of Cusa, *Selected Spiritual Writings*, 235.
3. Pseudo-Dionysius, *The Divine Names*, chap. 4, 712A, in *Complete Works*.
4. Ibid., 712B.
5. Julian of Norwich, *Showings*, 6.
6. See Pseudo Dionysius, *The Divine Names*, 712A.
7. Ibid., 709D.
8. Ibid., 712A.
9. Ibid.
10. Ibid.
11. Ibid., 712B.
12. Hadewijch, from letter 6, in Bowie, ed., *Beguine Spirituality*.
13. Julian of Norwich, *Showings*. See, for example, 257–67.
14. Ibid., 186.
15. Hadewijch, "To Learn Mary's Humility," in *Complete Works*.
16. This is one of the themes of Friedrich Schleiermacher's short work *Christmas Eve*.
17. This quotation comes from the children's video *The Polar Bear King*. This film (which I have watched at least 500,000 times with my youngest daughter) is a Norwegian film dubbed into English that retells several Norwegian folktales, listed in Norwegian in the final credits of the movie. Norwegian is not one of my languages, or I would have liked to track down the texts of these stories.
18. Euripides, *Hecuba*, 798–804.
19. Julian of Norwich, *Showings*, 220.

Chapter 7: Contemplation

1. Teresa of Avila, *Interior Castle*, 28.
2. Ibid., 29.
3. Ibid., 31.
4. Ibid., 33.
5. This discussion takes up one of the most vexed questions in Christian theology and rather glibly dismisses the conundrums. A bibliography of texts that address free will versus grace or the freedom and bondage of the will or true versus illusory freedom would be almost as extensive as Christian theology

itself. A synoptic introduction to the problem can be found in Hodgson and King, eds., *Christian Theology*, and its companion volume *Readings in Christian Theology*. Karl Rahner, Paul Tillich, Edward Farley, Simone Weil, and Nicolas Berdyaev are examples of more contemporary writers that grapple with this issue with great eloquence. The contemplative tradition tends to address this issue less theoretically and dogmatically but describes the odd paradox of feeling both utterly and exhaustingly active and utterly and blissfully passive as equally powerful components of religious practice. I am also aware that religious folk music would mostly qualify as "semi-Pelagian."

6. Bowie, ed., *Beguine Spirituality*, 90.
7. Mechthild of Magdeburg, *Flowing Light of the Godhead*, 4.12.
8. Hadewijch, *Complete Works*, "Poems in Couplets," 5.22.
9. Teresa of Avila, *Interior Castle*, 69.
10. Mechthild of Magdeburg, *Flowing Light of the Godhead*, 1.23
11. Ibid., 1.24.
12. This radical sense of grace is the great insight of the Reformers. I have wondered if it is not the intolerability of this magnitude of love that leads Luther and Calvin to disgrace immediately their insight with ideas of predestination, hell, and a malignant hostility toward those who disagree with them.
13. Murphy, ed., *Celtic Prayers*, 23.
14. Chodron, *Places That Scare You*, 75.
15. Ibid.
16. Athanasius, *Life of Saint Antony and the Letter to Marcellinus*.
17. Dorotheus of Gaza, *Discourses and Sayings*, 123. "No one is more wretched, no one is more easily caught unawares, than a man [sic] who has no one to guide him along the road to God," 122.
18. Teresa of Avila, *Interior Castle*, 53.
19. Hadewijch, *Complete Works*, letter 20.64.
20. A few examples of more detailed discussions of religious practices would include almost anything by Roberta Bondi, including *To Love as God Loves*; the writings of Thomas Keating, including *Open Mind, Open Heart* or *Invitation to Love*; the works of James Finley, including *The Contemplative Heart; Yoga: Discipline of Freedom: The Yoga Sutra Attributed to Patanjali*, trans. Barbara Miller; Indra Devi, *Yoga for You*; T. K. V. Desikachar, *The Heart of Yoga*; and His Holiness the Dalai Lama, *How to Practice*.
21. Keating's *Invitation to Love* provides a contemporary version of St. John's account of the "dark night."
22. John of the Cross, "The Dark Night," in *Collected Works*, 349–50.
23. Thomas Keating, *The Psychology of Centering Prayer*, Parts 1 and 2, and *The Method of Centering Prayer*, Parts 1 and 2.
24. John of the Cross, "The Dark Night," in *Collected Works*, 351.
25. Ibid., 350.
26. Ibid., 351.
27. Ibid., 317.
28. Ibid.
29. Ibid.
30. Meister Eckhart, *Meister Eckhart*, 25.
31. Weil, "The Love of God and Affliction," in *Simone Weil Reader*, 439.
32. Flinders's *Enduring Grace* is a particularly readable collection on the lives of women contemplatives. Bynam's *Holy Feast, Holy Fast*, Hollywood's *The Soul as*

Virgin Wife, or Jantzen's *Power, Gender, and Christian Mysticism* would be examples of more scholarly discussions of women's bodily practices and experiences.

33. This is quoted in Flinders's *Enduring Grace*, 137.
34. Williams, *Descent into Hell*, 207.
35. Ibid., 208.
36. Ibid., 209.

Chapter 8: "Christ Stripped Me of My Virtues"

1. Hopkins, "As kingfishers catch fire," in *A Selection*.
2. This image is drawn from Bergson's *Creative Evolution*.
3. This discussion of virtue is particularly influenced by Thomas Aquinas, *Treatise on the Virtues*. This work is excerpted from *Summa theologica*, first part of the second part, and Dorotheus of Gaza, "On Building Up Virtues and Their Harmony," *Discourses and Sayings*.
4. Chodron, *Places That Scare You*, 76.
5. The four immeasurables are a fundamental element of Buddhist ethics and liturgy, and recitation of the four immeasurables often accompanies certain meditation practices. See, for example, Harvey, *An Introduction to Buddhism*, 209, 245, 247, or Pabongka Rinpoche, *Liberation in the Palm of Your Hand*, 175.
6. See, for example, Shantideva, *Way of the Bodhisattva*, especially chap. 6, "Patience," and the Dalai Lama's redaction of Shantideva in *Healing Anger*. Also, Dorotheus of Gaza, "On Refusal to Judge Our Neighbor" and "On Rancor or Animosity," in *Discourses and Sayings*. Feminist theology is, by contrast, rife with much-needed criticism of these celebrations of patience.
7. Swan, "Introduction," *Forgotten Desert Mothers*, 54.
8. Swan, *Forgotten Desert Mothers*, 61.
9. Ibid.
10. Chodron, *Places That Scare You*, 80.
11. Ibid.
12. Swan, *Forgotten Desert Mothers*, 54.
13. Chodron, *Places That Scare You*, 82.
14. Bowie, ed., *Beguine Spirituality*, 99.
15. This little prayer is called St. Teresa's bookmark because it was found written in her breviary.
16. Schleiermacher's description of blessedness is similar to this. See *The Christian Faith*, particularly his discussion of "The Manner in which Fellowship with the Perfection and Blessedness of the Redeemer expresses itself in the Individual Soul." *Christmas Eve* gives more narrative expression to this idea in the women's stories. His "Sermon at Nathan's Grave," in which he is giving the graveside sermon at his beloved son's funeral, is a particularly poignant example of this "blessedness."
17. Dorotheus of Gaza, *Discourses and Sayings*, 94. See also Bondi's discussion of the role of humility in the writings of the desert ascetics in "Humility," *To Love as God Loves*.
18. Teresa of Avila, *Interior Castle*, 85.
19. Shantideva, *Way of the Bodhisattva*, 1.26.
20. Ibid., 10.57.
21. Shantideva, *Way of the Bodhisattva*, 3.1–2.
22. Ibid., 3.18–20, 22.

23. His Holiness the Dalai Lama et al., *Tantra in Tibet*, 48.
24. "Tibetan Buddhism, almost alone among Asian Buddhisms, preserved the huge treasury of Indian Buddhist Tantric traditions. . . . This Vehicle is the esoteric dimension of the Universal Vehicle [Mahayana Buddhism], and it emphasizes practices based on the cultivated sense of the immediate presence of the Buddha reality. It teaches methods for the attainment of complete Buddhahood in this very life, or at least within a few more lives, thus vastly accelerating the Universal Vehicle evolutionary path on which a Bodhisattva transforms from a human to a Buddha over three incalculable eons of self-transcending lifetimes," Thurman, *Essential Tibetan Buddhism*, 3.
25. His Holiness the Dalai Lama et al., *Tantra in Tibet*, 126.
26. Ibid., 198.
27. Ibid., 77.
28. Ibid.,124.
29. Ibid., 48.
30. Ibid., 121.
31. Rereading this, I realize it sounds as if Christ were the ultimate principle of reality that trumps all other religious principles. I do not mean this at all. I mean rather that for Christians, Christ is the chief name of the power of redemption. This power is everywhere, not only called by different names but understood in a wide variety of ways. As Christians, it is important to recognize that this power cannot be corralled into any single tradition, and we can appreciate the variety of ways liberation happens, even when it is in forms and represented by names and ideas we do not understand.
32. Fay Keys, Director of Green Bough House of Prayer.

Bibliography

This list reflects works directly quoted as well as those that I am aware of as exerting influence on the ideas developed in the work, even if not directly referred to in the body of the text.

Aquinas, Thomas. *Treatise on the Virtues*. Translated by John A. Oesterle. Notre Dame, IN: University of Notre Dame Press, 1984.

———."The Cause of Evil," *Summa theologica* 1a. Translated by the Fathers of the English Dominican Province. Westminster, MD: Christian Classics, 1981.

Athanasius. *The Life of Antony and the Letter to Marcellinus*. Translation and introduction by Robert C. Gregg. New York: Paulist Press, 1980.

Augustine. *Concerning the City of God against the Pagans*. Translation by Henry Bettenson. New York: Penguin Books, 1972.

———. *Confessions*. Translated with introduction by R.W. Pine-Coffin. New York: Penguin Books, 1961.

Berdyaev, Nicolas. *The Destiny of Man*. New York: Harper & Row Publishers, 1960.

Bergson, Henri. *Creative Evolution*. Translation by Arthur Mitchell. New York: Modern Library, Random House, 1944.

Bonaventura. *The Mind's Road to God*. Translated with an introduction by George Boas. New York: Macmillan Publishing Co., 1953.

Bondi, Roberta C. *To Love as God Loves: Conversations with the Early Church*. Philadelphia: Fortress Press, 1987.

Bowie, Fiona. *Beguine Spirituality: Mystical Writings of Mechthild of Magdeburg, Beatrice of Nazareth, and Hadewijch of Brabant*. Translated by Oliver Davies. New York: Crossroad, 1990.

Brother Lawrence. *The Practice of the Presence of God with Spiritual Maxims*. Grand Rapids, MI: Spire Books, 1967.

Bulfinch, Thomas. *Bulfinch's Mythology*. New York: Avenel Books, 1978 printing.

Bynam, Caroline Walker. *Holy Feast Holy Fast: Religious Significance of Food to Medieval Women*. Berkeley, CA: University of California Press, 1987.

Calvin, John. *Institutes of the Christian Religion*. Edited by John T. McNeill. Translated and indexed by Ford Lewis Battles. Philadelphia: Westminster Press, 1960.

Chodron, Pema. *The Places That Scare You: A Guide to Fearlessness in Difficult Times*. Boston: Shambhala Press, 2001.

———. *The Cloud of Unknowing*. Translated by Clifton Wolters. Baltimore: Penguin Books, 1961.

Cone, James H. *God of the Oppressed*. New York: Seabury Press, 1975.

De Caussade, Jean-Pierre. *Abandonment to Divine Providence*. Translated and introduced by John Beevers. New York: Doubleday, 1975.

Desikachar, T. K. V. *The Heart of Yoga: Developing a Personal Practice*. Rochester, VT: Inner Traditions International, 1995.

Desikachar, T. K. V. with R. H. Cravens. *Health, Healing, and Beyond: Yoga and the Living Tradition of Krishnamacharya*. New York: Aperture, 1998.

Devi, Indra. *Yoga for You*. Layton, UT: 2002. Originally published by Prentice Hall in 1959 as *Yoga for Americans*.

Dhamma, Venerable Rewata. *The First Discourse of the Buddha*. Boston: Wisdom Publications, 1997.

Dorotheus of Gaza. *Discourses and Sayings: Desert Humor and Humility*. Translated with an introduction by Eric P. Wheeler. Kalamazoo, MI: Cistercian Publications, 1977.

Dowman, Keith, trans. *Sky Dancer: The Secret Life and Songs of the Lady Yeshe Tsogyel*. Ithaca, NY: Snow Lion Publications, 1996.

Drolma, Delog Dawa. *Delog: Journey to Realms Beyond Death*. Translated by Richard Barron under the direction of His Eminence Chagdud Tulku Rinpoche. Junction City, CA: Padma Publishing, 1995.

Eckhart, Meister. *Meister Eckhart, from Whom God Hid Nothing: Sermons, Writings, and Sayings*. Edited by David O'Neal. Boston: Shambhala Press, 1996.

Eliot, George. *Middlemarch*. Edited by Bert G. Hornback. New York: W.W. Norton and Co., 1977.

Ellsberg, Robert. *All Saints: Daily Reflections on Saints, Prophets, and Witnesses for Our Time*. New York: Crossroad, 1999.

English, Elizabeth. *Vajrayogini: Her Visualizations, Rituals, and Forms*. Boston: Wisdom Publications, 2002.

Estes, Clarissa Pinkola, Ph.D. *Women Who Run With the Wolves: Myths and Stories of the Wild Woman Archetype*. New York: Ballantine Books, 1992.

Euripides, *Four Tragedies III*. Edited by David Grene and Richmond Lattimore. Chicago: University of Chicago Press, 1958.

Finley, James. *The Contemplative Heart*. Notre Dame, IN: Sorin Books, 2000.

Flinders, Carol Lee. *Enduring Grace: Living Portraits of Seven Women Mystics*. New York: HarperSanFrancisco, 1993.

Furlong, Monica. *Therese of Lisieux*. Maryknoll, NY: Orbis Books, 1987.

Getrude of Helfta. *The Herald of Divine Love*. Translated and edited by Margaret Winkworth. Mahwah, NJ: Paulist Press, 1993.

Gregory of Nyssa. *On the Soul and the Resurrection*. Translated and introduced by Catherine P. Roth. Crestwood, NY: St. Vladimir's Seminary Press, 1993.

Grimshaw, Anna. *Servants of the Buddha: Winter in a Himalayan Convent*. Cleveland, OH: Pilgrim Press, 1992.

Guenther, Herbert V. *The Life and Teaching of Naropa: Translated from the Original Tibetan with Philosophical Commentary Based on the Oral Transmission*. Boston: Shambhala Press, 1995.

Guru Rinpoche according to Karma Lingpa. *Tibetan Book of the Dead: The Great Liber-*

ation through Hearing in the Bardo. Translated with commentary by Francesca Fremantle and Chogyam Trungpa. Boston: Shambhala Press, 1987.

Gutiérrez, Gustavo. *A Theology of Liberation*. Translated and edited by Sister Caridad Inda and John Eagleson. Maryknoll, NY: Orbis Books, 1973.

Gyatso, Geshe Kelsang. *The Bodhisattva Vow: The Essential Practices of Mahayana Buddhism*. London: Tharpa Publications. 1991.

Gyatso, Veneral Lobsang. *The Four Noble Truths*. Translated by Venerable Sherabl Gyatso. Ithaca, NY: Snow Lion Publications, 1994.

Hadewijch of Brabant. *The Complete Works*. Translated and introduced by Mother Coluba Hart OSB. Mahwah, NJ: Paulist Press, 1980.

Harvey, Peter. *An Introduction to Buddhism: Teachings, History, and Practices*. New York: Cambridge University Press, 1990.

Hick, John. *Evil and the God of Love*. Revised edition. San Francisco: Harper & Row Publishers, 1977.

His Holiness the Dalai Lama. *Awakening the Mind, Lightening the Heart: Core Teachings of Tibetan Buddhism*. New York: HarperSanFrancisco, 1995.

———. *Healing Anger: The Power of Patience From a Buddhist Perspective*. Translated by Geshe Thupten Jinpa. Ithaca, NY: Snow Lion Publications, 1997.

———. *How to Practice: The Way to a Meaningful Life*. Translated and edited by Jeffrey Hopkins, Ph.D. New York: Pocket Books, 2002.

———. *The World of Tibetan Buddhism: An Overview of Its Philosophy and Practice*. Translated, edited, and annotated by Geshse Thupten Jinpa. Boston: Wisdom Publications, 1995.

———. *Path to Bliss: A Practical Guide to Stages of Meditation*. Translated by Gheshe Thubten Jinpa. Edited by Christine Cox. Ithaca, NY: Snow Lion Publications, 1991.

His Holiness the Dalai Lama and Alexander Berzin. *The Gelug/Kagyu Tradition of Mahamudra*. Ithaca, NY: Snow Lion Publications, 1997.

His Holiness the Dalai Lama, Tsong-ka-pa, and Jeffrey Hopkins. *Deity Yoga: In Action and Performance Tantra*. Ithaca, NY: Snow Lion Publications, 1981.

Hodgson, Peter C. and Robert H. King, eds. *Christian Theology: An Introduction to Its Traditions and Tasks*. Revised and enlarged edition. Philadelphia: Fortress Press, 1982.

———. *Readings in Christian Theology*. Philadelphia: Fortress Press, 1985.

Hollywood, Amy. *The Soul as Virgin Wife: Mechthild of Magdeburg, Marguerite Porete, and Meister Eckhart*. Notre Dame, IN: University of Notre Dame Press, 1995.

Hopkins, Gerard Manley. *A Selection of His Poems and Prose*. Edited by W. H. Gardner. Baltimore: Penguin Books, 1958.

Jantzen, Grace M. *Power, Gender, and Christian Mysticism*. New York: Cambridge University Press, 1995.

Jarrell, Randall. *Pictures from an Institution: A Comedy*. Chicago: University of Chicago Press, 1954.

John of the Cross. *The Collected Works of Saint John of the Cross*. Translated by Kieran Kavanaugh, OCD, and Otilio Rodriguez, OCD. Washington, DC: ICS Publications, Institute of Carmelite Studies, 1979.

Julian of Norwich. *Showings*. Translated with an introduction by Edmund Colledge, OSA, and James Walsch, SJ. New York: Paulist Press, 1978.

Kalsched, Donald. *The Inner World of Trauma: Archetypal Defenses of the Personal Spirit*. New York: Routledge, 1996.

Keating, Thomas. *Invitation to Love: The Way of Christian Contemplation*. New York: Continuum. 2002

————. *Open Mind, Open Heart: The Contemplative Dimension of the Gospel*. New York: Continuum, 2001.

Keats, John. "Ode to a Grecian Urn," *The Major Poets: English and American*. Edited by Charles M. Coffin. New York: Harcourt Brace & World, Inc., 1954.

Khoroche, Peter, trans. *Once the Buddha Was a Monkey: Arya Sura's Jatakamala*. Chicago: University of Chicago Press. 1989.

Large Sutra on Perfect Wisdom with the Divisions of the Abhisamahalankara. Translated by Edward Conze. Berkeley, CA: University of California Press.

Le Guin, Ursula. *A Wizard of Earthsea*. New York: Bantam Books, 1975.

Levinas, Emmanuel. *Totality and Infinity: An Essay on Exteriority*. Translated by Alphonso Lingis. Pittsburg, PA: Duquesne University Press, 1969.

————. *Collected Philosophical Papers*. Translated by Alphonso Lingis. Dordrecht: Martinus Nijhoff Publishers, 1987.

Luther, Martin. *Martin Luther: Selections from His Writings*. Edited with an introduction by John Dillenberger. Garden City, NY: Doubleday and Co., 1961.

Mechthild of Magdeburg. *The Flowing Light of the Godhead*. Translated and introduced by Frank Tobin. Mahwah, NJ: Paulist Press, 1998.

Miller, Barbara Stoller, trans. *Yoga: Discipline of Freedom: The Yoga Sutra Attributed to Patanjali*. New York: Bantam Books, 1998.

Murcott, Susan. *The First Buddhist Women: Translations and Commentary on the* Therigatha. Berkeley, CA: Parallax Press, 1991.

Murphy, Trace, ed. *Celtic Prayers*, Translated by Alexander Carmichael. New York: Doubleday, 1996.

Nelson, Gertrud Mueller. *Here All Dwell Free: Stories to Heal the Wounded Feminine*. Mahwah, NJ: Paulist Press, 1999.

Nicholas of Cusa. *Selected Spiritual Writings*. Translated and introduced by H. Lawrence Bond. Mahwah, NJ: Paulist Press, 1997.

Nomorua Yushi, trans. *Desert Wisdom: Sayings from the Desert Fathers*. Maryknoll, NY: Orbis Books, 2003.

Norbu, Chogyal Nahkahi. *Dzogchen: The Self-Perfected State*. Edited by Adriano Clemente. Translated by John Shane. Ithaca, NY: Snow Lion Publications, 1996.

Norbu, Padma Karpo Ngawang. *The Practice of the Co-Emergent Mahamudra*. Translated by Venerable Anzan Hoshin Sensei. Ottowa: Great Matter Publications, 1991.

Plaskow, Judith. *Sex, Sin and Grace: Women's Experience and the Theologies of Reinhold Neibuhr and Paul Tillich*. Lanham, MD: University Press of America, 1979.

Platform Sutra of the Sixth Patriarch: The Text of the Tun-Huang Manuscript. Translation, introduction, and notes by Philip B. Yampolsky. New York: Columbia University Press, 1967.

Plato. *Phaedrus*. Translated with an introduction and commentary by R. Hackforth. Cambridge: Cambridge University Press, 1952.

————. *The Republic of Plato*. Translated with introduction and notes by Francis MacDonald Cornford. London: Oxford University Press, 1945.

————. *Symposium*. Translated with introduction and notes by Alexander Nehamas and Paul Woodruff. Indianapolis: Hackett Publishing Co., 1989.

Ponticus, Evagrius. *The Praktikos and Chapters on Prayer*. Translated with an introduction and notes by John Eudes Bamberger OCSO. Kalamazoo, MI: Cistercian Publications, 1981.

Powers, John. *Introduction to Tibetan Buddhism*. Ithaca, NY: Snow Lion Publications, 1995.

Pseudo-Macarius. *The Fifty Spiritual Homilies and the Great Letter*. Translated, edited, and introduced by George A. Maloney, SJ. Mahwah, NJ: Paulist Press, 1992.

Pseudo-Dionysius. *The Complete Works*. Translation by Colm Luibheid. Mahwah, NJ: Paulist Press, 1987.

Rahner, Karl. *Foundations of Christian Faith: An Introduction to the Idea of Christianity*. Translated by William V. Dych. New York: Crossroad, 1984.

Rgyal, Tshe Ring Dbang. *The Tale of the Incomparable Prince*. Translated by Beth Newman. New York: HarperCollins, 1996.

Ricoeur, Paul. "The Myth of Punishment." In *Conflict of Interpretations: Essays in Hermeneutics*. Edited by Don Ihde. Evanston, IL: Northwestern University Press, 1974.

Rinpoche, Pabongka. *Liberation in the Palm of Your Hand: A Concise Discourse on the Path to Enlightenment*. Translated by Michael Richards. Edited by Trijang Rinpoche. Boston: Wisdom Publications, 1997 (paperback edition).

Ruether, Rosemary Radford. *Sexism and God-talk: Toward a Feminist Theology*. Boston: Beacon Press, 1983.

Schleiermacher, Friedrich. *The Christian Faith*. Edited by H. R. Mackintosh and J. S. Stewart. Philadelphia: Fortress Press, 1976.

———. *Christmas Eve: Dialogue on the Incarnation*. Translated with introduction and notes by Terence N. Tice. San Francisco: Edwin Mellon Press, 1990.

———. *On Religion: Speeches to Its Cultured Despisers*. Translated by John Oman, with a foreword by Jack Forstman. Louisville, KY: Westminster John Knox Press, 1994.

Shantideva. *The Way of the Bodhisattva*. Translated by the Padmakara Translation Group. Boston: Shambhala Publications, 1997.

Sogyal Rinpoche. *The Tibetan Book of Living and Dying*. New York: HarperSanFrancisco, 1993.

Swan, Laura. *The Forgotten Desert Mothers: Sayings, Lives, and Stories of Early Christian Women*. Mahwah, NJ: Paulist Press, 2001.

Taring, Rinchen Dolma. *Daughter of Tibet*. London: Wisdom Publications, 1970.

Tazewell, Charles. *The Littlest Angel*. Nashville, TN: Ideals Children's Books, 1991.

Teresa of Avila. *Interior Castle*. Translated and edited by E. Allison Peers. New York: Doubleday, 1989.

Therese of Lisieux. *The Autobiography of Saint Therese of Lisieux: The Story of a Soul*. Translated with an introduction by John Beevers. New York: Doubleday, 1989.

———. *Daily Readings with St. Therese of Lisieux*. Introduced and edited by Michael Hollings. Springfield, IL: Templegate Publishers, 1986.

Threefold Lotus Sutra: The Lotus of Innumerable Meanings, the Lotus Flower of the Wonderful Law, and Meditation on the Bodhisattva Universal Virtue. Translated by Bunno Kato, Yoshiro Tamura, and Kojiro Miyasaka. Tokyo: Kosei Publishing Co., 1975.

Thurman, Robert A. F. *Central Philosophy of Tibet: A Study and Translation of Jey Tsong Khapa's Essence of True Eloquence*. Princeton: Princeton University Press, 1984.

———. *Essential Tibetan Buddhism*. New York: HarperSan Francisco, 1995.

Tillich, Paul. *The Courage to Be*. New Haven, CT: Yale University Press, 1952.

Townes, Emilie M., ed. *A Troubling in My Soul: Womanist Perspectives on Evil and Suffering*. Maryknoll, NY: Orbis Books, 1996.

Tsong-ka-pa. *Tantra in Tibet*. Introduced by His Holiness the Dalai Lama. Translated and edited by Jeffrey Hopkins. Ithaca, NY: Snow Lion Publications, 1977.

Vimalakirti Sutra. Translated by Burton Watson. New York: Columbia University Press, 1997.

Ward, Benedicta, SLG, trans. *The Sayings of the Desert Fathers: The Alphabetical Collection*. Kalamazoo, MI: Cisercian Publications, 1975.

Weil, Simone. *Simone Weil Reader*. Edited by George A. Panichas. Wakefield, RI: Moyer Bell, 1977.

Welch, Sharon D. *A Feminist Ethic of Risk*. Minneapolis: Fortress Press, 1990.

Whitehead, Alfred North. *Process and Reality*. Edited by David Ray Griffin and Donald W. Sherburne. New York: Free Press, 1978.

Williams, Charles. *Descent into Hell*. London: Faber & Faber, 1937.

Williams, Robert R. *Recognition: Fichte and Hegel on the Other*. Albany, NY: State University of New York Press, 1992.

MUSIC, CDS, AND VIDEOS

Ailey, Alvin. *Revelations*. Disc 1. V2 Records, 1998. CD.

Anywhere with Jesus. MCC Discovery Team, Zambia, Canada, and the United States. Mennonite Central Committee. 1995. CD.

Best of Bluegrass: Preachin,' Prayin,' and Singin.' Polygram Records, 1996. CD.

Black, Mary. *Looking Back*. Curb Records, 1995. CD.

———. *Song for Ireland*. Gift Horse Records. CD.

Block, Rory. *Ain't I a Woman*. Rounder Records, 1992. CD.

———. *Confessions of a Blues Singer*. Rounder Records, 1998. CD.

———. *Rhinestones and Steel Strings*. Rounder Records, 1990. CD.

Bourgeault, Reverend Cynthia, Ph.D. *Singing the Psalms: How to Chant in the Christian Contemplative Tradition*. Sounds True, 1997. Audiocassettes.

Brumley, Albert E. "I'll Fly Away." Recorded by Liz McGeachy and Tim Merrima. *Some Bright Morning*. CD.

Chodron, Pema. *Pure Meditation*. Sounds True, 2002. Audiocassette.

"Climbing Up the Rough Side," *The Hopeful Gospel Quartet: Live*. High Bridge Company, 1997. CD.

Glover, Carla. *Hush My Restless Soul*. June Appal Recording, 1995. CD.

Hawker, Ginny and Kay Justice. *Come All You Tenderhearted*. June Appal Recording, 1993. CD.

How Can I Keep From Singing: Early American Religious Music and Song Classic Recordings from the 1920's and 1930's, vols. 1 and 2. Yazoo Records, 1996. CD.

Keating, Thomas. *The Christian Contemplative Heritage: Our Apophatic Tradition: The Psychology of the Centering Prayer*, Parts 1, 2, and 3. Contemplative Outreach, Ltd. St. Benedict's Monastery, Snowmass, CO, 1994. Video.

———. *The Christian Contemplative Heritage: Our Apophatic Tradition: The Method of Centering Prayer*, Parts 1 and 2. Contemplative Outreach, Ltd. St. Benedict's Monastary, Snowmass, CO, 1994. Video.

Kraus, Alison and Union Station. *So Long, So Wrong*. Rounder Records, 1997. CD.

———. *Now That I Found You*. Rounder Records, 1995. CD.

McGeachy, Liz and Tim Merrima. *Weaving Heaven and Earth*. www.lizandtim.com. CD.

Meeting in the Air: Sacred Music of the South Appalachians. John C. Campbell Folk School. Brasstown, NC, 1995. CD.

Nelson, Sonia. *Healing Chant from the Veda*. www.vedichantcenter.org. CD.

———. *Listen and Repeat: A Vedic Chant Tutorial Step 1*. www. vedicchantcenter.org. CD.

"Conversation with Death." Traditional. Recorded by Hazel Dickens, David Patrick Kelly and Bobby McMillon. *Songcatcher: Music from and Inspired by the Motion Picture*. Vanguard Records, 2001. CD.

O Brother Where Art Thou. Mercury Records, 2000. CD.

Odetta. *The Essential Odetta*. Vanguard Records, 1973, 1987. CD.

———. *Movin' It On*. Rose Quartz Records, 1987. CD.

———. *Odetta Sings Ballads and Blues*. Tradition, 1996 from original 1956 reprint. CD.

"Sweet Chariot." Emmy Lou Harris and Paul Kennerly. Sung by Emmy Lou Harris. *Portrait*, Disk 2. Reprise Records, 1996. Reprinted from *The Ballad of Sally Rose*. CD.

Sweet Honey and the Rock. *Sacred Ground*. Earthbeat Records, 1995. CD.

Williams, Robin and Linda and Their Fine Group. *Good News*. Sugar Hill Records, 1995. CD.

Index

CPSIA information can be obtained
at www.ICGtesting.com
Printed in the USA
LVHW040123240223
740256LV00001B/36